Studies in Liturgical Musicology
Edited by Dr. Robin A. Leaver

1. Frans Brouwer and Robin A. Leaver (eds.). *Ars et Musica in Liturgia: Essays Presented to Casper Honders on His Seventieth Birthday.* 1994.
2. Steven Plank. *"The Way to Heavens Doore": An Introduction to Liturgical Process and Musical Style.* 1994.

ARS ET MUSICA IN LITURGIA

Essays Presented to
Casper Honders
on His Seventieth Birthday

edited by
FRANS BROUWER
and
ROBIN A. LEAVER

Studies in Liturgical Musicology, No. 1

The Scarecrow Press, Inc.
Metuchen, N.J., & London
1994

British Library Cataloguing-in-Publication data available

Library of Congress Cataloging-in-Publication Data

Ars et musica in liturgia : essays presented to Casper Honders on his
   seventieth birthday / edited by Frans Brouwer and Robin A. Leaver.
         p.   cm. — (Studies in liturgical musicology ; no. 1)
      Chiefly in English; some contributions also in Dutch and German.
      Includes bibliographical references.
      ISBN 0-8108-2948-7
      1. Church music. 2. Liturgics. I. Honders, Casper.
   II. Brouwer, Frans. III. Leaver, Robin A. IV. Series.
   ML3000.A74 1994
   781.71—dc20   94-33862

Contents

Editor's Foreword

Ars et musica in liturgia is the first volume to be published in the series Studies in Liturgical Musicology. Although future titles will normally be by one author, this first volume, by its composite and international authorship, encapsulates in many respects the intended scope of the series.

Studies in Liturgical Musicology is devised as an international series that will explore biblical foundations, theological presuppositions, and liturgical functions of worship music in Judeo-Christian traditions. Individual titles will therefore investigate the cantoral, congregational, and choral aspects of the music of historical and contemporary worship, with a particular emphasis on primary source material, bibliography, and reference.

Ars et musica in liturgia is a celebratory volume marking the seventieth birthday of the Dutch Emeritus Professor Dr. Casper Honders, the first Director of the Liturgical Institute, State University of Groningen. He is known, both within the Netherlands and internationally, as a leading liturgical scholar in the Reformed tradition who in the course of his career has explored the interplay between music and liturgy from the perspectives of theology, history, and contemporary practice.

The contributions have been written by colleagues, former students, and others who have been associated with Casper Honders and reflect many of his own concerns. Most of the chapters appear in English, but those written in German or Dutch are followed by summaries in English. The volume is being simultaneously issued in the series Kerkmusiek en Liturgie (Church Music and Liturgy), published by the Netherlands Institute for Church Music, which forms part of the Faculty of Music within the School of the Arts, Utrecht. The final stages of the production of the book were completed in some haste—in order that it should appear in print in the Netherlands on Casper Honders's 70th birthday on 6 June 1993. In the process one or two typographical errors were overlooked, notably opening question marks, which sometimes follow Dutch usage and appear elsewhere according to English usage. Hopefully these small imperfections will not detract from the substance of the book itself. As the volume was prepared entirely without the knowledge of Casper Honders—he only knew of it when a copy of the Dutch edition was put into his hands on his 70th birthday—some of the more important writings were omitted from the bibliography; they are included in this American edition, in the Addendum of page 205.

Robin A. Leaver
Series Editor
Westminster Choir College, Princeton, and
Drew University, Madison, New Jersey

Preface

"I am still a pastor at heart," are words that Casper Honders repeated often during his lectures and seminars when he was Professor of Liturgiology at Groningen University. They characterize the way he conducted his scholarship. He once wrote in a personal letter: "Those ministers who do not experience the coming-together of heaven and earth in this field of liturgiology will miss the mark."

Most of the writing and teaching of Casper Honders combine both theory and practice, both principles of worship and liturgical usage. Instead of only talking and writing about liturgy and its music in a more or less cold scholarly way, heavily footnoted with lists of data and structural diagrams, he attempts to join the Bride and the Bridegroom, the cognitive with the intuitive, to explore the emotional with the rational. This is clearly demonstrated in the recent columns he contributed to the *Groninger Kerkblad* (Groningen Church Newspaper).[1] They focus on some of his former parishioners in Zeeuws-Vlaanderen and Betuwe (respectively in south-west and central Netherlands), who are described as typical religious people with the deepest feelings for liturgy and life.

In these "low-church" essays we recognize Casper Honders the pastoral scholar who brought many of his parishioners, colleagues, students and friends into contact with the inspiring world of, for example, the music of Johann Sebastian Bach, or the sometimes surprising stanzas of nineteenth-century hymnody. For him liturgy is necessarily associated with the visual arts, poetry and music if it is to give concrete forms to biblical principles. These are the human tools which enable us to understand what lies beneath the surface, to hear what echoes beyond words and sounds, to see more directly into the visions of others, whether they be from the past or the present. The reciprocity between liturgy and the arts is for Casper Honders the con-

---

1 *Groninger Kerkblad*, 6 September 1992, 6 ("Bertus"; 1 November 1992, 11 ("Dirk"); 29 November 1992, 11 ("Guus"); 13 December 1992, 11 ("Jan"); 20 March 1993, 5 ("Herman"); 25 April 1993, 6 ("Marien").

comitant of the interaction between religion and the common life. Thus for him liturgiology is focused in the fertilization of arts and sciences within people's hearts.

It is for this reason that we have chosen *Ars et musica in liturgia* for the title of this Festschrift which we, all the contributors, present to our *praeceptor et amicus* Casper Honders on the occasion of his seventieth birthday. By honouring him in this way we trust that these contributions will lead to a deeper understanding of worship on the part of scholars, artists, pastors and, fundamentally, worshippers themselves.

In keeping with his pastoral approach to liturgiology, the photograph of Casper Honders that faces his bibliography (see page 4) does not depict the university professor in bands and gown lecturing at a podium. Instead we see the scholar in his sweater working with an open mind towards new possibilities and carrying with ease his years, experience and knowledge.

This is not the first collection of articles, etc., to be dedicated to Casper Honders. In 1984 a section of the September issue of the *Mededelingen van het Instituut voor Liturgiewetenschap van de Rijksuniversiteit te Groningen*[2] was reserved to honour his retirement as Professor of Liturgiology, and in 1987, when Casper Honders resigned the editorship of the *Bulletin Internationale Arbeitsgemeinschaft für Hymnologie*, several colleagues gave him a collection of personal letters at the end of the IAH congress in Lund, Sweden.[3]

We offer our sincere thanks to all the authors represented in this volume for their willingness to contribute. We are particularly pleased that most of the articles are in English or German so that they will be accessible to readers beyond the borders of the Netherlands. We are also grateful to Thomas Remenschneider and Brian Middleton for their help with translations, and to Jacqueline Huisman for intensive assistance in preparing the final form of the manuscript for publication. We are most grateful to the Stichting Steunfonds Nederlands Instituut voor Kerkmuziek (Foundation Support-Fund of the Nether-

---

2 *Mededelingen van het Instituut voor Liturgiewetenschap van de Rijksuniversiteit te Groningen* 18 (September 1984), 1-84.

3 They were reproduced, under the title "Letters to the Editor... A. Casper Honders, Editor IAH Bulletin 1974-1987", in: *Bulletin Internationale Arbeitsgemeinschaft für Hymnologie* 18 (June 1988), 208-247.

lands Institute for Church Music) for underwriting a substantial portion of the production costs, and to Scarecrow Press, Metuchen (U.S.A.) for publishing the North American edition of this volume.

It is obvious that there is a broader circle of colleagues, students and friends than can be represented in this Festschrift who are also grateful to Casper Honders for his inspirational teaching, supervision, friendship, and his interest in their personal lives as well as their professional and artistic achievements. It was a labour of love and respect for us to plan and compile this book, which hopefully represents the gratitude of all these colleagues and friends of Casper Honders, our "singing professor".

Frans Brouwer   *Robin A. Leaver*

Bibliography
The publications of Casper Honders

Frans Brouwer and Jan R. Luth

Adriaan Casper Honders was born on June 6, 1923 in Zoeterwoude, the Netherlands. After his education at the secondary grammar school (Rijnlands Lyceum) in Wassenaar he studied theology in Leiden (1945-1951), Zürich (1948), with Karl Barth in Basle (1948) and at the University of Amsterdam (1951). He studied organ playing with Dr. Hendrik Leendert Oussoren (1937-1942), Dr. Fritz Morel (Basle, 1948) and Adriaan C. Schuurman (1949-1951). At the end of the forties he attended courses with Dr. Ina Lohr, in Basle as well as in Wassenaar. It was through her influence that Casper Honders became interested in the revival of the church modes. Casper Honders promoted as Doctor of Theology at the University of Amsterdam in December 1963, with a dissertation entitled *Doen en laten in Ernst en Vrede: Notities over een broederkring en een tijdschrift.*
Casper Honders was ordained into the ministry of the Dutch Reformed Church (Nederlandse Hervormde Kerk) and served as the minister of Sas van Gent and Philippine from 1951 to 1956, and of Oosterhout and Slijk-Ewijk, from 1956 to 1963. He was then asked to inaugurate the newly-founded Instituut voor Liturgiewetenschap at the Rijksuniversiteit in Groningen, where he was appointed successively principal tutor (wetenschappelijk hoofdmedewerker, 1963-1978), lecturer (1978-1980), and professor (1980-1984) for liturgiology. Casper Honders taught liturgy and hymnology at the Groningen Conservatory of Music from 1972 to 1982 and at the Nederlands Instituut voor Kerkmuziek from 1979 to 1980.
He was president of the Commission for Church Music of the Dutch Reformed Church for five years (1965-1970), during which period many pioneering activities were undertaken; president of the Commission for Organ Affairs of this Church (1972-1977); member of the Vorstand of the Internationale Arbeitsgemeinschaft für Hymnologie (IAH) for fourteen years (1971-1985); first editor of the *Bulletin IAH* for thirteen years (1974-

1987) and founder-member of the Internationale Arbeits-gemeinschaft für theologische Bachforschung (from 1976). The following is a listing of his principal scholarly publications (until March 1993).

Abbreviations:

Bulletin IAH	Bulletin Internationale Arbeitsgemeinschaft für Hymnologie, Instituut voor Liturgiewetenschap Groningen
JLO	Jaarboek voor Liturgie-Onderzoek, Instituut voor Liturgiewetenschap Groningen
KT	Kerk en Theologie
MILW	Mededelingen van het Instituut voor Liturgie-wetenschap van de Rijksuniversiteit te Groningen
MuG	Musik und Gottesdienst
MuK	Musik und Kirche
NAK	Nederlands Archief voor Kerkgeschiedenis

1960

Doen en laten in Ernst en Vrede: Notities over een broederkring en een tijdschrift (The Hague 1963), 208 pp. (diss. Amsterdam).

Literaturberichte Liturgik und Hymnologie. In: *Jahrbuch für Liturgik und Hymnologie* (Kassel 1955-). These reports appear in the volumes published between 1963 and 1983.

De "Markus-Passion" van Bach. In: KT 16 (1965), 147-152.

Bach's "Siebzehn Choräle": Musica sub communione? In: *Jaarboek voor de eredienst 1965-1966* ('s-Gravenhage [s.d.]), 135-145.

Kohlbrugge en de liturgie. In: NAK XLIX (1969), 220-241.

Bachs Fughetta over "Dies sind die heilgen zehn Gebot". In: KT 20 (1969), 192-198.

Bachs grote voorspel voor orgel over "Vater unser im Himmel-reich." In: *Vox theologica* 39 (1969), 35-41.

1970

Valerandus Pollanus Liturgia Sacra (1551-1555): Opnieuw uit-gegeven en van een inleiding voorzien [Kerkhistorische Bijdragen onder red. van J.N. Bakhuizen van den Brink, et al.: No. I] (Lei-den 1970), 270 pp.

Collectanea funebria. In: MILW 5 (Feb. 1970), 1-12.

Voorbereiding voor het avondmaal. In: MILW 6 (April 1971), 1-11.

Een Nederlandsch liturgisch tijdschrift uit het begin van de 19e eeuw. In: KT 23 (1972), 162-175.

Laten wij onze zonden belijden. In: *Concilium* (1973), 91-102.

Het nieuwe Liedboek en de theologie. In: *Rondom het Woord: Theologische etherleergang van de NCRV* 15 (1973), 63-73.

Het nieuwe Liedboek en de liturgie. In: idem, 74-83.

Het nieuwe Liedboek en de kerkgeschiedenis. In: idem, 84-94.

Bachs großes Vorspiel für Orgel über "Christ, unser Herr, zum Jordan kam." In: MuK 44 (1974), 124-129.

Liturgie en bevrijding. In: *Rondom het Woord: Theologische etherleergang van de NCRV* 16 (1974), 49-60.

"Allein Gott in der Höh sei Ehr" BWV 663: Van dank naar troost. In: A.C. Honders, R. Steensma, J. Wit (ed.), *Gratias agimus: Opstellen over Danken en Loven, aangeboden aan Prof. Dr. W.F. Dankbaar* [Studies van het Instituut voor Liturgie-wetenschap No. 2] (Groningen 1975), 149-155.

Bach en de kerk. In: E. Pruim (ed.), *Klein Bachboek* (Baarn 1975), 62-72.

Op zoek naar de theologische struktuur van het Réveil. In: KT 27 (1976), 1-17.

"Allein Gott in der Höh' sei Ehr" BWV 663: Vom Dank zum Trost. In: MuG 29 (1975), 106-110.

Een Nederlands liturgisch tijdschrift uit het begin van de 19e eeuw. In: KT 27 (1976), 162-175.

Liturgie tussen verval en vernieuwing: Enkele stemmen uit de tijd rond 1800. In: MILW 10 (April 1976), 16-28.

Liturgie. In: *Documentatieblad voor de Nederlandse Kerkgeschiedenis van de negentiende eeuw* (Feb. 1977), 26-36.

Roelof Bennink Janssonius: Een Nederlands hymnoloog uit de 19de eeuw. In: A.C. Honders, R. Steensma, J. Wit (ed.), *Het lied en de kerk: Hymnologische opstellen* [Studies van het Instituut voor Liturgiewetenschap No. 3] (Groningen 1977), 305-317.

Abraham im Kirchenlied: Einige skizzenhafte Notizen. In: *Bulletin IAH* 4 (April 1977), 29-35.

Een Compendium van achtergrondinformatie bij de 491 gezangen uit het Liedboek voor de Kerken (Amsterdam 1977, ²1978). Includes several contributions of Casper Honders:
1) Articles written on the following hymns: Nos. 14, 26, 68, 78, 110, 179, 221, 231, 257, 258, 259, 291, 292, 293, 304, 312, 314, 358, 390, 394, 399, 451, 452, 462, 464, 465, 466, 468, 469, 470, 471, 472, 474.
2) Biographical articles on N. Beets (cols. 1143-1144), A. van den Berg (cols. 1144-1146), P.L. van den Kasteele (col. 1195), J.J.L. ten Kate (cols. 1196-1197), J.J. Thomson (col. 1257), and J.E. van der Waals (cols. 1268-1269).

En wat zij zong hoorde ik dat psalmen waren (M. Nijhoff). In: A.C. Honders (ed.), *Klinkend geloof* (The Hague 1978), 97-103.

8

Una voce canentes...? Bemerkungen und Fragen zu 'Adoro devote..'. In: *Bulletin IAH* 7 (May 1979), 39-45.

Er zit muziek in: Enkele opmerkingen over de wetenschap der liturgie. Rede uitgesproken bij de aanvaarding van het ambt van gewoon lector in de liturgiewetenschap aan de Rijksuniversiteit te Groningen op 22 mei 1979 (The Hague [1979]), 18 pp.

1980

Het Reveil en het lied: Een eerste verkenning. In: J. van den Berg, P.L. Schram, S.L. Verheus (ed.), *Aspecten van het Reveil: opstellen ter gelegenheid van het vijftigjarig bestaan van de Stichting Reveil-Archief* (Kampen 1980), 106-125.

De uitgave van de werken van O. Noordmans. In: MILW 14 (April 1980), 44-48.

Remarks on the Postcommunio in some Reformed Liturgies. In: B.D. Spinks (ed.), *The Sacrifice of Praise: Studies on the Themes of Thanksgiving and Redemption in the Central Prayers of the Eucharist and Baptismal Liturgies, in Honour of Arthur Herbert Couratin* [Bibliotheca 'Ephemerides Liturgicae' "Subsidia" 19] (Rome 1981), 143-157.

Psalm 1 in de liturgie. In: J. D'Hollander (ed.), *Liber Amicorum Prof. Ignace de Sutter 1911-1981* (Sint-Niklaas 1981), 174-179.

Psalm singing in London 1550-1553. In: *Bulletin IAH* 9 (May 1981), 64-69.

Een liturgie voor een passie-dienst. In: MILW 15 (Sept. 1981), 9-14.

Een vrouw achter het Liedboek. In: MILW 15 (Sept. 1981), 21-28.

De taal in de liturgie. In: *Kosmos en Oekumene* (1981), 123-127.

Veranderingen in de liturgie: Voorstellen uit de tijd rond 1850. In: MILW 16 (Sept. 1982), 12-25.

Kerkelijk jaar en zondagse pericopen. In: MILW 16 (Sept. 1982), 26-32.

Einige Gedanken und Überlegungen zu BWV 685. In: MuK 53 (1983), 187-192.

Das Abendmahl nach der Antwerpener Ordnung 1567 und (1579) 1672. In: I. Pahl (ed.) *Coena Domini I: Die Abendmahlsliturgie der Reformationskirchen im 16./17. Jahrhundert* [Spicilegium Friburgense: Texte zur Geschichte des kirchlichen Lebens 29] (Freiburg [Switzerland] 1983), 273-298.

Das Abendmahl nach den Ordnungen Johannes a Lascos (1550) 1555 und Marten Microns (1554). In: idem, 431-460.

Das Abendmahl nach der Ordnung des Petrus Dathenus 1566. In: idem, 525-535.

Das Abendmahl nach der Ordnung der Remonstraten 1640. In: idem, 563-599.

Het Reveil en het lied: Voortgezette verkenning. In: MILW 17 (Sept. 1983), 11-23.

Over ranken en vruchten: Opmerkingen bij gezang 78 uit het Liedboek. In: MILW 17 (Sept. 1983), 41-45.

Karl Barth over kerkmuziek. In: MILW 17 (Sept. 1983), 46.

Blik op de hymnologie. In: MILW 18 (Sept. 1984), 92-114.

Anglice omnia Fiunt... Een brief van 10 November 1550 van Valerandus Pollanus (Londen) aan Heinrich Bullinger (Zürich). In: MILW 18 (Sept. 1984), 115-118.

"Het oude jaar is nu voorbij", BWV 614. In: W.H. Morel van Mourik (ed.), *Feestbundel aangeboden aan Adriaan Cornelis Schuurman ter gelegenheid van zijn 80e verjaardag* (Den Haag [1984]), 53-57.

10

Kerkmuziek na 1945: Een tocht door een deel van de protestantse Achterhoek. In: *Werkmap voor Liturgie* 18 (Hilversum 1984), 94-104.

De klank der woorden. In: *Preludium/Concertgebouwnieuws* (April 1984), 2-4.

Hinter den Kulissen... In: *Bulletin IAH* 13 (1985), 9-11.

Ach! Liebe Seele, bitte du... In: *In de Waagschaal* 14 (1985), 495-500.

Van Groningen naar Bach. In: *Met in zijn jaszak 17 eendeëieren: 17 essays ter gelegenheid van de 300ste verjaardag van Johann Sebastian Bach* (Groningen 1985), 65-69.

Tekst en Uitleg. In: *Het Orgel* 81 (1985), 265-269.

Over Bachs schouder... Een bundel opstellen (Groningen 1985), 148 pp.

Nieuwe Kerkmuziek. In: K. Hoek, W. Oosterwal, H. Ruiter (ed.), *Nieuwe muziek in de liturgie* (Harlingen 1987), 9-14.

...In deiner Mitte, Jerusalem!... (Ps. 116). In: *Bulletin IAH* [Sondernummer: Dankesgabe an Markus Jenny] (Nov. 1987), 43-53.

Liturgie: Barsten en breuken (Kampen 1988), 188 pp.

Het "Orgel-Büchlein" gehoord vanuit de teksten. In: *Bachs "Orgel-Büchlein" in nieuw perspectief: Studies over Bachs "Orgel-Büchlein". Verslag van het Internationale Bach-Congres van de Nederlandse Organistenvereniging 1985 te Groningen* [Kerkmuziek & Liturgie No. 1] (Voorburg 1988), 21-51.

Mijn lief is mijn... Over het Hooglied in het werk van J.S. Bach [Kerkmuziek & Liturgie No. 2] (Voorburg 1988), 64 pp.

Vergleich von BWV 79^2 mit BWV 234^5. In: R. Steiger (ed.), *Parodie und Vorlage: Zum Bachschen Parodieverfahren und seiner*

Bedeutung für die Hermeneutik. Bericht über die Tagung Heidelberg 1988. [Internationale Arbeitsgemeinschaft für theologische Bachforschung, Bulletin 2] (Heidelberg 1988), 146-149.

"Als troostte ons niet eenzelfde lied": Over de "Zondagsliederen" van Allard Pierson. In: JLO 5 (1989), 213-226.

Super flumina Babylonis... Bemerkungen zu BWV 653b. In: *Bulletin IAH* 17 (June 1989), 53-60.

1990

Crematie: met en zonder vraagteken. In: A. Blijlevens et al.: (ed.), *Op dood en leven*, vol. 3: *Crematie: Elementen voor begrafenisliturgie, theologie en pastoraat rond de dood uit 20 jaar werkmap Liturgie (1966-1985)* (Hilversum 1990), 77-81.

Crematie en pastoraat. In: idem, 82-86.

Der Choralkantatenjahrgang (1724-25): Einige Überlegungen und Bemerkungen. In: R. Steiger (ed.), *Johann Sebastian Bachs Choralkantaten als Choral-bearbeitungen. Bericht über die Tagung Leipzig 1990* [Internationale Arbeitsgemeinschaft für theologische Bachforschung, Bulletin 3] (Heidelberg 1991), 101-108.

"Mein Seel auf Rosen geht..." In: *Tijdschrift voor Oude Muziek* (Feb. 1991), 14-17.

J.S. Bach en het kerklied. In: JLO 7 (1991), 185-195.

"Zo doe Hij ook aan mij...": De psalmberijming van Datheen (1566) en de staatsberijming (1773). In: J. de Bruin (ed.), *Psalmzingen in de Nederlanden: Vanaf de zestiende eeuw tot heden* (Kampen 1991), 201-213.

In der Welt habt ihr Angst: Über Leben und Werk Hugo Distlers (1908-1942). In: *Der Kirchenmusiker* 44 (1993), 1-13.

The Reformers on Church Music. Forthcoming in the Howard G. Hageman Festschrift (1993).

Church Music in Iceland during the Nineteenth Century[1]

Frans Brouwer

Introduction

"Eene eeuw van worsteling" ("a century of wrestling"), was the way the Utrecht professor of church history, S.D. van Veen typified the history of Christianity in the nineteenth century.[2] After the break with the past through various revolutions and the general effects of the Enlightenment, people were looking for new directions in different disciplines. Reorientation of frontiers, forms of government, cultures and technology went hand in hand with a renewal of the ancient into new forms of expression for the "most individual emotion." Great personalities assumed or demonstrated the power of genius: Napoleon and Bismarck as military heroes, Ludwig van Beethoven and Richard Wagner in the world of music, Friedrich Hegel and Charles Darwin as scientists, artists like Francisco Goya and Auguste Rodin, just to mention a few. It was a transitional period that did not pass without struggle: a century of wrestling, understood spiritually as well as physically.

Recent published results of research into the musical aspects of congregational singing in the Reformation churches of Europe during the nineteenth century[3] have generally omitted any des-

---

1 I am grateful to Mr. Arni Eymundsson of Odijk, the Netherlands, who at my request made several working-translations of prefaces from Icelandic hymn- and chorale books in 1989.

2 S.D. van Veen: *Eene eeuw van worsteling: Overzicht van de geschiedenis van het Christendom in de negentiende eeuw* (Groningen 1904).

3 For example, F. Blume, *Geschichte der evangelischen Kirchenmusik* (Kassel ²1965), especially 217-269; N. Temperley, *The Music of the English Parish Church*, 2 vols. (Cambridge 1979); G. Oost, *Een beschouwing over de kerkmuziek in Nederland gedurende de 19e eeuw* (Den Haag 1982); J.R. Luth, *"Daer wert om 't seerste uytgekreten..." Bijdragen tot een geschiedenis van de gemeentezang in het Nederlandse Gereformeerde protestantisme ± 1550 - ± 1852*, 2 vols. (Kampen 1986), especially 243-399; F. Brouwer, *Vernieuwing in drieklank: Een onderzoek naar de liturgische ontwikkelingen in Denemarken (± 1800 tot ± 1950)* (Utrecht 1990), especially 345-

13

cription of the Icelandic church music of the period.[4] But in a special way developments in Iceland can be characterized as a "wrestling" that reveals interesting facets that need to be compared with church music traditions in other countries. Territories such as Iceland, which have been in a relatively isolated position, geographically and historically, often enshrine a long-conserved cultural heritage.

This chapter is a brief overview of Icelandic congregational singing and its accompaniment until the earliest years of the twentieth century. It is based on four primary sources, the work of three Icelandic musicians: a unison melody book and a three-part chorale book by Pétur Guðjonsson (1861[5] and 1878[6], respectively), the first four-part chorale book in Iceland by Jónas Helgason (1885[7]) and the four-part chorale book by Bjarni Þorsteinsson (1903[8]).

Survey of the History of Icelandic Church Music Until the Nineteenth Century

No music other than congregational singing and liturgical chant (the so-called "messusaung" sung by the minister) was heard during the regular services of the Lutheran Church of Iceland until the twentieth century. The development from the beginnings of polyphony mediated through music from the Netherlands and Italy to the church music styles of the Baroque, Classic and Romantic periods passed Iceland by. Icelanders knew nothing of vocal or instrumental accompaniment of congregational singing, except the use, probably from around

---

402; see also Luth's chapter concerning organ accompaniment in Germany during the nineteenth century elsewhere in this volume.

4   In an unpublished German State Examination Church Music A thesis Hörður Askelsson surveyed the church music history of Iceland from the Reformation to 1972: *Lutherlieder in Island, Bestandteil der isländischen Kirchenmusikgeschichte* ([Heidelberg] 1981). Some of the information presented here is taken from Askelsson's essay.

5   Pétur Guðjonsson, *Íslenzk Sálmasaungs- og messubók* (København 1861).

6   Pétur Guðjonsson, *Sálmasöngsbók* (Reykjavík 1878).

7   Jónas Helgason, *Kirkjusöngsbók* (København 1885, Reykjavík ²1906).

8   Bjarni Þorsteinsson, *Íslenzk Sálmasöngbók með fjorum röddum* (Reykjavík 1903, ²1926).

1835,[9] of the "langspil" (a "psaltery" with three strings), and the harmonium and its predecessor. In 1800 there was just one harmonium in the country,[10] but from around 1865 a slow increase in the number of instruments began to occur. However, by 1906 only ten churches are reported as possessing an harmonium.[11] The development of choirs with their four-part singing, which acquired a fixed liturgical place in the Sunday morning service around the turn of the century (through the influence of Jónas Helgason's four-part chorale book of 1885), became so influential that congregational singing was quickly eliminated. Only in recent decades has there been a return to the practice of congregational song. Most churches obtained harmoniums for accompanying their congregations sometime around 1940. Pipe organs became more general in Iceland only after 1950.[12]

What were the conditions that created this limited tradition of church music in Iceland over the centuries? To begin with, the cultural heritage of the Icelanders of the Middle Ages emphasized other artistic expressions, namely, the poetry and narrative craft of their epic songs and sagas. During the long years

---

9 The "langspil" seems related to the Norwegian "langleik," which had tonic and dominant drone strings. This instrument originated in Northern Europe during the 1830s and was used for singing lessons in schools and churches. See A. Buchner, *Handboek van de muziek-instrumenten* (Zutphen 1985), 278. In 1855 Ari Sæmundsen published the first collection of hymn melodies issued since 1594 - in a letter notation - under the title: *Leiðarvísir til að spila á langspil og til að læra sálmalög eptir notum og Nótur med Bókstöfum* ("Instruction on How to Play the 'Langspil' and to Learn Hymn Melodies by Notes and Notes with Letters") (Akureyri 1855).

10 There is a tradition that suggests that Magnús Stephensen brought the first harmonium to Iceland in 1800. It was placed in the church of Leirá (north of Reykjavík, on the Borgarfjord) and was used for worship. This instrument, however, cannot have been a harmonium, because the harmonium, with vibrating reeds rather than the usual pipes and resonators of the organ, was first made by the Viennese instrument maker Anton Häckl in 1818, after the "orgue expressif" by the Frenchmen Gabriel Joseph Grenié and Alexandre François Debain in 1810. The instrument which was brought to Iceland by Magnús Stephensen, could have been an "Aeoline" or something similar: a free-reed keyboard instrument with vibrating reeds and resonators above; see C. Sachs, *De geschiedenis van de muziekinstrumenten* (Utrecht 1969), 460; T. Willemze, *Algemene Muziekleer* (Utrecht 1979), 366-367 and Buchner, op. cit., 149.

11 Communication from Kristján Valur Ingólfsson in Ísafjörður, dated 7 May 1986.

12 The Hallgrímskirkja, Reykjavík, the largest church in Iceland, installed a new 72-rank organ, the work of the German organ builder Hans Gerd Klais of Bonn, in 1992.

of Danish domination (1387-1918/1944) the political and cultural needs of conserving Icelandic identity created conservation skills that maintained and developed national characteristics. On the one hand, the all-pervasive Icelandic literary influence erected a barrier to the development of other artistic practices, such as music. On the other hand, resistance of the Icelanders to all Danish influences on their country perpetuated their artistic insularity. Thus the liturgical prescriptions for the Danish monarchy, authorized by the Danish king, were invalid for Iceland. Similarly, the authorized Danish hymnals were useless in Iceland because of the obduracy of the Icelandic bishops and ministers who insisted that only Icelandic was the authentic ecclesiastical language for the worship of their churches.[13] Thus Danish church music practices had no influence in Iceland until the second half of the nineteenth century.

Another cause of Icelandic insularity has been the general poverty of the Icelandic population. Danish economic dominance coupled with periodic destruction caused by volcanic eruptions produced an economic situation in which there was no surplus to purchase expensive items such as organs. In brief, Iceland was in an isolated position geographically, economically, and also musically.

Within this musical insularity singing developed in a particular way from the sixteenth until late in the nineteenth century, especially because of the absence of instrumental accompaniment. This singing approximates to the local, improvisational style, the so-called "Kingosang" in certain territories of Norway, Denmark and on the Faroe Islands.[14] At first the Icelandic hymn repertory consisted of 328 hymns, expanded to 379 in 1619. The basic corpus was for the most part collected by bishop Guðbrandur Þorláksson (1571-1627) in *Ein Ny Psalma Bok* (1589)[15] and in *Graduale: Ein Almeneleg Messusöngs Bók*

---

13 This was not the case in other areas that came under the rule of Denmark. For example, the church in Norway had to use Danish for all spoken and sung texts in worship until 1813/1840, and also in the church in the Faroe Islands until 1930/1960.

14 See F. Brouwer, op. cit., 353-360.

15 Guðbrandur Þorláksson, *Ein Ny Psalma Bok* (Hólar 1589, ²1619, facs. Reykjavík 1948).

$(1594)^{16}$ — in common Icelandic parlance known as "Grallarinn" (pronounced as "gràtlarin"). This repertory consisted of sixteenth-century texts, translated into Icelandic either directly from German and Latin or from Danish translations, and was essentially the same as the basic Reformation hymn repertory in Germany and the other Nordic countries. The melodies associated with these Icelandic hymn texts are essentially those that originated in Reformation and post-Reformation Germany. The musical notation of the "Grallarinn" is clear and exhibits few variations from the forms found in German and Danish sources. The sixteenth-century Icelandic hymn repertory gave rise to the development of the so-called "Grallarinn" singing, which continued until the early nineteenth century. A distinctive feature of this singing was the "Tvísöngur" (literally: two-songs), a kind of organum practice with a tenor, the *vox principalis*, the melody of the hymn, and a so-called "bassus", the *vox organalis*, an improvised counter-melody in fifths, and occasionally in primes and thirds, above and beneath the melody. "Tvísöngur" were sung from the beginning of the seventeenth century, at first in the home or at work, but from the end of the eighteenth century also in the Sunday morning service. When this singing entered the church it was customary for the minister to sing the "bassus" (if he could sing!), and the deacon to lead the congregation in singing the melody.[17] A preference for the lydian mode meant that dorian melodies were transmuted into the lydian mode. "Grallarinn" singing became chaotic, and at the end of the nineteenth century was described as being "sung" by screaming voices.[18]

One example of a "Tvísaung" is *Gef þinni kristni góðan frið*, with

16 Guðbrandur Þorláksson, *Graduale: Ein Almeneleg Messusöngs Bók* (Hólar 1594, ^{2}1607).

17 Bjarni Þorsteinsson, *Íslenzk Þjóðlög* (København 1906-1909), 770.

18 M. Stephensen, *Evangelisk-kristileg Messusaungs- og Sálma-Bók* (Leirargørdum 1801), 282-283. Magnús Stephensen states that the people sing with booming and wavering voices, and do not keep good time or observe rests. Some try to sing faster than the rest and gasp for breath, while others lengthen-out the melody, drawling more and more. Magnús Stephenson continues: "the most beautiful way of singing is obtained when one sings by the notes." He adds further: "It is terrible to hear and see singers force a scream from their throats, with swollen veins on their foreheads and faces." (I thank Mrs. Paula Vermeyden of Amsterdam for assistance in translating this passage.)

the melody of *Verleih uns Frieden gnädiglich*,[19] following the authentic form of the melody as found in the 1594 "Grallarin". This "Tvísaung" was transcribed at the end of the nineteenth century from the oral practice of the people by Bjarni Þorsteinsson (see Ex. 1).[20]

Example 1

19 See *Evangelisches Kirchengesangbuch*, No. 139, according to the version of Wittenberg 1529/Leipzig 1545.
20 Bjarni Þorsteinsson, *Íslenzk Þjóðlög* (København 1906-1909), 796.

18

The addition of a second leading note and melismas are significant. The "bassus" crosses above and below the cantus firmus and therefore differs from the organum practice of the eleventh century. From around 1835 "Tvísöngur" might be accompanied by the "langspil" (see above).[21]

Pétur Guðjonsson

During the second half of the nineteenth century the practice of Icelandic church music, which had been strongly determined by tradition and region, went through a turbulent process of renewal that extended until about 1940. In the preface to the 1936 chorale book the editors, Sigfús Einarsson and Páll Ísolfsson, draw attention to the work of the primary motivator of this renewal, Pétur Guðjonsson,[22] and the fact that for his hundredth birthday, commemorated in 1912, two compositions were specifically written.[23] In other words, the importance of Pétur Guðjonsson in connection with the development of Icelandic church music has been obvious and greatly valued in his own country.

Pétur Guðjonsson[24] was born in Hrafnagili (in the Eyjafjarðar area, west of Akureyri), on 29 November 1812, the son of a farmer. In 1832 he left the northern part of Iceland to attend the Latin school of Bessastaðir (near Reykjavík), the academic

---

21 On the "Tvísöngur," see Hallgrímur Helgason, Íslenzkar Tónmenntir: Kvæðalög, fordaga peirra, bygging og flutningsháttur (Reykjavík 1980), 134 et seq.; Bjarni Þorsteinsson, Íslenzk Þjóðlög.

22 Sigfús Einarsson og Páll Ísolfsson, Sálmasöngsbók til Kirkju (...) (Reykjavík 1936), iv.

23 A composition for soprano-solo, choir and organ (harmonium), a setting of a poem by Guðmundur Guðmundsson, by Sigfús Einarsson, and a four-part harmonization of three stanzas by Einar P. Jónsson.

24 Biographical information relating Pétur Guðjonsson (sometimes written as Pjetur Guðjohnsen) is scarce. One will search in vain for his name in the three best-known Icelandic biographical dictionaries, such as Dansk Biografisk Leksikon, neither in The New Grove Dictionary of Music and Musicians, and in Musik in Geschichte und Gegenwart. Gösta Morin, et. al. (ed.), Sohlmans Musiklexikon: Nordiskt och allmänt uppslagsverk för tonkunst, musikliv och dans, vol. 2 (Stockholm 1950), 768, has an entry written by Jón Þórarinsson. Einar Jónsson wrote a more extended biography in the preface to Pétur Guðjonsson's chorale book, Sálmasöngsbók (Reykjavík 1878), v-xiv.

centre of Iceland in those days, where he stayed for two and a half years. Later on, in 1846, Guðjonsson became a teacher in this school and taught candidates for the ordained ministry. From 1837 to 1840 he made himself conversant with congregational singing and playing the harmonium at a Danish teachers' seminary.[25] In Denmark he was impressed by the practice of church music, especially congregational singing in Copenhagen. It was in Copenhagen that he encountered the work of the Danish leader of church and folk music at that time, the organist and pedagogue A.P. Berggreen (1801-1880). On his return to Iceland Pétur Guðjonsson became an elementary school teacher and an advocate of singing hymns according to the Danish manner. He therefore supported the purchase of a harmonium for Reykjavík Domkirkja, where he was appointed organist in 1840, a position he retained until his death on 25 August 1877. For almost forty years Pétur Guðjonsson was considered to be *the* church musician and music pedagogue of Iceland.

Pétur Guðjonsson's Danish publications exerted a determining influence on his work in Iceland. First, he supplied the need of a theory of music,[26] because a basic knowledge of music, such as staff notation, was either imperfect or non-existent.[27] The distribution of his melody book (1861) and his three-part chorale book (published posthumously in 1878) was an important ad-

---

25 Einar Jónsson, in Pétur Guðjonsson, *Sálmasöngsbók*, vii, mentions the village "Joenstrup" on Sjælland where Pétur Guðjonsson is supposed to have studied, but "Joenstrup" is not a Danish place-name. This should be "Jonstrup", near Copenhagen, which had a teacher's seminary. It was at this seminary that Pétur Guðjonsson came into contact with A.P. Berggreen's musical practice.

26 Pétur Guðjonsson, *Leiðarvísir til þekkingar á saunglistinni* (Reykjavík 1870). This was an adaptation of *Musikens Katechismus* from 1864, published by the Copenhagen organist Johan Chr. Gebauer (1808-1884), which was itself a Danish translation of one of the most common German music theoretical manuals, namely, J.C. Lobe, *Katechismus der Musik* (Leipzig 1851). See Pétur Guðjonsson, *Sálmasöngsbók*, xiv, and N. Schiørring, *Musikkens Historie i Danmark*, vol. 2 (København 1978), 238.

27 In 1801 Magnús Stephensen remarked: "(It should) be desirable that everyone, especially the ministers themselves, should seriously introduce and maintain good singing in their churches, so that public worship can be experienced in a dignified way; with regard to this they should pay close attention to the relevant instruction in the back of this book, concerning the three new hymns with musical notation, and general congregational singing as it ought to be"; Magnús Stephensen, *Evangelisk-kristeleg Messusaungs- og Sálma-Bók* (Leirargørdum 1801), xviii.

vance in practical Icelandic church music. This becomes obvious when these two publications are compared with the later chorale books of Jónas Helgason (1885) and Bjarni Þorsteinsson (1903). Within a period of almost forty years the traditional Icelandic "Tvísöngur" gave place to "restored" melodies, mostly in three or four-part harmonizations, accompanied by an harmonium or sung by a choir. Considering that Iceland was a very sparsely populated area, with poor communications between the remote churches, these radical changes were accomplished within a relatively short period of time.

Pétur Guðjonsson's *Sálmasaungs- og messubók* (1861)[28] contains 110 unison melodies for the hymn texts found in the *Evangelisk-kristeleg Messusaungs- og Sálma-Bók* of Magnús Stephensen (1801), and for a few texts from older hymnals. In the preface Pétur Guðjonsson expounds the motivation for his twenty years of "restoration work," and describes his working method. It begins with a beautiful panegyric on the Italian art of singing and composition during the time of Palestrina:

Since Iceland missed all the fine arts,[29] except poetry, from the beginning, one can say this above all with regard to the art of singing. We are now, in 1860, at the same stage as the people in Italy were five hundred years ago, with just one difference: the Italians loved this art passionately and when there was someone among them who showed an exceptional talent for that art, everyone was ready not only to help him along the road to the practice of the art, but also to shower him with titles and riches. They founded schools for this art in almost every town of Italy, and attracted the best musicians and masters from other countries (Spain, France and The Netherlands) as teachers who often gave free lessons to young people.[30]

---

28 See previous note. There is no direct relationship between the publication of the melody book of 1861 and the *Nýr Vidbætir*, a supplement to the 1801 hymnal, published in the same year, 1861. On page 5 of the preface to his melody book Pétur Guðjonsson explains his decision to issue only the melodies. Although he would have preferred to have published the melodies in two, three or four-part harmonizations, such an edition would have cost twice as much and therefore would not have been an economic proposition. However, he emphasizes the didactic advantage of including only the unison melody, that is, concentrating the attention more on the melody itself than would be the case in a multi-part harmonization.

29 With regard to the word "íþrótt" which is used by the author here, see the concluding paragraph of this chapter.

30 Pétur Guðjonsson, *Sálmasaung*, 1.

Thus Pétur Guðjonsson characterizes the culturally isolated position of Iceland until the second half of the last century. Further, he considers the failure to provide singing lessons in both dioceses, Hólar and Skálholt, as well as the decay and mutilation of the original melodies from the pre- and post-Reformation periods, the primary causes of poor congregational singing: pre-Reformation decay as the result of the musical ignorance of the priests; post-Reformation mutilation through an oral tradition that rendered the melodies formless — because the people could not read music even if it was provided: "It cannot be disguised that (...) the melodies of Grallarinn (...) had become monsters (...) by the oral tradition of the people, [monsters] by which all pure feelings are put to rout," he wrote concerning the "Grallarinn singing." To improve Icelandic congregational singing he believed that singing lessons in all the schools was essential, after having first made available the original, simple forms of the melodies in clear staff notation. For his restoration work Pétur Guðjonsson ordered sources to be sent from Germany and Denmark (including, among others, Niels Jesperssøn's *Graduale* of 1573). In his annotations on the hymns he often refers to G. Fr. von Tucher's *Schatz des evangelischen Kirchengesangs im ersten Jahrhundert der Reformation*,[31] and to the Danish chorale books of F. Chr. Breitendich,[32] and H.O.C. Zinck.[33] In addition to "old" melodies in relatively simplified versions with regard to rhythm and melodic form, which are tonal rather than modal, Pétur Guðjonsson also incorporated some hymn melodies by Danish composers of the day, for instance, A.P. Berggreen, among others. In his "melody reconstructions" he endeavored to bring textual accents into line with musical accents as much as possible (see Ex. 2).

Although the introduction of the practical outcome of his ideas found much opposition, Pétur Guðjonsson's church music agenda was approved of and implemented in many places.[34]

Pétur Guðjonsson's various reforms in Iceland were in sympathy with Danish practices of congregational singing which were also

---

31 G. Fr. von Tucher, *Schatz des evangelischen Kirchengesangs im ersten Jahrhundert der Reformation*, 2 vols. (Leipzig 1848-1867).
32 F. Chr. Breitendich, *Fuldstændig Choral-Bog (...)* (København 1764).
33 H.O.C. Zinck, *Koral-Melodier til den Evangelisk-christelige Psalmebog* (København 1801).
34 Pétur Guðjonsson, *Sálmasaung*, 2-5.

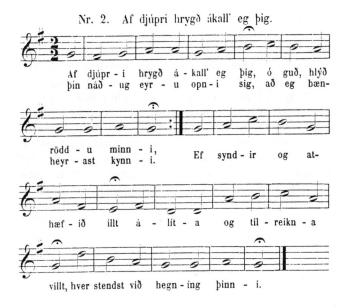

Nr. 2. Af djúpri hrygð ákall' eg þig.

Af djúpr - i hrygð á - kall' eg þig, ó guð, hlýð
þín náð - ug eyr - u opn - i sig, að eg bæn-

rödd - u minn - i,
heyr - ast kynn - i.   Ef synd - ir og at-

hæf - ið illt á - lít - a og til - reikn - a

villt, hver stendst við hegn - íng þinn - i.

Example 2

common in other countries of nineteenth-century Europe: namely, the demise of the isorhythmic "Grallarinn singing" and the
"Tvísöngur"; the first beginnings of a return to modal melodies;[35] and the improvement of the teaching of singing. All of
this was achieved under the adage: "Back to the sources of the
Reformation period."

Two Chorale Books (1878 and 1885)

The first (three-part) chorale book of Iceland was published
almost one year after the death of its composer, Pétur Guðjonsson. In 1878 a student of theology, Einar Jónsson, edited and
published posthumously Pétur Guðjonsson's work, dating from

---

35 See his explanation of the phrygian and mixolydian modes in his preface; *Sálmasaung*, 11.

23

the period 1861-1877.[36] Einar Jónsson explains in the preface that it had become necessary to publish harmonizations of the melodies because there were already "small organs (harmonia)" in many churches. According to Pétur Guðjonsson, four-part harmonizations do not serve the development of the singing as do three-part settings, because neither in churches nor in people's homes were there "enough singers for well sounding three-part singing, more problems are created by four-part singing"; for it is "better to sing well with fewer voice-parts than worse with more voices."[37] This chorale book was designed for use with the 1801 hymnal, together with some hymns from the new 1871 hymnal by Helgi Hálfdánarson (1826-1894).[38] The musical repertory of the 1878 chorale book comprised around 120 melodies, of which there were a greater number of Danish melodies than in the 1861 collection. The influence of Danish congregational singing in Iceland, begun by Pétur Guðjonsson's importation of A.P. Berggreens ideas on the practice, led to the steady increase in popularity of a number of Danish romantic melodies.[39]

A.P. Berggreen's influence on Pétur Guðjonsson is evident. When Berggreen's four-part harmonization of *Aus tiefer Not* (1875)[40] is compared with the Icelandic three-part harmonization (1878),[41] it will be seen that the notation is almost identical, including the fermatas and punctuation marks between the musical phrases (see Ex. 3a and b).

Major differences between the two harmonizations occur at the beginning of the penultimate melodic line, where Pétur Guð-

---

36 According to Einar Jónsson's own words, with much respect to A.P. Berggreen's comments on the original version of Pétur Guðjonsson; Pétur Guðjonsson, *Sálmasöngsbók*, iii, xv.

37 Pétur Guðjonsson, *Sálmasöngsbók*, xiv.

38 Helgi Hálfdánarson, *Sálma-bók til að hafa við guðsþjónustugjørð í kirkjum og heimahúsum* (Reykjavík 1871).

39 From the 1830s a unique genre of church hymn developed in Denmark, the so-called "romance". C.E.F. Weyse, H. Rung, J.P.E. Hartmann and Chr. Barnekow were the leading composers who wrote in this style. A.P. Berggreen, however, enriched Danish congregational singing with romantic melodies which had more in common with the traditional chorale tradition than with the romances; see F. Brouwer, op. cit., 363-402.

40 *Af Dybsens Nöd*; A.P. Berggreen, *Melodier til (...) "Evangelisk-christelig Psalmebog" (...)* (København 1875), 96.

41 *Af djúpri hryggð ákalla' eg þig*; Pétur Guðjonsson, *Sálmasöngsbók*, 2-3 (No. 2b).

Example 3a

jonsson deviates significantly from Berggreen, and at the beginning, where Pétur begins in e minor and Berggreen with an E major seventh chord; other differences are infinitesimally small. This comparison shows that Pétur Guðjonsson's pursuits were focused on a return to the chorale of the Reformation, which therefore ran contrary to his only non-Icelandic church music reference, the four-part harmonizations of his teacher, A.P. Berggreen.

Viggo Sanne (1840-1896) cooperated with the publisher of the first four-part chorale book of dom organist Jónas Helgason (1839-1903) in 1885. It is likely that Jónas Helgason requested the assistance of the Danish organist because Sanne had become Berggreen's successor as "Sanginspektør" (1880), and had edited the sixth edition of Berggreen's chorale book (1883). In addition, in 1875 Sanne had documented the melody repertory of Vartov Kirke in Copenhagen, which may have been the primary reason for his involvement with the Icelandic chorale book be-

Nr. 2 b. Af djúpri hryggð ákalla' eg þig.

Example 3b

cause of the Danish romance melodies which were introduced in Iceland from around 1870.[42]

Jónas Helgason's chorale book comprises 178 harmonizations and 22 unison-notated melodies, and forms a musical repertory suitable for 533 of the 535 hymn texts of the 1871 hymnal. The relationship between textual and musical accents was determined by the criterion of the metrical foot, as was usual in the nineteenth century: 2/4 for a trochaic metre; 3/4 for a dactylic metre,

---

42 See F. Brouwer, op. cit., 396-400.

26

etc. The matching of the meaning of the text by suitable music was a secondary concern. In his preface to the 1885 chorale book Jónas Helgason indicates that the harmonizations can be used as organ, harmonium or "fortepiano" accompaniments, but that they are also suitable for a capella four-part singing.[43] Jónas Helgason's chorale book was the first publication in Iceland to include Danish, or Danish-orientated, romance melodies in staff notation. Although most of the melodies appear in isometric forms, some small concessions were made towards a more rhythmic variation in melody and harmony. From the metronome indications, however, it is clear that the tempo of the singing remained slow (♩ = 50 with C) (see Ex. 4).

Nr. 57. Ó Jesú, brunnur blessunar (Af djúpri hrygð ákalla' eg þig.

Example 4

---

43 Jónas Helgason, *Kirkjusöngsbók*, 1. The 1871 hymnal consists of 267 texts from Magnús Stephensen's collection (1801), 200 from the supplement (1861), and 67 new hymn texts.

Bjarni Þorsteinsson's chorale book (1903)

Bjarni Þorsteinsson (1861-1938), minister and musician in Siglufjörður (north west from Akureyri), concentrated his energies towards the improvement of Icelandic congregational singing, and did so by building on the work of the minister and hymn writer Stefán Þorarensen (1831-1892).[44] He argued for the building of good organs and the provision of more institutions for the education of church organists, who, in his opinion, should also teach hymn-singing in elementary schools.

His remark that "congregational singing in our churches is without question mostly very poor"[45] indicates that Þorsteinsson was aware of the practice in foreign countries. Most of his examples probably derived from his Danish experiences while he was a theological student. This hypothesis is confirmed by the presence in his chorale book (1903) of a great number of Danish melodies and harmonizations by such nineteenth-century romance composers as J.P.E. Hartmann (1805-1900), C.E.F. Weyse (1774-1842), H. Matthison-Hansen (1807-1890) and others. Similarly, many of his sources were Danish, notably A.P. Berggreen's chorale book. But he also introduced some Swedish and English melodies into Iceland. According to Þorsteinsson's preface, the English melodies are tender and charming, and simply learned. He quotes a sentence of Stefán Þorarensen, from his supplement to Jónas Helgason's chorale book (1891): "Our singing is already dull enough, so that one need not look for more of those heavy melodies than is necessary."[46]

Bjarni Þorsteinsson's contribution to the improvement of Icelandic congregational singing includes, in addition to the above-mentioned aspects, a thorough "sanitation" of the melodies and their harmonizations, which had become necessary following the publication of a new hymnal in 1886.[47] Bjarni Þorsteinsson reproached Jónas Helgason, who had published his chorale book just one year before (1885), for not having consulted with the hymnal commission. The chairman of this commission was Helgi

---

44 Bjarni Þorsteinsson was referred to above in connection with his transcription of old Icelandic folk songs and "Tvísöngur".
45 Bjarni Þorsteinsson, *Sálmasöngbók*, viii.
46 Ibid., vi.
47 *Sálmabók til kirkju- og heima-söngs* (Reykjavík 1886, [7]1903, [9]1907, [19]1929).

Hálfdánarson, who contributed 210 of his own texts to the new hymnal book, but Jónas Helgason's chorale book gave no melody indications for these texts, nor for the 140 or so new hymn texts by Valdemar Briem (1848-1930) also included in the new hymnal. Bjarni Þorsteinsson also criticized the great number and quality of the melodies included in Jónas Helgason's chorale book of 1885. Therefore for his chorale book Bjarni Þorsteinsson eliminated, altered or renewed well-known melodies and added some new ones.[48] With regard to the four-part harmonizations, he simplified the voice-parts of old harmonizations and corrected the typographical errors of the 1885 chorale book. He also transposed some melodies into other keys to improve their singability by the congregation[49] (see Ex. 5). Bjarni Þorsteinsson's chorale book comprised in 174 four-part harmonizations for the 650 texts of the 1886 hymnal.

Bjarni Þorsteinsson built on the influence of Berggreen, which had become known in Iceland through the work of Pétur Guðjonsson, and extended the Icelandic hymn repertory by the inclusion of more Danish romance melodies. Chorale melodies of the Reformation era continued to be given in isorhythmic form but with romantic harmonizations. It took a long time, almost exactly one hundred years, before the fruits of the German and Danish church music renewal movements[50] completed the endeavors of Pétur Guðjonsson, who had worked for the ideal of the Reformation chorale in Iceland. It was only late in this century that sixteenth-century melodies began to be sung in more or less original rhythmic forms.

The preface of the chorale book of 1903 mentions some interesting data concerning the tempo of the Icelandic congregational singing around 1900. It was Bjarni Þorsteinsson's experience that organists simply did not observe the tempo indications found in the chorale books; he therefore gave up the Berggreen tradition of including metronome markings. Instead he prescribed just four rough guides for the singing tempi, indicated by the letters a-d: fast and lively (a); moderately fast (b); moderately slow (c); and slow (d). These indications reveal the general tendency to quicken the singing tempo, in contrast to the established prac-

---

48 Bjarni Þorsteinsson, *Sálmasöngbók*, v-vi.
49 Ibid., vii.
50 See F. Brouwer, op. cit., 412-438.

29

tice of the time. Bjarni Þorsteinsson wanted the content of the text and the context of the occasion to determine the singing tempo. The congregation should "practice two things: singing not too loud, and not too slow." By this explicit statement, taken together with his comment that "in the churches of other countries the singing tempo is faster than here," it is clear that Iceland experienced a slower development with regard to the renewal of church music, from the second half of the nineteenth century, than most other Reformation churches of Europe.

Nr. 78. Af djúpri hryggð ákalla' eg þig.

Úr hryggð - ar djúp - i háтt til þín, ó herr - a guð, jeg kvein - - a;
þitt bless - að eyr - a beyg til mín, svo bót jeg fá - i mein - - a. Ef reikn - a

vilt - u mis - gjörð manns og mun - a gjörv - öll brot - in hans, hver stund fær stað - izt ein - - a?

Example 5

Appendix: the Concept "íþrótt"

Reading the introductions by Pétur Guðjonsson, Einar Jónsson and Bjarni Þorsteinsson, that stand at the beginning of their respective melody and chorale books, being a devotee of athletics, I was struck by the word "íþrótt", which is often now translated as "sport(s)". Using that translation one could render the following sentences thus: "This piece [Palestrina's *Stabat mater dolorosa*) is still considered one of the greatest masterpieces of this 'sport'";[51] and "But when you (...) see the beauty and the 'sport' of congregational singing (...)."[52] But this is not acceptable. Equally, the word cannot be translated as "music", because Icelanders use the word "tónlist" for "music." After consulting the dictionary my need for an adequate translation was not only satisfied, but I found much *more*. In the old-nordic saga literature the word "íþrótt" denotes physical and mental skills, accomplishment, and art; the plural "íþróttir" means training, or sport. For the Icelanders in the Middle Ages the word also embraced poetry (versification), playing the harp, and other skills such as swimming, rowing, shooting, horse riding, wrestling and playing chess.[53] The original meaning of the term "íþrótt" is "way of living".[54] Those involved in sports recognize a well-balanced, coherent scale of conceptions in this word "íþrótt", but so do musicians. Perhaps many theologians — even the church as a whole — could derive benefit from connecting these several meanings, echoing overtones of the word "íþrótt"; a word that was used by Pétur Guðjonsson, Einar Jónsson and Bjarni Þorsteinsson to denote *"the Arts"*. A word should be *heard* in its pure forms — as should music — if there are to be echoes in the ear and mind of the listener.

Thus writing about "Eene eeuw van worsteling" ("a century of wrestling") in connection with the history of Icelandic church music in this celebratory volume in honor of Casper Honders — which has the title *Ars et musica in liturgia* — one cannot avoid the ideas of the one who is celebrated here. With his head inclined a little, his ears acutely attuned, we hear him saying: "Of course, there is more echoing in this..."!

---

51 Pétur Guðjonsson, *Sálmasaung*, 1.
52 Bjarni Þorsteinsson, *Sálmasöngbók*, viii.
53 R. Cleasby, G. Vigfusson, and W.A. Craigie, *An Icelandic-English Dictionary* (Oxford 1969), 320.
54 J. de Vries, *Altnordisches Ethymologisches Wörterbuch* (Leiden 1961), 288.

A Case of Liturgical Practice in Johann Sebastian Bach's Home?
The four Duets BWV 802-805

Albert Clement

One of the many intriguing issues with which Bach scholarship has been occupied for years is the question why Johann Sebastian Bach included the four Duets BWV 802-805 in the third part of his *Clavier Übung*.[1] Already in 1950 Hermann Keller regarded that the four Duets as being so unique and to some extent so difficult to comprehend, that one might indeed presume that Bach wanted to express something exceptional with them, but as yet no-one has found the right key to understand them.[2]
More than thirty-five years later the situation was obviously unchanged, since in his book *Over Bachs schouder... Een bundel opstellen*, which appeared in 1986, Casper Honders drew attention to the fact that no satisfactory explanation had yet been found for their origin and place within the framework of the Clavierübung as a whole. Nevertheless, it seemed to him possible that resulting from further research a connection with Luther's *Haustafel* (included in Luther's Small Catechism), might become apparent, because as a musician Bach can be placed right next to both the preacher and the catechist: the man of music stood next to the man of the word.[3] This supposition does not seem strange when one considers that, besides vocal and instrumental works linked to the chorale, there are also

---

1 This is not the place to present a comprehensive and critical survey of the opinions hitherto advanced by other authors; this will be done in my forthcoming book on the Third Part of Bach's Clavierübung. A German version of this article appears simultaneously in *Bulletin Internationale Arbeitsgemeinschaft für theologische Bachforschung* 4.

2 Hermann Keller, *Die Klavierwerke Bachs: Ein Beitrag zu ihrer Geschichte, Form, Deutung und Wiedergabe* (Leipzig 1950), 210.

3 Casper Honders, *Over Bachs schouder... Een bundel opstellen* (Groningen 1986), 20.

purely instrumental compositions of Bach which carry a deeper significance. A well-known example of this is formed by the pieces framing the Clavierübung III: the prelude and fugue in E flat major (BWV 552). Even if individual interpretations differ partially from one another, there is general agreement in the musicological literature that both pieces exhibit trinitarian relationships.[4]

It seems obvious to conclude that the meaning of the four Duets will be found within the context of the publication in which they appear. Let us then firstly examine this context.

The four Duets were published in Bach's Clavierübung III which appeared in Nuremberg and Leipzig in 1739, probably at the time of the Michaelmas fair.[5] It is noteworthy that the collection appeared in a year in which no less than three Reformation festivals were celebrated, namely, on May 25th, the bicentenary of Martin Luther's preaching on Whitsunday in the Thomaskirche, on August 12th, the bicentenary of the Augsburg Confession, and on October 31st, the usual Reformation Festival.[6] The complete title of the collection reads as follows:

Dritter Theil der Clavier Übung bestehend in verschiedenen Vorspielen über die Catechismus- und andere Gesaenge, vor die Orgel: Denen Liebhabern, und besonders denen Kennern von dergleichen Arbeiten, zur Gemüths Ergezung, verfertiget von Johann Sebastian Bach, Koenigl. Pohlnischen, und Churfürstl. Saechs. Hoff-Compositeur, Capellmeister, und Directore Chori Musici in Leipzig. In Verlegung des Authoris.[7]

(Third Part of the Keyboard Practice consisting in Various Preludes on the Catechism and Other Hymns, for the Organ: For music lovers, and especially for Connoisseurs of such Work, to refresh their Spirits, composed by Johann Sebas-

---

4   Apart from the Clavierübung III one also finds that for certain instrumental compositions there are theological interpretations which, at all events, are stimulating. To give just one example, I refer here Ulrich Siegele's analysis of the sinfonia in F minor: cf. his study "Erfahrungen bei der Analyse Bachscher Musik". In: Reinhold Brinkmann (ed.), *Bachforschung und Bachinterpretation heute: Bericht über das Bachfest-Symposium 1978 der Philipps-Universität Marburg* (Leipzig 1981), 136-145, esp. 143-144.

5   Cf. *Bach-Dokumente* II (Kassel 1969), No. 455.

6   Cf. Robin A. Leaver, "Bach's 'Clavierübung III': Some Historical and Theological Considerations". In: *The Organ Yearbook* 6 (1975), 17-32, esp. 17; see also Peter Williams, *The Organ Music of J.S. Bach* II (Cambridge 1980), 175 (without reference to Leaver). Regarding the *Festum Reformationis Lutheri* in Leipzig during Bach's time, see also Günther Stiller, *Johann Sebastian Bach and Liturgical Life in Leipzig*, ed. by Robin A. Leaver (St. Louis 1984), 57.

7   Cf. the Facsimile edition, ed. by Christoph Wolff (Leipzig/Dresden 1984).

tian Bach, Royal Polish Court-Composer, and Director Chori Musici in Leipzig. Published by the Author.[8])

Despite its diffuseness, the title does not give any precise information about the contents nor its instrumental and liturgical purpose. In any case the title should already be a warning against the completely inappropriate designation of the Clavierübung III as an "Orgelmesse" ("Organ Mass"), which is often found in the literature,[9] for it expressly speaks of "Catechismus- und andere Gesaenge" ("Catechism and Other Hymns"). For the same reason a definition such as "Orgelkatechismus" ("Organ Catechism") or something similar would also be misleading because of its excessive one-sidedness. All the same, the title is incomplete, since the prelude and fugue in E flat as well as the four Duets, that is, the purely instrumental works of the collection, receive no mention whatsoever. The prelude and fugue in E flat form the frame of this collection, which Christoph Wolff describes as Bach's "most extensive" and also "most significant organ work"; Wolff even characterizes it as "the quintessence of his (= Bach's) art of organ composition and performance".[10] It is not possible here to undertake a detailed examination of the brilliant structure of this microcosmos,[11] which is the only part of Bach's entire Clavierübung to be intended not only for music-lovers but "besonders denen Kennern von dergleichen Arbeit" ("especially for Connoisseurs of such Work"). To be sure, even a superficial consideration cannot fail to reveal that the Clavierübung III was in fact assembled according to a carefully constructed plan. What concerns us at the moment is the question of the location of the four Duets in the overall scheme. Reinhold Birk remarks correctly that the Duets

---

8   Translations based on Hans T. David and Arthur Mendel (ed.), *The Bach Reader: A Life of Johann Sebastian Bach in Letters and Documents*, revised edition (New York 1966), 164.

9   (a) It offers more than a *Missa Brevis*; (b) it is not an organ mass in the sense of a "Messe pour l'orgue"; and (c) there is no evidence for stating that the works BWV 802-805 were intended as *musica sub communione*. Compare Williams, op. cit., 177, as well as my book announced in note 1 above.

10 Cf. respectively Wolf, op. cit., 42, and "Johann Sebastian Bach's Third Part of the *Clavier-Übung*", in: Fenner Douglass, Owen Jander and Barbara Owen (ed.), *Charles Brenton Fisk - Organ Builder*, Vol. I: *Essays in his Honour* (Easthampton, Massachusetts 1986), 291.

11 Cf. the book announced in note 1.

34

represent a self-contained section of the collection, just like the "Missa" and the catechism chorales.[12] During the 1989 Leipzig Bach conference, Markus Schiffner asserted that the four Duets constituted a group of their own in the formal arrangement of the whole. On this point he noted: "Ihr Erscheinen an der Stelle vor der Schlußfuge gab zu den merkwürdigsten Deutungsversuchen Anlaß, es fehlt ein wirklich überzeugender Nachweis einer evidenten inneren Beziehung zum Gesamtwerk"[13] ("Their appearance in the position just before the closing fugue has caused most peculiar interpretational attempts; a really convincing proof of a manifestly inner relationship to the entire work is lacking").

As stated before, it seems obvious to conclude that the meaning of the four Duets will be found from within the context in which they were published.

The Contents of Clavierübung III

Praeludium	*pro organo pleno*
Kyrie, Gott Vater	c.f. in soprano
Christe, aller Welt Trost	c.f. in tenor
Kyrie, Gott heiliger Geist	c.f. in pedal
	(*con organo pleno*)
Kyrie, Gott Vater	$^3/_4$ *manualiter*
Christe, aller Welt Trost	$^6/_8$ *manualiter*
Kyrie, Gott heiliger Geist	$^9/_8$ *manualiter*
Allein Gott in der Höh'	Trio in F, *manualiter*
Allein Gott in der Höh'	Trio in G
Allein Gott in der Höh'	Trio in A, *manualiter*
Diess sind die heil'gen zehn Gebot'	c.f. in canon
Diess sind die heil'gen zehn Gebot'	*manualiter*

12 Reinhold Birk, "Die Bedeutung der 'Vier Duette' in Bachs 'Klavierübung III'". In: *Musik und Kirche* 46 (1976), 63-69, esp. 69. However, I cannot follow the arguments supporting his description of them as "ein selbständiger, *christologischer* Teil" ("a self-contained, *Christological* section") (my emphasis).

13 Markus Schiffner, "Werk – Sammlung – Zyklus: Bachs Klavierübung III", in: *Beiträge zur Bachforschung* 9/10 (Leipzig 1991), 77-84, esp. 81-82.

Wir glauben all' an einen Gott	*in organo pleno*
Wir glauben all' an einen Gott	*manualiter*
Vater unser im Himmelreich	c.f. in canon
Vater unser im Himmelreich	*manualiter*
Christ, unser Herr, zum Jordan kam	c.f in pedal
Christ, unser Herr, zum Jordan kam	*manualiter*
Aus tiefer Noth schrei' ich zu dir	*in organo pleno*
Aus tiefer Noth schrei' ich zu dir	*manualiter*
Jesus Christus, unser Heiland	c.f in pedal
Jesus Christus, unser Heiland	*manualiter*
Duetto I	$^3/_8$ E minor
Duetto II	$^2/_4$ F major
Duetto III	$^{12}/_8$ G major
Duetto IV	$^2/_2$ A minor
Fuga	*pro organo pleno*

From the above overview of the contents of the Clavierübung, it is clear, in the first place, that the Mass chorales, the Catechism chorales, and the Duets, are consistantly grouped within the overall structure. The German Kyrie and Gloria chorales are contrasted: the Kyrie settings maintain a stylistically retrospective vocal polyphony (the cantus firmus proceeds successively from the soprano to the tenor to the bass in the three settings), while the Gloria is presented in concertato trio movements (in order of ascending keys: F-G-A). The six Catechism chorales can be divided – as far as the pedaliter settings are concerned (each of which is always followed by a manualiter prelude) – into two groups, each consisting of three pieces with an organo pleno movement invariably in the middle. Two settings of canonic cantus firmus design entwine around the first plenum piece, whilst the second group is framed by two chorales with the cantus firmus in the tenor and virtuosic interweaving of the upper voices (BWV 684 and 688). The Duets are arranged in the order of ascending keys, namely, E minor - F major - G major - A minor, whereby the pieces in minor keys represent the frame and thus enclose the two Duets written in major keys. If one portrays the contents of Clavierübung III as a circular structure it is noticeable further that the four Duets represent the tonal counterpart of the Kyrie settings – in E minor – and the

ensuing Gloria movements in F major - G major - A major.[14]
In examining the collection from a theological perspective, one
sees that the first section shows itself to be connected with the
church service: it is a Missa brevis. The second section, a Catechismus Sonorus, directs attention both to the church and the
domestic circle, because, in Bach's time, catechetical instruction
took place not only in church (for youth and adults)[15] but also
in the home. Besides, one can point to the tradition of the so-
called "Katechismusbeten" (Catechism prayer services) in Leipzig,[16] as well as to the many Catechism instruction services during certain fixed periods of the church year.[17]
If we now consider the subdivisions of Clavierübung III and,
more especially, consider how its first section stands in connection with the church and the second with church and home, we
would logically expect an association with the domestic circle for
the third section.
Two additional pieces of evidence appear to support this supposition. Firstly, I would draw attention to the fact that in this
collection Bach not only included pedaliter as well as manualiter
pieces which are tied to the cantus firmus, but also represented
both categories by purely instrumental works, that is, that the
four Duets therefore form the counterbalance to the E-flat
major prelude and fugue. While these paired movements of
prelude and fugue were undoubtedly written for church use, the
four Duets might equally have been intended for music-making
in the home. Secondly, it is to be remembered that the musical
idiom of the Duets implies, above all, a keyboard instrument
with strings rather than pipes. This therefore suggests domestic
music, similar in character to Bach's Inventions BWV 772-786.

---

14 As far as I am aware, this was first suggested in the booklet accompanying Ton
   Koopman's LP recording of Clavierübung III (Harlekijn Holland, No. 2454
   501/502 [1976?]), which was brought to my attention by the Australian harpsichor-
   dist, organist and musicologist David Collyer.
15 The Catechism was taught on Sundays in connection with the Vespers services
   (Johann Christoph Rost, verger of the Thomaskirche in Bach's time, testifies to
   the fact that in Leipzig the catechism was expounded during Vespers in Advent;
   see Stiller, op. cit., 59), and also during the week (Ibid., 45-46, 50).
16 Ibid., 113.
17 In 1723 there were no less than eleven weekly catechetical instruction services. By
   preference, the chief chorales appropriate to the relevant sections of the catechism
   were sung in these services. Cf. Honders, *Over Bachs schouder...*, 19.

Further, Bach's nephew, private secretary and "Hauslehrer", Johann Elias Bach (1705-1755), broached the subject of the collection in a letter dated January 10th 1739:

> So ist es auch an dem, daß mein Herr Vetter einige *Clavier* Sachen, die hauptsächlich (!) vor die Herrn *Organi*sten gehören u. überaus gut *componirt* sind, heraus wird geben (...).[18]
> (Thus it happens that my honored Cousin will bring out some *Clavier* pieces which are mostly for *organi*sts and are exceedingly well *composed* [...].[19])

The words "*Clavier* Sachen" ("*Clavier* pieces") and "hauptsächlich" ("mostly") are crucial here. They appear to indicate that not all the pieces are expressly meant for the organ. The Duets in particular are hereby brought into question, and it is worth recalling that the title page with the indication "vor die Orgel" mentions only the chorale preludes. According also to the latest insights, which suggest that the collection might have come into being in several stages, the collection contained *manualiter* preludes already in its first stage.[20]
The constructional plan of the Clavierübung III, plus other considerations, indicates therefore that the four Duets BWV 802-805 were most probably intended for music-making in the home. In this context I would draw attention to a source which has as yet not been consulted in connection with the Duets, and which might not only lend support to the thoughts I have presented, but may possibly even contain Bach's original basis for the compositions in question. This source is a book of Heinrich Müller (1631-1675). With the exceptions of M. Luther and the orthodox theologian August Pfeiffer, Müller – the Rostock theologian and author of devotional books who enjoyed contemporary fame and adhered to the views of Johann Arndt – was the most prominently represented religious writer in Bach's library. As is well known, Bach held this professor of theology in high regard and owned at least five of his works including, in all probability, the *Geistliche Erquick=stunden/ Oder Dreyhundert Haus= und*

18 *Bach-Dokumente* II, No. 434.
19 *The Bach Reader*, 162.
20 See Gregory Butler, *Bach's Clavier-Übung III: The Making of a Print* (Durham NC 1990), and my forthcoming review of this study in *Musik und Kirche* 63 (1993).

Tisch=Andachten (Rostock 1666, and many later editions).[21]
If one calls to mind Bach's lively interest in the Bible, in didactic-pastoral writings and in theological thought in general –
compare for instance his marginal notes in the Calov commentary, his theological remarks and significantly his musical compositions, which are themselves frequently profoundly her-
meneutical – it can be assumed that he seriously took note of
the *Haus= und Tisch=Andachten*. It even seems highly likely
that this work was read regularly in the Bach family circle. As a
result of Elke Axmacher's spectacular discovery that ap-
proximately half of Picander's poetic sections in the *Matthäus-
Passion*, BWV 244, were based on Müller's Passion sermons, we
should not in any way underestimate Bach's interest in the writings of Heinrich Müller.[22]
The title of one of the *Haus= und Tisch=Andachten*, namely
number CXCIV, is: "Von vier süßen Dingen" ("Of four sweet
things"). (See Fig. 1). The four things of which Müller treats
are:

1. The word of God (in particular the contrast "food for the
   soul – food for the body")
2. The cross ("The longer I bear it, the lighter it becomes")
3. Death, especially the fact that one need not fear death
   ("In Christ, death is not death but the doorway to life")
4. Heaven, particularly the yearning for heaven ("O that we
   were there!")

Is it possible to demonstrate certain relationships between these
four "sweet things" and the four Duets? I think it is, and to this
end I would first discuss the second Duet in F major, which
proves to have the most clarity of organization of the four.

---

21 See Robin A. Leaver, *Bachs theologische Bibliothek / Bach's theological Library*
   [Beiträge zur theologischen Bachforschung 1] (Neuhausen-Stuttgart 1983), 157-
   159; and Thomas Wilhelmi, "Bachs Bibliothek: Eine Weiterführung der Arbeit
   von Hans Preuß". In: *Bach-Jahrbuch* 65 (1979), 107-129, esp. 122.
22 Elke Axmacher, *"Aus Liebe will mein Heyland sterben": Untersuchungen zum Wan-
   del des Passionsverständnisses im frühen 18. Jahrhundert* [Beiträge zur theologischen
   Bachforschung 2] (Neuhausen-Stuttgart 1984); cf. Elke Axmacher, "Ein Quellen-
   fund zum Text der Matthäus-Passion". In: *Bach-Jahrbuch* 64 (1978), 181-191.

Duetto II in F major (BWV 803)

Kurt von Fischer speaks of this work as a high point in Bachian constructional form;[23] according to Hermann Keller the layout of the piece shows "verblüffende Symmetrien" ("amazing symmetries"),[24] and although Van Huystee initially condemns the search for such interpretations with regard to the Duets, the structure of this "Meisterwerk" induces him finally to assert: "Und darum enthält meines Erachtens der 'Dritte Theil der Clavier Übung' (...) kein einziges profanes Werk"[25] ("And therefore according to my judgement the Clavier Übung Part III [...] contains not a single secular work") (see Ex. 1).

BWV 803

Example 1

In examining Duetto II we see immediately that it is a da capo work. The middle section is, with its 75 bars, almost exactly as long as the two outer sections taken together; each outer section contains 37 bars. In the middle section two almost identical blocks of 31 bars enclose a central block of 13 bars. The structure of the whole is accordingly symmetrical, and can be shown thus:

A (37)   B (31)   C (13)   B (31)   A (37)

Ulrich Meyer has drawn attention to the fact that the A-sections both contain three simple developments of the theme, the B-sections two, and the central C-section one, in which the theme is inverted. He establishes that for the number of thematic de-

23 Kurt von Fischer, "Zum Formproblem bei Bach: Studien an den Inventionen, Sinfonien und Duetten". In: Karl Matthaei (ed.), *Bach-Gedenkschrift 1950* (Zürich 1950), 150-162, esp. 162.
24 Keller, op. cit., 211.
25 Th. van Huijstee, "Die vier Duette aus Bachs 'Drittem Theil der Clavier Übung'". In: *Musik und Kirche* 43 (1973), 275-282, esp. 281.

velopments per section the succession 3-2-1-2-3 is produced and he concludes: "Diese von der 3 zur zentralen 1 hin und wieder zurückführende Zahlenfolge kann unmittelbar von lutherisch-spätbarocker Musikanschauung her verstanden werden"[26] ("This numerical series leading from the 3 to the central 1 and back again can be understood directly from a Lutheran/late-baroque view of music").

Two years after Meyer submitted his dissertation, an interesting specialized study by Ulrich Siegele on Bach's theological concept of form and BWV 803 appeared. After having discussed the compositional characteristics of the middle section of the Duet he writes:

Beim Übergang vom Original zur Umkehrung werden die Stimmen vertauscht; das Thema wechselt von der Unter- zur Oberstimme, der Kontrapunkt von der Ober- zur Unterstimme. Ich lese diesen satztechnischen Tatbestand des Stimmtauschs als Figur des Kreuzes. Man wird mit Recht einwenden, der Stimmtausch sei ein übliches satztechnisches Mittel, die eine Figur des Kreuzes sage also nicht viel. Nun gibt es aber in diesem Stück noch andere Figuren des Kreuzes; sie folgen aus der Lesung auch anderer satztechnischer Tatbestände. Und diese Figuren des Kreuzes ordnen sich selbst wieder zur Figur.[27]
(At the transition from the original to the retrograde the voices are exchanged: the theme changes from the lower to the upper voice, and the counterpoint, from the upper to the lower. I take this compositional technique – the voice exchange – as a figure of the cross. One may correctly interject that the voice exchange is a typical technical device, that a single cross figure does not say much. There are, however, other figures of the cross in this piece; they are the consequences of yet other compositional techniques. And these figures of the cross take their own place within a figure once more.)

Siegele establishes convincingly that every one of the five sections draws the figure of the cross, "die inneren Rahmenteile und der Mittelteil durch den Stimmtausch, die äußeren Rahmenteile durch die Anordnung der Einsatzstufen und die Lage der Einsatztöne"[28] ("the inner sections of the framework and the middle section by the exchange of voices, the outer sections of the framework by the order of the steps of the entries and the position of the notes of each entry"). The number five itself points to the wounds of Christ, and therefore to his crucifixion

---

26 Ulrich Meyer, *J.S. Bachs Musik als theonome Kunst* (Wiesbaden 1979), 85.
27 Ulrich Siegele, *Bachs theologischer Formbegriff und das Duett F-Dur* (Neuhausen-Stuttgart 1978), 23.
28 Ibid., 28.

and the redemption of our guilt.[29] In Duetto II Bach also makes use of canon technique, in the context of which Siegele remarks that the canon is the figure of the active obedience with which Christ fulfilled the law in our stead, and that the cross is the figure of the suffering obedience with which he died in our stead.[30] And in reference to Leonhard Hutter's *Compendium locorum theologicorum* he amplifies this as follows:

(...) wo Gott das Kreuz (...) zu tragen gibt, da gibt er auch seine Tröstungen. Unter den Beweisen der Schrift steht die gewisse Zuversicht auf die Vergebung der Sünden in Christus, die macht, daß wir sind in der Gnade Gottes, in welcher Trübsal wir schließlich auch immer geübt werden (Hutter XXIV, 9, auch 5).[31]
([...] where God [...] gives a cross to bear, there also he gives his comfort. Among the proofs of Scripture is the certain confidence in the forgiveness of sins in Christ, which sets us in the grace of God, no matter what affliction we suffer.)

In the context of this composition Siegele does not fail, lastly, to remind us what distress Bach suffered, both outwardly and inwardly, from at least the summer of 1730 until the autumn of 1737, during his own long years of 'cross' and tribulation.[32] At the same time I would not exclude the idea that the presence of the *passus duriusculus* in this Duet was also inspired by the thought of cross-bearing.

Following these observations it will not be difficult to realise that a relation between Bach's second Duet and the second "sweet thing" of Müller's *Haus= und Tisch=Andachten* can be quite easily demonstrated, for both music and text deal with the cross and in both cases one should bear in mind that, with the help of God, the carrying of the cross is not hard. That one should carry it confidently is something which Bach knew very well, also on May 24th 1738 – that is, precisely at the time he prepared Clavierübung III – when he wrote in his letter to Johann Friedrich Klemm about his son Johann Gottfried Bernhard Bach:

Da keine Vermahnung, ja gar keine liebreiche Vorsorge und *assistence* mehr zureichen will, so muß mein Creütz in Gedult tragen, meinen ungerathenen Sohn aber lediglich Göttlicher Barmhertzigkeit überlaßen, nicht zweiflend, Dieselbe werde mein wehmüthiges Flehen erhören, und endlich nach seinem heiligen Wil-

---

29 Ibid., 28-29.
30 Ibid., 30.
31 Ibid.
32 Ibid., 33-34.

len an selbigem arbeiten, daß er lerne erkennen, wie die Bekehrung einig und allein Göttlicher Güte zuzuschreiben.[33]

(Since no admonition, nor even any loving care and *assistance* will suffice any more, I must bear my cross in patience, and leave my unruly son to God's mercy alone, doubting not that He will hear my sorrowful pleading, and in the end will so work upon him, according to His Holy Will, that he will learn to acknowledge that the lesson is owing wholly and alone to Divine Goodness.[34])

Duetto III in G major (BWV 804)

If we turn next to the following Duet in G major, a few comments may suffice for now. Christian Brückner characterizes the second Duet in F as an example of arithmetical calculation of exact symmetry, and according to Brückner Bach shows in BWV 804 "wieviel Wohlklang und Lieblichkeit" (how much euphony and charm) can be attained in a composition such as this.[35] Such a description is, in my estimation, not inapt. In this regard I would like to point out that BWV 804 is the only one of the four Duets which exhibits no prominent chromatic element, a remarkable fact which to my mind – in view of Müller's expositions in question – must be seen as significant. The following observation of Humphreys on BWV 804 is also quite pertinent: "Its most immediately striking feature is its gentle 12/8 metre" [36] (see Ex. 2).

BWV 804

Example 2

---

33 *Bach-Dokumente* I (Kassel etc./Leipzig 1963), No. 42.
34 *The Bach Reader*, 160.
35 Christian Brückner, "J.S. Bachs 'Dritter Theil der Clavier Übung'". In: *Musik und Gottesdienst* 27 (1973), 62-66; 83-95, esp. 89. Yet, his use of the term "Orgelkomposition" (ibid.) with regard to this work seems to me to be incorrect.
36 David Humphreys, *The Esoteric Structure of Bach's Clavierübung III* (Cardiff 1983), 15; in respect of BWV 804 he speaks also of "warmth and lyricism which contrasts pleasantly with the brittle virtuosity of the latter" (= Duetto II).

Regarding Bach's interpretation of the 12/8 metre, Renate Steiger has demonstrated that Bach uses this metre to proclaim the presence of the promised salvation. Among other things, she draws attention to the eschatological motivation for the idea of death in several of Bach's cantata movements – including the opening choral movement of BWV 8, *Liebster Gott, wenn werd ich sterben* – which, with their 12/8 metre, "das selige Sterben als Wunder, als eschatologische Gabe beschreiben"[37] (describe blessed death as a miracle, as an eschatological gift). In 1989 I pointed out an example of this metre in Bach's organ works, to wit *Variatio 7* of the chorale partita *O Jesu, du edle Gabe* BWV 768.[38] The text on which this variation is based reads:

> Wenn der Tod mir grauen machet/
> dein Blut JEsu ihn verlachet/
> weil er an mir und mein Orden
> durch dein Blut zu schanden worden
> dein Blut mich von Sünden wäschet/
> und der Höllen=Gluth auslöschet.
> (When Death comes to horrify me,
> Your blood, Jesu, derides it;
> for through your blood it has been
> destroyed before me and my lineage;
> your blood washes my sins from me
> and extinguishes the glow of hell.)

The central thought here also is the elimination of the fear of death through the blood of Christ.[39] As it turns out, it is exactly this particular thought that forms the theme of the third of Müller's four "sweet things". The "Lieblichkeit" with which Brückner styled the quality of the third Duet is found again also in Müller's exposition on the concept of death when he writes:

---

37 Renate Steiger, "'Die Welt ist euch ein Himmelreich' / Zu Bachs Deutung des Pastoralen". In: *Musik und Kirche* 41 (1971) 1-8; 69-79, esp. 77.

38 Albert Clement, *"O Jesu, du edle Gabe"*. *Studien zum Verhältnis von Text und Musik in den Choralpartiten und den Kanonischen Veränderungen von Johann Sebastian Bach* (Utrecht 1989), 129-132.

39 This point was first evinced in Clement, op. cit.; cf. Albert Clement, "Eine bemerkenswerte Übereinstimmung dreier Orgelchoralbearbeitungen J.S. Bachs (BWV 617; 736; 768, Var. 8)". In: *Johann Sebastian Bachs Choralkantaten als Choral-Bearbeitungen* [= Bulletin 3 der Internationalen Arbeitsgemeinschaft für theologische Bachforschung: Bericht über die Tagung Leipzig 1990] (Heidelberg 1991), 180-192; see also Albert Clement, "'Alsdann ich gantz freudig sterbe...': Zu J.S. Bachs Deutung des 24/16 Taktes". In: *Musik und Kirche* 61 (1991), 303-311.

Andern ist der Tod ein solch Schröckbild/ daß ihnen auch für dem Anblick grauet;
Mir ist diß Bild so lieblich/ daß ich mich nit satt dran sehen kann. In Christo ist
der Tod kein Tod/ sondern eine Thür zum Leben/ nicht schröcklich/ sondern
lieblich/ nicht heßlich/ sondern herrlich/ nicht bitter/ sondern süsse. Durch tägliche
Sterbens=Gedanken befreund ich mich mit dem Tod/ gute Freunde reisen gern
mit ein ander.[40]
(For others, death is such a horrifying prospect that they fear even to look at it.
For me this prospect is so dear that I cannot see enough of it. In Christ death is
not death, but rather a door to life; not frightening, but lovely; not ugly, but glorious; not bitter, but sweet. Through daily thoughts of dying I befriend death. Good
friends like to travel together.)

The character of Duetto III seems to correspond completely to
these didactic-pastoral statements of Müller.

Following these two Duets in major keys, the two Duets in
minor keys which enclose them will now come under discussion.

Duetto I in E minor (BWV 802)

Müller begins his 'Haus- und Tischandacht' CXCIV with an
exposition on the word of God. If one wonders how a composer
could confer musical shape on such a concept, it is worth bear-
ing in mind that since olden times the word of God was connected with the concept of 'Vollkommenheit' (perfection). And
this is exactly where Bach seems to be aiming with his musical
theme – a theme which, according to Van Huijstee, attracts all
attention to itself in this Duet.[41] With its head Bach draws a
circolo, a circle, the symbol of perfection – in the original printing this can be seen much more beautifully than in the modern
editions. This circle has the range of an octave, the interval
which encompasses the whole tonal area. That, also, may be
understood as a symbol of perfection and all-encompassing
universality. In this light it is also significant that in Duetto I the
whole extension $C-c^3$ is used.[42]

Moreover, the theme of BWV 802 contains the most notes of
the four Duets. It cannot be ruled out that Bach was thinking
hereby of the idea of 'becoming filled with food for the soul', of
which there is mention in Müller's text (see Ex. 3, and below).

---

40 Müller, op. cit., 568.
41 Van Huijstee, op. cit., 277.
42 Cf. ibid.

Example 3

The second subject which contrasts with this theme contains the interval of the chromatic fourth – the *passus duriusculus* – and also even larger leaps – *saltus duriusculi*. Keller regarded BWV 802 as a "Meister-Invention" (masterly Invention) in which a whole number of opposing elements of expression can be demonstrated.[43] In fact the contrastin 'Affekte' in BWV 802 are noteworthy. In taking a second look at the relevant text in Müller, we are nevertheless struck by the fact that here contrast likewise plays an important role, namely in the sense of the antithesis between food for the soul and food for the body. Almost right at the beginning we read (my emphasis):

> Gottes Wort soll der Seelen Speise seyn. Ach wie vielen ist es so fremd und un-bekandt/ daß es ihnen *mehr eine Artzney als Speise* zu sein scheinet: der *leiblichen Speise* wil *niemand entbehren/* aber die geringste Ursach macht oft/ daß wir die *Seelen=Speise versäumen.*[44]
> (The Word of God should be the food of the soul. Alas, to how many people is it [the Word] so strange and unknown, that for them it appears to be *more of a medicine than nourishment*: *no one* wants *to miss* the *bodily meal,* but the least little thing will often cause us *to miss the meal of the soul.*)

And later the following:

> Je mehr man von leiblicher Speise zu sich nimmt/ je satter wird man/ aber je mehr man sich an Gottes Wort erlustigt/ je begieriger und hungriger wird die Seele.[45]
> (The more one eats at a bodily meal, the fuller one becomes; but the more one partakes of the Word of God, the more desirous and hungry the soul becomes.)

Thus it appears possible to explain the opposing 'Affekte' of this composition from these textual passages. A remarkable development occurs in bar 61. The tonal entry here is unusual in that it represents a caesura between bars 1-60 and the last 13 bars.

---

43 Keller, op. cit., 210.
44 Müller, op. cit., 567.
45 Ibid.

Was Bach here pursuing a certain aim? The number six was traditionally the sign of *perfectio*, while the thirteen signifies the relationship between Old and New Testament. In this regard it must be said that the final thirteen bars can in fact be divided into ten plus three. My idea of the caesura seems to be reinforced by the number of notes, for the first sixty bars contain exactly 830 notes, which gematrically could indicate 'Immanuel' [= 83], while the last thirteen bars are comprised of 158 notes: gematrically this stands for 'Johann Sebastian Bach'. Whether these conjectures are right cannot, of course, be said with certainty. The numerical relationships, however, might allow that they at least be expressed.

Duetto IV in A minor (BWV 805)

We turn finally to BWV 805. As several authors have remarked, this piece is conceived as a fugue.[46] And as has likewise been established, the form of this Duet employs to some extent the plan of Duet I.[47] Hence BWV 802 and BWV 805 form the frame of the four Duets, not only because they are both pieces in minor keys but also as a result of the conformities in their basic plan; thus a complete, rounded-off whole is created.

Like Duet I, Duet IV is built of three sections. Firstly we see an A section which, as in the first Duet, is repeated with voices interchanged as a second A'; this whole section is indeed lengthened with sequences and a repetition of the theme which give it a structure corresponding with the first two sections of BWV 802. As in the case of the latter, the first group of the first two sections in BWV 805 is not repeated in the third section. The first section (A) is made up of 2 x 16 bars; the second section (A') contains 45 bars and can be subdivided into three groups of 16, 14 and 15 bars respectively; the third section (B) of 31 bars consists of two groups of 8 and 23 bars respectively.

Ernst Kurth calls the theme of Duetto IV an example of a fugal theme which in itself conceals polyphonic effects, and which in

46 Cf. Brückner, op. cit., 89; Humphreys, op. cit., 16; cf. however, in addition ("regular fugue"), Peter Williams, *The Organ Music of J.S. Bach* I (Cambridge 1980, ²1982), 326.
47 On this point see Von Fischer, op. cit., 161; Van Huijstee, op. cit., 278-279.

addition can serve in permitting a heightening of the polyphonic sonority of a fugue "ins Ungemessene" (beyond all bounds).[48] Van Huijstee describes it as the most extraordinary theme of all four Duets, and points further to the unique thematic exposition in the lower voice and to what he terms the "Gipfelmelodie" (ascending melody) which can be traced in the theme.[49] A second, very characteristic subject – which contains a 'Seufzer'- enters for the first time on the fourth quarter of bar 17. The three places in which this subject occurs can be regarded as interludes; they are found in bars 17-24 [-32], 49-56 [-62] and 78-85.[50]

In enquiring about possible relationships with Müller's expositions concerning heaven and the desire to enter heaven, one should refer in the first place – as with Duetto III – to the total concept of the piece. Humphreys believes: "Again, the choice of the fugue form (*fuga* = flight) is surely no coincidence."[51] In my opinion this observation is correct, even if I do not – as does Humphreys – start from an association with Luther's words "von selbst gelaufen und gerennet" (running helter-skelter of one's own accord) found in his Small Catechism,[52] but on the contrary interpret this idea of flight as an allusion to the 'going up into heaven'. (Incidentally, Luther's words occur in a passage which describes exactly the situation when one does *not* hold the Sacrament in high regard; consequently, Humphreys' interpretation must already for this reason be considered to be unlikely.[53])

The theme may support this viewpoint. It seems to contain a suggestion of the 'earth-heaven' relationship whereby the striking "Gipfelmelodie" points as *anabasis* in the direction of heaven. This relationship of 'below' and 'above' possibly comes out already in the exposition, where the theme is found – exceptionally – in the lower voice.

The characteristic second subject with 'sighs' ('Seufzer') gives us cause to ask just what Bach might have intended by it. Had the 'Seufzer' appeared only sporadically in this piece it might be obvious to seek reference to a title such as: "Tägliche Seuffzer

---

48 Ernst Kurth, *Grundlagen des linearen Kontrapunkts (...)* (Berlin ²1922), 311.
49 Van Huijstee, op. cit., 279.
50 Cf. ibid., 278.
51 Humphreys, op. cit., 18.
52 Ibid., 17.
53 WA 30/1, 352.

um ein seliges Ende" (Daily sighings about a blessed end) from Johann Olearius' book entitled *Christliche Bet=Schule*, with which Bach was most probably acquainted.[54] However, such is not the case. The supplicatory figure is always found in several bars in succession, and indeed constantly at melodic highpoints which are arrived at by a preceding ascending leap of a sixth or a seventh. If we study the part of the *Haus= und Tisch=Andachten* related to this, there seems to be an amazing correspondence with Müller's words when he writes: "(...) der Schmack zündet die Himmelslust an/ und treibt ein Seufftzerlein nach dem andern hinauf"[55] ("[...] the taste kindles the joy of heaven and impels one little sigh after another on high") (see Ex. 4).

BWV 805

Example 4

Finally, a comment about the bar groupings is in order. In the middle of the Duet there is a group of 14 bars. As is known, 14 stands gematrically for 'Bach'. Could this number be interpreted in this manner here? This does actually appear to be the case because the final section contains 31 bars: read gematrically, 31 signifies 'J-O-H'. The two 16-bar groups of the first section and

---

54 Renate Steiger, "'Auf allerley Fälle des Lebens': Trost und Ermahnung". In: *Ex Libris Bachianis* II (Heidelberg 1985), 32-34, here 32.

55 Müller, op. cit., 569.

– related to them – the outer groups of the middle section which contain 16 and 15 bars respectively, form together 63 bars; 63 signifies 'Sebast'.

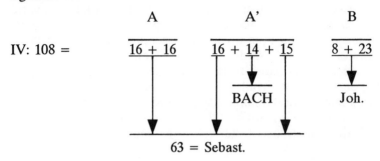

In the number of bars of Duetto IV we thus find Bach's signature written in the same way as he signed, for instance, his famous letter of October 28th 1730 to Georg Erdmann,[56] and also in the same way he now 'signs' the last of the three groups of pieces of Clavierübung III.

The term 'Duetto'

Following this account of certain issues dealing with the four Duets it is appropriate to devote some attention to the term Duetto. Keller's opinion that the word Duet was used because it was a 'neutral' title-statement is in no way conclusive.[57] This has already been demonstrated by Robin Leaver when he recalls that Bach applies the word "Dialogus" to various cantata movements in order to indicate a conversation between Christ and the believing soul, and therewith the activity of prayer.[58] Leaver's observation can nevertheless be made even more precise, for we find that Bach employs not only the word "Dialogus" but also indeed, in several vocal works, the indication "Duetto". Besides, it is not always just a matter of a

56 *Bach-Dokumente* I [see note 33], No. 23. Cf. for example Bach's letter to Tobias Rothschier of May 2nd 1735 (ibid., No. 30) as well as his letters to the council of the city of Leipzig dated 12th August 1736 (ibid., No. 32) and 15th August 1736 (ibid., No. 34).
57 Keller, op. cit., 210.
58 Leaver, op. cit. (see note 6), 28.

conversation between the soul and Christ. In the fifth movement of the cantata entitled *Unser Mund sei voll Lachens* BWV 110, the soprano and tenor sing the words: "Ehre sei Gott in der Höhe und Friede auf Erden und den Menschen ein Wohlgefallen!" ("Glory to God in the highest and peace on earth and delightful contentment to all men!") And in the fifth movement of the cantata *Erschallet, ihr Lieder* BWV 172, the Duetto consists of a soprano ("Seele" ["soul"]) and a contralto ("Heiliger Geist" ["Holy Ghost"]).

It cannot be doubted that Bach could have found sufficient grounds in Müller's *Haus=* und *Tisch=Andacht* CXCIV for using the term Duetto as the title of the four compositions under discussion. Each Duetto actually deals with the longings of the soul, that is, the love between soul and a concept. I will give a few quotations here as examples:

– "Je mehr man sich an Gottes Wort erlustigt/ je begieriger wird die Seele" ("the more one takes pleasure in God's word/ the more eager the soul becomes")
– "Das Creutz hat mich so lieb/ es läst mich nicht" ("The cross loves me so much/ it never leaves me")
– "Mir ist der Tod so lieblich/ daß ich mich nit satt dran sehen kan" ("To me death is so delightful/ that I never tire of looking at it").

Furthermore, on several occasions there is talk of two friends (p. 567, bottom of page and p. 568, middle and bottom of page).[59] It seems superfluous to point out that Müller is referring to the Song of Solomon in his picture of the sweetnesses – he himself draws attention to this on p. 566 – and it may be equally unnecessary to mention that Bach often composed in dialogue or duet form precisely in connection with the Song of Solomon. For the sake of giving an example I cite BWV 172, 5th movement, where the *Anima* sings: "Liebste Liebe, die so süße, Aller Wollust Überfluß!" (Dearest beloved, O most sweet, overflowing with all delights!). Casper Honders has examined this in detail in his book on Bach and the Song of Solomon.[60]

---

59 Cf. e.g. BWV 140.6: Soprano "Mein Freund ist mein" – Bass "Und ich bin sein".
60 Casper Honders, *Mijn lief is mijn... Over het Hooglied in het werk van J.S. Bach* [Kerkmuziek & Liturgie 2] (Voorburg 1988).

By way of summary it seems plausible to consider the four Duets, following as they do the *Missa Brevis* and the *Catechismus Sonorus*, as a part of the Clavierübung III which is connected with the domestic circle. In this sense they also form the counterpart to the other free works in the collection, namely the paired movements BWV 552. This supposition is underpinned not only by the indication of a stringed musical idiom (cf. here the communication of Johann Elias Bach), but also by the clear relationship between the Duets and the relevant expositions of Heinrich Müller in his *Haus= und Tisch=Andacht* CXCIV. Moreover, it is noteworthy that these expositions occur *in the same order* as the Duets. The didactic-pastoral practice of the time, which we encounter in Müller, seems to be reflected in those compositions of Bach to which he significantly gave the title Duetto. The possibility that the foundation for Bach's four Duets actually exists in this *Haus= und Tisch=Andacht* of Heinrich Müller should be given serious consideration as a result of these reflections, in which case the pieces might be considered as an example of liturgical practice (in the sense of worship) in the home of Johann Sebastian Bach.

Erquickstunden. 565

Meide die Gesellschafft der Bösen / sie
ist verführisch /betäube deinen Leib/daß
er nicht geil und lüstern werde/halt maß
in Speis und Tranck/an dürren Orten
findet der Satan keine Ruhe / bey nas-
sen Brüdern nistet er gemeiniglich ein.
Arbeite / denn beym nichts thun lernet
man böses thun / hasse niemand mehr
als dich selbst um deiner Unart willen /
und fürchte dich vor keinem mehr als
vor deinem eignen Hertzen / denn es ist
dein Verräther / traust du ihm/ so wirst
du betrogen. Folge dem Geist / er ist
der rechte Führer / sein Fuß geht Himmel an. Gott helffe streiten!

CXCIV.
Von vier süssen Dingen.
Je länger/ je lieber.

Vier Dinge meyne ich. Erstlich das
Wort Gottes. Je länger man
eine süsse Speise käuet/je süsser schmeckt
sie. Gottes Wort soll der Seelen Speise seyn. Ach wie vielen ist es so frembd
und unbekandt / daß es ihnen mehr eine
Artzney als Speise zu seyn scheinet: der
leiblichen Speise wil niemand entbe-

Aa 7 ren/

Figure 1-6. Heinrich Müller, Geistliche Erquick=stunden / Oder Dreyhundert Haus= und Tisch=Andachten (Frankfurt a.M. 1672), Titelseite und S. 565-569. Reproduced with kind permission of the Herzog
August Bibliothek in Wolfenbüttel (Th 1835).

53

ren/aber die geringste Ursach macht oft/ daß wir die Seelen-Speise versäumen. Wie? ist sie denn so saur/ daß man einen Eckel dafür haben möcht? Ach nein/ süsser deñ Honig und Honigseim. Milch und Honig ist unter Jesus Kälen/ und Rosenzucker trägt er auf seinen Lippen/ wie das Lied Salomons zeugt. Die natürliche Speise erquickt/weil sie dem hungrigen Magen eine Zufriedenheit bringt/ drumb sagt die Schrifft / daß GOTT erfülle unsre Hertzen mit Speis und Freuden/ Ap.Gesch.14/ 17. Wär ein geistlicher Hunger bey uns/ ach! wie würden wir uns an dem Wort GOttes erquicken / mehr dann ein Kindlein an den Milch-Brüsten. Wann wir der irdischen Speis geniessen / finden wir eine solche Lieblichkeit drinn / daß der Appetit zur Speise immer zunimt / da zeucht ein süsser Biß den andern nach sich; wann die Krafft und Süssigkeit Göttliches Worte gekostet wird/wächst in der Fülle der Hunger/ und können wir sein nicht satt werden/denn der Glaube ergreifft die tröstliche

liche Verheissungen nicht nur als warhafftig zur Beystimmung / sondern auch als gut und lieblich zu vestem Anhang/ wil die Brüste nicht lassen / weil die Milch so süß ist. Je mehr man von leiblicher Speise zu sich nimt/je satter wird man/ aber je mehr man sich an Gottes Wort erlustigt/ je begieriger und hungriger wird die Seele. Drum/ mein Hertz/wann dich dünckt/Gottes Wort sey dir leyd geworden/ so hör und lies es desto fleissiger/ denn im lesen und hören fällt dir ein süß Tröpflein nach dem andern ins Hertz / da gewinnestu wieder lieb/was dir vor leyd war.Vors ander das Creutz. Je länger ichs trage / je leichter wirds/ (die Gewonheit macht alles leicht) und je leichter je lieber. In dem es bey mir wohnt/werd ich bekand mit ihm/ und verlieb mich immer mehr und mehr drin: je länger 2. gute Freund mit einander umgehen / je lieber haben sie einander/und je schmertzlicher ist das scheiden.Das Creutz hat mich so lieb/es läst mich nicht/ und lieff ich zum Thor hinauß: so hab ichs auch wiederum so lieb/ daß

daß ichs umb Welt/ Gold und Silber
nicht geben wolt/ niemand als der Tod
sol uns trennen. Was Gott zusammen
fügt/ muß kein Mensch scheiden. Vors
dritte den Tod. Je länger ich an ihn
gedencke / je lieber wird er mir. Andern ist der Tod ein solch Schröckbild/
daß ihnen auch für dem Anblick grauet;
Mir ist diß Bild so lieblich/ daß ich mich
nit satt dran sehen kan. In Christo ist
der Tod kein Tod / sondern eine Thür
zum Leben/ nicht schröcklich / sondern
lieblich/ nicht heßlich / sondern herrlich/
nicht bitter / sondern süsse. Durch tägliche Sterbens-Gedancken befreund ich
mich mit dem Tod/ gute Freunde reisen
gern mit ein ander.   Spannt der Tod
an/ ich fahre mit / und spreche mit Simeon: Herr nun / ach nun / in diesem nun/ in diesem Pünctlein/ laß
deinen Diener im Frieden fahren/
gönne mir doch Feyrabend / daß ich
meinem guten Freunde das Geleit ge-
be/ der Tod wil fort/ ich muß mit/ ach
Herr/ halt mich nicht auff. Viertens
den Himmel.   Je länger hinauff/ je
lieber

lieber hinein.   Himmlische Gedancken
haben eine Magnetische Krafft/ entzü-
cken das Hertz im Geist/ in solcher Ent-
zückung wirds mit himlischer Wollust
gelabet/ der Schmack zündet die Himmelslust an/ und treibt ein Seufftzerlein nach dem andern hinauff? Eya /
wären wir da ! je krässtiger wir die
Süssigkeit deß Himmels schmäcken /
je brünstiger ist das Verlangen in uns
nach der Offenbahrung der Kindschaft
Gottes.   Wie ein Kind / wanns ein
Bißlein Zuckers gekostet hat / immer
nach Zucker schreyt und weynt/ so seh-
nen wir uns nach der völligen Erndte/
wann wir die Erstlinge haben bekommen. Ach nim mich in den Himmel /
Herr Jesu balde.

CXCV.
Von den Wegen Gottes und der
Menschen.

Gerad zu.

Ist der kürtzte Weg. Eine gerade Linie hält man für die kürtzte.
Mein Hertz/ fehlet was ? drückt was?
gerad zu Gott/ das treugt nicht. Du
er-

Gegenwartskunst im Gottesdienst der Kirche

Philipp Harnoncourt

Es gibt nur wenige Universitätsinstitute, an denen in der Liturgiewissenschaft der Gegenstand *Liturgie* (= Gottesdienst) in seinem ganzen Umfang als lebendiges Ereignis des Glaubensvollzugs, also in seinem rituellen Vollzug mit Sprechhandlungen und körpersprachlichen Ausdrucksformen, mit Musik und Gesang, mit seinem Raum und seiner künstlerischen Gestalt, in die Forschung einbezogen ist. Zu diesen wenigen Instituten gehören das von Casper Honders, dem Empfänger dieser Festschrift, ausgebaute Institut an der Rijksuniversiteit Groningen und das vom Verfasser dieses Beitrags gegründete Institut an der Karl-Franzens-Universität Graz, ersteres an einer reformierten theologischen Fakultät, letzteres an einer katholischen theologischen Fakultät. Als Kollegen und Freunde arbeiten wir seit mehr als 25 Jahren zusammen.

Bisher waren es vor allem ökumenische und hymnologische Fragen, die wir gemeinsam besprochen haben, und wenn auch der Gegenwartsbezug immer im Vordergrund stand, so waren es doch meistens Fakten und Phänomene aus der Geschichte der Liturgie, die wir beraten haben. Hier will ich einmal ein anderes Problem skizzieren und zur Diskussion stellen, das mir von größter Aktualität zu sein scheint: das Problem der zeitgenössischen Kunst für die Kirche im allgemeinen und von deren Einbeziehung in die Liturgie der Kirche im besonderen.

Ich möchte meine Überlegungen in drei Schritten vorlegen:
1. Worum geht es in der zeitgenössischen Kunst?
2. Warum müssen sich die Kirchen mit zeitgenössischer Kunst befassen?
3. Warum bedarf die Liturgie der zeitgenössischen Kunst?

Natürlich gehört auch die Musik zur Kunst, darum gelten die hier vorgelegten Gedanken prinzipiell auch bezüglich der zeitgenössischen Musik. Aber der zur Verfügung stehende Raum erlaubt nur die Befassung mit der bildenden Kunst, einschließlich der Architektur. Meine Überlegungen zur Notwendigkeit von zeitgenössischer Musik in der Liturgie, die ich im März 1992 an der Akademie für Kirchen- und Schulmusik in Luzern vorgetragen habe, werden demnächst dort veröffentlicht.

Worum geht es in der zeitgenössischen Kunst?

Kunst ist eine besondere Weise des persönlichen und schöpferischen Ausdrucks, die von anderen wahrgenommen und erfaßt werden kann, also eine der Sprache vergleichbare Form von Kommunikation. Das Ergebnis des schöpferischen Prozesses – das Kunstwerk – bleibt, wenn es materialisiert ist, in der folgenden Zeit bestehen, oder es geht sofort wieder unter, wie etwa Sprache, Gesang, Musik, die keiner Materie bedürfen, hinterläßt aber mehr oder weniger deutliche Spuren im Gedächtnis sowohl der Künstler wie auch der Wahrnehmenden. Jedes Kunstwerk bringt etwas "zur Sprache", bildet etwas ab oder stellt etwas für andere wahrnehmbar und erfaßbar dar. Der Künstler sagt durch sein Werk "etwas" aus, beziehungsweise er stellt "etwas" dar:
– ein bestimmtes Objekt, das heißt einen Gegenstand oder einen Sachverhalt;
– ein Gefühl oder eine Impression;
– etwas über sich selbst;
– etwas über die je gegenwärtige Situation der Welt oder der Gesellschaft, wie sie vom Künstler – bewußt oder unbewußt – wahrgenommen wird.

Wer seine Gegenwart in umfassender Weise erfahren und begreifen will, darf sich nicht damit begnügen, scharfsinnige Analysen darüber zu lesen oder vielleicht auch selbst anzustellen. Dem Verstand und der klaren sprachlichen Darlegung ist immer nur ein Teil der Wirklichkeit zugänglich. Weitere Teile – und das sind in der Regel die für das Leben und Überleben wichtigeren – werden gefühlsmäßig oder auch intuitiv erfaßt, sei es von allen oder auch nur von einigen besonders sensiblen Zeitgenossen, unter denen immer die Künstler eine besondere Rolle gespielt haben.
Die Gegenwartskunst enthält, wenn auch oft kompliziert und verschlüsselt, tatsächlich erlebte und persönlich erfahrene Gegenwärtigkeit. Sie vermittelt – über alle Ich-Aussagen hinaus – Botschaften an die Gesellschaft, Diagnosen der Zeit-Situation, Appelle zur Änderung oder auch zur Stabilisierung. Wer an der

Gegenwartskunst achtlos vorübergeht, verschließt sich selbst einer wichtigen Selbstdarstellung seiner "Gegenwart".

Was freilich die Beschäftigung mit der Gegenwartskunst, ihre Interpretation oder ihre "Lesbarkeit" empfindlich erschwert, ist die Tatsache, daß in unserem Jahrhundert die aus der Geschichte bekannten Zeit-Stile – das sind allgemein verwendete und darum auch verstandene Ausdrucksformen bestimmter Epochen – mehr und mehr zugunsten von Personal-Stilen verschwunden sind. Es herrscht heute der Eindruck vor, daß beinahe jeder Künstler seine eigene Sprache erfindet und gebraucht, die vom Empfänger nicht selten erst mühsam erlernt werden muß, um verstanden werden zu können. Vor dieser Mühe schrecken nicht wenige zurück und begnügen sich mit dem, was ihnen seit jeher vertraut ist, und mit dem aus dem Gegenwartsschaffen, was ihnen gefällt, das heißt mit dem "Gefälligen".

Wichtige Zeugnisse der Gegenwartsdeutung bleiben ihnen daher verschlossen. Wer sich mit der zeitgenössischen Kunst ernsthaft befaßt, muß bereit sein, "fremde Sprachen lesen" zu lernen, immer wieder aufs neue "lesen" zu lernen. Auch erfahrene Kenner tun sich mit einzelnen Künstlern oder Kunstrichtungen oft lange Zeit schwer. Aber es lohnt sich, diese Mühe auf sich zu nehmen. Neue Welten können sich plötzlich öffnen. Das Leben wird reicher und tiefer.

Warum müssen sich die Kirchen mit der zeitgenössischen Kunst befassen?

Beim ad-limina-Besuch in Rom im April 1992 wurden die österreichischen Bischöfe von Papst Johannes Paul II. ausdrücklich aufgefordert, sich sehr eingehend mit der Kultur der Gegenwart zu befassen, einerseits weil die Kirche selbst ein Teil eben dieser Gegenwartskultur ist, andererseits weil diese die Situation der Gesellschaft und der einzelnen Menschen bestimmt, in die hinein die Kirche ihre Sendung heute zu erfüllen hat. Sie sollten – so wurden sie vom Papst ermuntert – eine kritische Analyse der gegenwärtigen kulturellen Strömungen vornehmen, mit repräsentativen Vertretern beziehungsweise Trägern der Gegenwartskultur in Dialog treten und schließlich um die "Verchristlichung" dieser Kultur sich bemühen in Verantwortung gegenüber einer bald zweitausendjährigen Tradition in Europa.

Dieser Appell des Papstes schließt die nachdrückliche Ermahnung ein, sich mit der zeitgenössischen Kunst in allen ihren Formen gründlich auseinanderzusetzen, stellt sie doch einen wesentlichen Bestandteil der Gegenwartskultur dar. Die Kirchen würden ihre Aufgabe, der Welt und mit ihr der Gesellschaft und dem Menschen "heute" zu dienen, in unverantwortlicher Weise vernachlässigen, wenn sie die Werke und die Tendenzen der zeitgenössischen Kunst nicht mit leidenschaftlichem Interesse beachten wollten.

Darüber hinaus dokumentieren vor allem die bildende Kunst und die Musik, das heißt die nicht-verbalen Formen künstlerischen Ausdrucks, daß die uns umfassende Wirklichkeit immer, also auch heute, das rational Verstehbare und das verbal Erklärbare und Aussagbare weit übersteigt. Kunst läßt erfahren, daß unsere Welt "offen" ist – nach oben und in die Tiefe. Sie erschließt somit einen Weg zur Transzendenz, ohne daß aber deshalb jede Kunst schon als "religiös" vereinnahmt werden dürfte. Jede Kunst ist aber überzeugender Ausdruck dafür, daß die Wirklichkeit, und zwar sowohl die uns umgebende Wirklichkeit wie auch die Wirklichkeit unserer selbst, etwas Umfassenderes ist als das Rationale. Und jedenfalls ist die Kunst ihrer eigentümlichen "Offenheit" wegen ein unverzichtbares Phänomen für jede "Religion" als eine Beziehung zum Heiligen und als Zeugnis für das Heilige.

Wollten sich die Kirchen damit begnügen, daß die Kunst vergangener Epochen so viele herrliche Zeugnisse tiefen Glaubens und bedeutungsvolle Darstellungen der Glaubensverkündigung hervorgebracht habe, daß sie auf zeitgenössische Kunst gut verzichten könnten, so würden sie vielen Menschen, die sehr bewußt in der Gegenwart leben und Gegenwärtigkeit erfahren, den Eindruck vermitteln, man müsse aus der Gegenwart "aussteigen" und gewissermaßen in die (heile?) Vergangenheit fliehen, um überhaupt Christ sein zu können. Manchen Menschen, die ohnehin in der heutigen Zeit nichts Schönes erkennen, wäre das vielleicht angenehm und willkommen, aber für viele und gerade für Menschen, die die Gegenwart mitbestimmen, ist das ein Grund die Kirche zu verlassen, weil diese heute und für heute nichts mehr zu sagen hätte. Ihrer Verantwortung im Hinblick auf die zeitgenössische Kunst kommen die Kirchen nicht schon dadurch nach, daß da und dort Kunstpreise gestiftet oder einzelne Künstler gefördert werden. Das können auch Alibi-Handlungen sein. Es geht vor allem darum, glaubwürdig ein ganz existentielles Interesse an Kunst und Künstlern der Gegenwart zu zeigen und ernsthaft in den Dialog einzutreten. Es geht darum, Möglichkeiten der Begegnung und des Gespräches mit Künstlern zu schaffen – zum Beispiel durch Ausstellungen, Atelier-Führungen, Kunstreisen, Diskussionen undsoweiter – und es geht schließlich auch darum, bei den Christen bis hin auf die Gemeinde-Ebene Interesse an der zeitgenössischen Kunst zu wecken und ihnen Zugänge zu ermöglichen. Und wenn es dabei zu Infrage-Stellen, zu Widerstand und vielleicht sogar zu heftigen Protesten kommt, so ist das noch immer besser als interesselose Ignoranz.

Warum bedarf die Liturgie der Kirche der zeitgenössischen Kunst?

Seit es Liturgie der Christen gibt, und das ist seit den Tagen der Apostel der Fall, gibt es auch Kunst in der Liturgie. Es wird gesungen, und sobald es die äußeren Umstände erlauben, werden eigene Räume für den Gottesdienst reserviert, und diese erhalten eine besondere Gestaltung, die zum Ausdruck bringt, worum es den Christen hier geht: in der liturgischen Versammlung erfahren sie die Gegenwart des erhöhten Herrn, in Wort und Sakrament, erfahren sie Gottes gnädige Zuwendung, als Kirche erfahren sie, daß die Vollendung, in die ihr Herr durch Tod und Auferstehung eingegangen ist, auch für sie selbst schon angebrochen ist, wenn auch noch verborgen.
Im Lauf der Geschichte der Kirche(n), haben die bildenden Künste im Hinblick auf den Gottesdienst einige Gattungen hervorgebracht, die immer in jeweils zeitgenössischen Formen anzutreffen sind. Dazu gehören vor allem: Bau und Ausstattung von Kirchen, Ikonen, liturgisches Gerät und Paramente. Auf uns gekommene Stücke dieser Gattungen lassen erkennen, wie die jeweilige Kirche in der entsprechenden Zeit sich selbst und ihren Gottesdienst verstanden hat, wie stark und lebendig geglaubt worden ist, welche Besonderheiten christlicher Frömmigkeit gerade entstanden und praktiziert worden sind, wie sie ihre Umwelt interpretiert und sich ihr gegenüber verhalten hat und noch vieles mehr.
Wenn nun Christsein und Glauben, Gottesdienstfeier und Gebet, auch in der Gegenwart lebendig, also "zeitgemäß" sind, dann muß sich das auch in zeitgenössischer sakraler Kunst aus-

60

drücken. Es bedarf dieses Zeugnisses, um zu zeigen, daß die Kirche und ihr Gottesdienst ganz existentiell in die Gegenwart gehören. Jegliches Sich-Begnügen mit dem Althergebrachten erweckt den Eindruck, daß die Liturgie der Kirche eigentlich schon "veraltet" und nur noch als ein Relikt der Vergangenheit vorhanden ist, oder daß die Gemeinde der Glaubenden aus der Gegenwart ausziehen und in die Vergangenheit flüchten muß, um ihren Glauben gemeinsam leben und feiern zu können. Wird die Botschaft des Heils "hier und heute" existentiell erfahren, angenommen und feiernd kundgetan, so muß das auch in Ausdrucksformen von "hier und heute" geschehen. Die Kirche und ihre Botschaft sind und bleiben freilich immer unwiderruflich gegeben, und die in Jesus Christus vollendete Erlösung ist ein für allemal geschehen. Da somit auch der Gottesdienst der Kirche seinem Wesen nach von Generation zu Generation und von Ort zu Ort derselbe bleibt, ist es auch sinnvoll und notwendig, daß alte Formen brauchbar bleiben und immer neu vollzogen werden können.

Es kann also nicht darum gehen, Neues gegen Altes, zeitgenössische Kunst gegen traditionelle Kunst, auszuspielen, sondern es geht um die glaubwürdige und lebendige liturgische Tradition. Tradition heißt ja nicht Vergangenes unverändert aufbewahren oder am Vergangenen um jeden Preis festhalten, wie es manche gerne verstehen möchten, sondern es heißt wörtlich (lateinisch: *tradere = trans-dare*) weitergeben, also hier und heute etwas annehmen, sich zueigen machen und damit leben und schließlich so weitergeben, daß auch andere es sich zueigen machen und damit leben können. Daraus ergibt sich sehr konsequent, daß zeitgenössische Kunst für den Gottesdienst der Kirche nicht einfach autonom sein kann, sondern immer auch solcher Tradition verpflichtet sein muß. Es geht also nicht darum, Künstlern der Gegenwart die Möglichkeit zu geben, "etwas" für die Kirche zu schaffen oder sich selbst irgendwie zum Ausdruck zu bringen, sondern – und das ist der besondere Dienst der Künstler an Kirche und Glauben, wenn sie eingeladen werden, für die Liturgie zu schaffen – sie stellen einer Christengemeinde Werke und Formen zur Verfügung, in denen und mit denen diese Gemeinde ihren Glauben artikulieren und feiern kann.

Zeitgenössische Kunst für den Gottesdienst darf den Christen nicht gegen ihren Willen und gegen ihre Überzeugung aufgezwungen werden, sondern sie muß ihnen die Möglichkeit zur Verfügung stellen, sich selbst damit ausdrücken zu können. Für den Gottesdienst bestimmte Kunst ist daher nicht nur Kunst für die Kirche, sondern im tiefsten Grund Kunst der Kirche selbst. Darüber muß sich jeder Künstler im klaren sein, der für die Liturgie der Kirche schafft.

Die Kirche als Auftraggeber für gottesdienstliche Kunst muß natürlich mit den Künstlern das Gespräch suchen, mit ihnen im Gespräch bleiben und ihnen plausibel machen, worum es in solchen Aufträgen geht. Es muß zum Beispiel darüber gesprochen werden, was eine Kirche (als Raum und als Gemeinde) ist und was darin geschieht, was ein Altar ist und was auf ihm geschieht, was den Christen das Evangelium und die Sakramente bedeuten, warum sie und wie sie Gott loben, welche Bedeutung die Verehrung der Heiligen hat, um nur einige wichtige Fragen anzuführen. Für die zufriedenstellende Erfüllung des Auftrags ist somit auch der Auftraggeber mitverantwortlich.

Die Kirche als Auftraggeber und Verantwortungsträger ist aber auch verpflichtet, den Christen und den Gemeinden zu helfen, eine ihnen zunächst noch nicht vertraute Formensprache lesen, erfassen und gebrauchen zu lernen. Leider wird gerade dieser Dienst nicht selten sträflich vernachlässigt. Manche Gemeinde fühlt sich gewissermaßen verurteilt, in einer "modernen Kirche" oder mit "moderner Kunst" feiern zu müssen, obwohl doch letzlich sie selbst einen Anspruch darauf hätte, in "ihrer Kirche" und mit "ihren Ausdrucksformen" zu feiern. Was oder wem nützt es, wenn zwar die internationale Fachpresse und bedeutende Kunstexperten zeitgenössische Werke der Sakralkunst anerkennen und in den höchsten Tönen loben, jene aber, für die sie geschaffen sind, nichts damit anfangen können, vielleicht sogar deshalb auswandern.

Gott sei Dank gibt es Erfahrungen, die dazu ermutigen, solche Gespräche zu beginnen. Es gibt sowohl das vermittelnde Gespräch, das heißt das Gespräch des Auftraggebers einerseits mit den Künstlern und andererseits mit der Gemeinde, es gibt aber auch das direkte Gespräch zwischen Künstlern und Gemeinden, in welchem beide Partner – und das ist wohl eine Voraussetzung für jedes ernstzunehmende Gespräch – sowohl Gebende wie auch Empfangende sind. Das kommt nicht nur beiden Gesprächspartnern zugute, das kommt auch die Kirche von heute, dem Gottesdienst von heute und nicht zuletzt der Welt und dem Menschen von heute zugute, die so oft vergeblich ein zeitgenössisches Zeugnis des Glaubens von der Kirche erwarten.

Summary

In this contribution three questions are posed in relation to modern art in the worship of the church. First, what is contemporary art all about? Second, why should the church be concerned with it? Third, why is contemporary art needed in the liturgy of the church? In contrast to the implied negatives these question appear to promote, the author explores some of the positive reasons for the church's involvement with contemporary art, notably the common concern to understand and communicate what is sacred in human experience.

Der Engadiner Kirchengesang im 17. und 18. Jahrhundert – ein kulturhistorisches Unikum[1]

Markus Jenny

Seit 1537 treten alljährlich die evangelischen Prädikanten Graubündens (Schweiz) zu ihrer Synode zusammen. Während fünf Tagen sind sie jedes Jahr wieder in einer anderen Gemeinde des weitverzweigten Berglandes zu Gast, lernen Landschaft und Leute jener Gegend kennen und bekommen Einblick in das dortige kirchliche Leben. Diese Eindrücke mögen bisweilen stärker gewesen sein als das, was der Einzelne von den Verhandlungen und vom kollegialen Beisammensein der Pfarrer mit nach Hause nahm. Es klang so:

Pseaume 108

Paratum cor meum, Deus

T. D. B.- M. P.

Mon cœur est dispos, ô mon Dieu, Mon cœur est tout prest en ce lieu

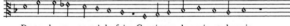

De te chanter tout à la fois Cantiques de main et de voix:

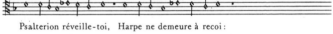

Psalterion réveille-toi, Harpe ne demeure à recoi:

Car je veux debout comparoistre, Dés que le jour vient à paroistre.

---

1 Radiovortrag DRS 2 vom 4. Juli 1972. Die Musikbeispiele wurden damals vom Radiochor unter Leitung von Prof. Martin Flämig gesungen. Diese gedruckte Fassung erschien zuerst in: *Bündner Monatsblatt. Zeitschrift für bündnerische Geschichte und Landeskunde* 1992, 375-388.

CANTUS — Mon cœur est dispos, ô mon Dieu, — Mon cœur est dis-pos,

QUINTUS (Cantus II) — Mon cœur est dispos, ô mon Dieu, — Mon cœur est dis-

ALTUS — Mon cœur est dispos, ô mon Dieu, — Mon cœur est dis -

SEXTUS (Tenor II) — Mon cœur est dispos, ô mon Dieu,

TENOR — Mon cœur est dispos, ô mon Dieu, — Mon cœur___ est dis-

BASSUS — Mon cœur est dispos, ô mon Dieu,

ô mon Dieu, — Mon cœur est tout prest en

- pos, ô mon Dieu, Mon cœur est dis-pos, ô mon Dieu, ___ Mon cœur est

- pos, ô mon Dieu, Mon cœur est dis-pos, ô mon Dieu,

Mon cœur est dis - pos, ô mon Dieu,

- pos, ô mon Dieu, Mon cœur est tout

Mon cœur___ est dis- pos, ô mon Dieu,

65

Abb. 1. Aus: R. Lagas (ed.), *Jan Pieterszoon Sweelinck: Opera omnia* II (Amsterdam 1965), 289-290.

Jedenfalls im Jahre 1712, als sich die Synode in Samedan versammelte, muß das so gewesen sein. Es dürften nur wenige Synodalen gewesen sein, die etwas ähnliches wie das, was sie hier im Gottesdienst als Musik zu hören bekamen, schon gehört hatten.

Es handelte sich um die erste Strophe einer Vertonung des Liedes zum 108. Genfer Psalm von Jan Pieterszoon Sweelinck aus dem Jahre 1623. Der Chor sang diese Psalmliedstrophe natürlich nicht mit dem originalen französischen Text, sondern so, wie sie im damals im Gebrauch stehenden ladinischen Kirchengesangbuch von 1661 zu finden war:

Mieu cor eis appino o Dieu
da celebrar il saench nom tieu,
et cun ma lengua voelg cantaer,
lo tiers sunand voelg te lodaer.
Ma cytt'r e psalter sü's sdaschdè
et cun voss tuns bain 's accordè,
ch'eau da m'sdaschdaer nu'm' voelg artegner,
manvalg per gnir avaunt il Segner.

Wer sich aufgrund der in Abbildung 1 wiedergegebenen Partitur ein hinlängliches Bild von dieser Musik machen kann, wird sagen, Ähnliches hätte er von Schallplatten, am Radio oder bei Kirchenkonzerten von hiesigen Kirchenchören auch schon gehört, und auch der Kenner wird sagen, Sweelinck sei zwar schöne Musik, aber ihr Auftreten im Engadin des 18. Jahrhunderts verdiene doch nicht, als Sensation eingestuft zu werden. Anders war das für die damaligen Hörer anläßlich der Synode, die aus allen reformierten Gemeinden der drei Bünde nach Samedan gereist waren. Einer unter ihnen war der erst 23 jährige Pfarrer von Churwalden, der drei Jahre zuvor in die Synode aufgenommen worden war, ein gebürtiger Engadiner aus Zernez, Nicolin Sererhard. Er sollte später noch öfter Gelegenheit bekommen, die Kirchenchöre seines Heimattales auf Synoden und wohl auch bei anderen Gelegenheiten zu hören. Und er wußte auch Bescheid über sie. Als Pfarrer von Seewis hat er später, im Jahre 1742, seine große Bündner Landeskunde, die *Einfalte Delineation aller Gemeinden gemeiner dreyen Bünden*, geschrieben und sich dabei seiner kirchenmusikalischen Erlebnisse im Hochtale der Ladiner erinnert. So schreibt er über den Flecken Zuoz, damals das politische und kulturelle Zentrum des Oberen Engadin:

Dies ist ein ansehnliches, großes und gleichsam städtisch erbautes Dorf, an einem zugleich anmuhtigen Ort situirt, hat auch ob ihme einen großen, lieblichen Berg. (...) Zu Zuz findet sich das rahreste Kirchen Gesang im ganzen Land, ja in vielen Ländern. Ein Zuzer Schulmeister hatte diese rare Singkunst von den Musicanten des Prinzen von Oranien in Holland erlehrnet und in seinem Vaterland schon vor ziemlich vielen Jahren durch Hilf der Herren Planta als Liebhabern der Music, die das gemeine Volk darzu mit allem Fleiß angetrieben, endlich in Übung bringen können. Der ganze Lobwasserische Psalter ist nur in 24 besondere Melodeyen gebracht, mit denen sie alterniren, die ganze Singer-Gesellschaft ist in sieben Chören abgetheilt, jeder Chor singt nur wenig Worte, der folgende empfacht dessen Stimm in der Eyl, da indessen der erstere pausirt, und also circuliren sie, und wechseln immer mit einandern ab auf die seltsammste Weiß, bis das Gesang vollendet ist. Hab mich auf dem Synodo zu Zuz über die Rarität dieser Music und über die Fertigkeit der Singern beyderley Geschlechts nicht wenig verwundern müssen, und darbey gedacht: Omnia conandi docilis solertia vincit [Der gelehrige Eifer, das Ganze zu wagen, wird siegen!], auch zugleich, wie noch weit herrlicher die Chören der himlischen Musicanten seyn werden.

Zu diesem Bericht ist nun allerhand zu bemerken. Zunächst dies: Aus nichts kam diese hohe Singkunst natürlich nicht. Früher als die meisten Orte der benachbarten und befreundeten Eidgenossenschaft kannte das Engadin den evangelischen Gemeindegesang, wahrscheinlich schon seit 1530. Das zweite Buch, das in einem der rätoromanischen Idiome gedruckt wurde, war das ladinische Kirchengesangbuch, eine getreue Übersetzung des in Zürich gedruckten Konstanzer Gesangbuches. Der Pfarrer von Susch, Duri Champell, hatte es geschaffen und auf eigene Kosten 1562 in Basel drucken lassen.

Mit dem Beginn des 17. Jahrhunderts begann sich in der deutschsprachigen evangelischen Eidgenossenschaft das reformierte Einheitsgesangbuch (wie man heute sagen würde), der Genfer Psalter, durchzusetzen. Ein Rechtsgelehrter im fernen Königsberg mit Namen Ambrosius Lobwasser hatte diese französische Bereimung sämtlicher 150 Psalmen ins Deutsche übertragen und mit diesem Werk einen beispiellosen Erfolg erzielt, wie ihn nur wenige Werke der Literatur zu verzeichnen haben; die Nachdrucke dieser Psalmliedersammlung sind ungezählt. Und weil man nicht nur in Genf, wo ab und zu Bündner Prädikanten studierten, und im reformierten Holland, wohin militärische Beziehungen bestanden, sondern auch in Bern, Basel und Zürich, den Vororten der reformierten Eidgenossenschaft, wo auch die Ausbildungsstätten der Theologen Bündens waren, diesen Psalter brauchte, sah der Zuozer Jurist Lurainz Wiezel sich veranlaßt, die Arbeit seines Königsberger Berufskollegen ins Ladinische weiterzuübersetzen. Es handelt sich also um eine Enkelübersetzung des französischen Urtextes der Genfer Dichter Clément Marot und Théodore de Bèze. Wiezel sagt das in seinem Titel ausdrücklich:

Ils Psalms da David, suainter la melodia francesa, schantaeda eir in tudaisch traes Dr. Ambrosium Lobwasser. (...) Da noef vertieus et schantos in vers romaunschs da cantaer, traes Lurainz Wietzel, Dr. da Ledscha.

(Die Psalmen Davids nach der französischen Melodie, auch deutsch übertragen durch Dr. Ambrosius Lobwasser. [...] Erneut übersetzt und in romanisch singbare Strophen gesetzt, durch Lurainz Wietzel, Doktor der Rechte.)

Der Engadiner Kirchengesang des 16. Jahrhunderts war einstimmig. Und auch dieses zweite Engadiner Gesangbuch, 99 Jahre nach dem ersten erschienen, enthält nur die einstimmigen Melodien. Der vierstimmige Kirchengesang kam in der Schweiz in eben jenen Jahren erst langsam auf.

Wer nun denkt, das Engadin, fernab von den großen Kultur-

und Musikzentren, hätte mit derselben Verzögerung, mit der es den Lobwasser-Psalter in ladinischer Fassung einführte, dann auch den vierstimmigen Kirchengesang im Anfang des 18. Jahrhunderts langsam aus dem Unterland importiert, täuscht sich. Im Gegenteil: Zu einem Zeitpunkt, da in den Unterländer Dörfern von der Größe von Zuoz, Samedan, S-chanf oder Puntraschigna mit Mühe wenigstens der einstimmige Psalmengesang eingeführt wurde, hörte man im Engadin schon vierstimmige Psalmenmusik. In den *Aschantamaints*, der Gemeindeordnung von Zuoz, wird der Kirchengesang schon 1666 erwähnt. Es heißt dort (in deutscher Übersetzung):

Eine Person aus jedem Hause ist verpflichtet, anwesend zu sein bei einer Busse von 6 Kreuzern. Wenn in der Kirche gesungen wird, so muß aus jedem Hause eine Person ihren Psalm [gemeint ist das Gesangbuch, M.J.] mitnehmen und singen; und diejenigen, die nicht singen können, sollen mit Andacht nachlesen, bei oben erwähnter Busse. Bei der gleichen Busse wird verboten, daß weder Männer noch Frauen die Kirche verlassen, solange der Gesang nicht beendet ist, und ist er beendet, so sollen die Frauen vor den Männern hinausgehen.

Zwei Jahre später heißt es in den Gemeindestatuten von Samedan:

Tuots aquels, chi haun Ig dunn da chianter, es dessen lascher tiers et continuar tuot Ig ann oura a chianter, nonobstante chia muriss Iur qualche prossem paraint, u ün otra persuna, schi per aque nun dessane interlaschar da der Iod al Segner cun Ig public chianter.
(All diejenigen, die des Singens mächtig sind, sollen [am Gottesdienst] teilnehmen und mit Singen das ganze Jahr durch fortfahren, auch wenn irgendeiner ihrer nächsten Angehörigen sterben sollte, oder eine andere Person, so sollen sie um dessentwillen nicht unterlassen, dem Herrn mit dem öffentlichen Singen zu preisen.)

So ernst wird der Gesang im Gottesdienst also genommen, daß die Verpflichtung zur Mitwirkung auch durch einen Todesfall in der Familie nicht aufgehoben wird. Zwar ist in beiden Fällen vom mehrstimmigen Gesang nicht die Rede. Aber die Strenge dieser Bestimmungen wird uns eigentlich nur verständlich, wenn wir an eigentlichen Chorgesang denken. Spätere Statuten, die ihn ausdrücklich erwähnen, lassen uns dasselbe vermuten. Wir haben aber sogar einen Beweis. Er führt uns nach S-chanf. Vor mir liegt ein seltenes Gesangbuch, das wohl musikalisch reichste und bemerkenswerteste Kirchengesangbuch, das im 17. Jahrhun-

dert in der Schweiz gedruckt wurde.[2] Die Textilfabrikanten
Gebrüder Gonzenbach von St. Gallen haben es bezahlt und die
Witwe Genath in Basel hat es 1669 gedruckt. Es enthält – so der
Kupfertitel – *Ambrosij Lobwassers D. Psalmen Davids. Mit IV
und V Stimmen des kunstreichen Claudin le Jeune. Sambt anderen
Geistreichen Gesängen vnd Gebetten In Verlag Hs. Jacob und
Bartholome Gontzenbach*. Claude le Jeune ist einer der besten
und fruchtbarsten Komponisten Frankreichs im 16. Jahrhundert
gewesen. Er starb 1600 in Paris als "compositeur de la musique
de la Chambre du Roy", obwohl er sich zum evangelischen
Glauben bekannte. Wie die meisten seiner Werke sind auch
seine vier- bis fünfstimmigen einfachen Liedsätze zu den Genfer
Psalmen nach seinem Tode von seiner Nichte herausgegeben
worden. 1648 erschienen sie dann in Amsterdam auch mit dem
deutschen Text Lobwassers. Und diese Ausgabe haben die Brü-
der Gonzenbach in Basel nachdrucken lassen. Das Vorsatzblatt
des mir vorliegenden Exemplars nun sagt in schön verzierten
Buchstaben:

Aquaist psalm oda alla honorata Uschina Unchia da Schianf cunpro anno 1674.
Inüs dals cantaduors chia Dieu voeglia chia que ludabel et bell Exercici da
chianter piglia tiers. Plü invia et plü et chia serva al Lod da Dieu et in sallüd da
nus tuots. Amen.
(Dieses Psalmenbuch [= Gesangbuch] gehört der ehrsamen Ursina Mengia
[Domenica] von S-chanf zu Nutzen, Anno 1674. Im Gebrauch der Sänger-
gemeinschaft. Schenke es Gott, daß diese löbliche und schöne Übung des Singens
zunehmen möchte, immer mehr, und daß sie dem Lob Gottes und dem Heil von
uns allen diene. Amen.)

Der erste Teil mit den Lobwasser-Psalmen im Tonsatz Le Jeunes zeigt sehr starke Gebrauchsspuren, während der zweite Teil
völlig unberührt ist. Seit 1674 singt man also in S-chanf – und
gewiß auch in den anderen Oberengadiner Gemeinden – Le
Jeunes Psalmsätze. Von keinem anderen Ort der Schweiz haben
wir den geringsten Hinweis auf den Gebrauch dieses Gesangbuches und seiner herrlich klingenden Musik. Die ungleich viel
stärker verbreiteten Psalmsätze des um eine Generation älteren
andern großen französischen Psalmkomponisten Claude Goudimel, waren im Engadin auch nicht unbekannt. In den Hand-

---

2 Vergleiche Markus Jenny, "Die beiden bedeutendsten deutschschweizerischen Kir-
   chengesangbücher des 17. Jahrhunderts", in: *Jahrbuch für Liturgik und Hymnologie*
   1 (Kassel 1955), 63-71.

schriften, von denen noch die Rede sein wird, finden wir neben Abschriften aus dem Le Jeune-Psalter auch Stimmen aus den Goudimel-Sätzen. Es war eine verlegerische und typografische Großleistung, daß Landammann Johann Batista Rascher von Zuoz dann 1733 diese Le Jeune-Sätze zu den 150 Genfer Psalmen mit dem romanischen Text Wietzels in einem fast 800 Seiten starken Quartband neu herausgab, von Johan Nuot Janet 1733 in dem kleinen Unterengadiner Dorf Strada gedruckt[3] – der bedeutendste Musikdruck in rätoromanischer Sprache, den es gibt. 1776 erschienen auch die Goudimel-Sätze im Druck mit ladinischem Text; aber für diesen wesentlich weniger schönen Druck von allerdings nun über 1000 Seiten brauchte es gleich vier Landammänner als "promotuors" und nicht weniger als drei Drucker!

Abb. 2a und 2b. Die Druckerpresse und der Setzkasten, die zur Herstellung des Engadiner Le Jeune-Psalters von 1733 dienten, im Rätischen Museum Chur (Foto E. Heer, Winterthur).

Während die französischen Hugenotten in ihren Gottesdiensten ausschließlich – auch an den Festtagen – Psalmen sangen, ent-

---

3 Das Haus, in welchem Janet druckte, steht noch heute, an der Firmen-Inschrift zu erkennen, und die Druckerpresse, auf der das Buch hergestellt wurde, hat sich erhalten; sie steht im Rätischen Museum in Chur (siehe Abb. 2).

hielten die Gesangbücher der deutschsprachigen Reformierten immer auch einen zweiten Teil mit Festliedern und anderen geistlichen Liedern. So auch die Engadiner Gesangbücher. Während man sich aber im Unterland damit begnügte, von dritt- und viertklassigen Notenbastlern Sätze im Stil Goudimels zu diesen Melodien schreiben zu lassen, gingen die Oberengadiner Kirchenchöre auch hier anspruchsvollere Wege. Das konnte freilich nicht dadurch geschehen, daß diese Gemeinden mit ihren wenigen tausend Einwohnern noch weitere Musik für ihre Chöre druckten; die Kosten dafür wären zu hoch gewesen. Die Chorsänger mußten sich vielmehr ihre Stimmen von Hand abschreiben und dann mit den romanischen Texten versehen. Von den Notenbüchern, welche auf diese Weise entstanden sind, ist eine größere Anzahl erhalten geblieben. Allein das Bündner Staatsarchiv in Chur verwahrt deren 28;[4] weitere befinden sich in den anderen Archiven und in Privatbesitz. Die ältesten beiden, die wir kennen, stammen aus S-chanf und sind schon 1667 und 1677 begonnen worden.[5] Da die Schreiber oft die benützte Quelle angeben – manchmal sogar mit der genauen Seitenzahl –, läßt sich relativ leicht feststellen, woher die Tonsätze stammen. So finden wir einige Sätze von Giovanni Battista Beria, der 1651 bis 1671 Organist in Novara war. Wohl aus einer 1597 in Heidelberg gedruckten Sammlung von Sätzen verschiedener französischen Meister zu den Genfer Psalmen ist ein sechsstimmiger Satz des ebenfalls kaum bekannten französischen Komponisten Jean de Maletty übernommen worden. Und um noch einen deutschen Komponisten zu nennen: Aus der 1622 in Neuauflage durch den Kantor von Rothenburg ob der Tauber, Erasmus Widmann, herausgegebenen Sammlung des Balthasar Musculus, die unter diesem letzteren Namen lief, übernahmen die Engadiner einen fünfstimmigen reizvollen Satz von Melchior Vulpius, dem Schöpfer mehrerer noch heute gesungener Kirchenliedmelodien. Der deutsche Text ist ein Weihnachtslied. Die Engadiner haben ein schon im 16. Jahrhundert romanisch gesungenes Osterlied von Thomas Blarer untergelegt, was einiges Geschick erforderte.

---

4 Sie sind verzeichnet und ausführlich beschrieben in: Rudolf Jenny, *Staatsarchiv Graubünden*, Bd. II: *Handschriften aus Privatbesitz. Repertorium mit Regesten* (Chur 1974), 525-575 und 611-625.
5 Ms. A 306, Ms. A 30 (vgl. Abb. 2b).

Zeigen schon diese drei Namen, wie weltoffen die Engadiner Kirchenmusik des ausgehenden 17. Jahrhunderts war – von Süden, Westen und Norden bezog man Werke von Format –, so wird uns die Fortsetzung im 18. Jahrhundert vollends in Staunen versetzen. Auch der Kenner der Musikgeschichte wird die drei genannten Namen im Lexikon nachschlagen müssen. In den Notenbüchern der Kirchenchöre aus dem 18. Jahrhundert aber taucht nun in überaus auffallender Häufigkeit ein Name auf, der Klang hat: Sweelinck. Jan Pieterszoon Sweelinck, geboren in Deventer in Holland 1562 und gestorben als Organist an der Oude Kerk zu Amsterdam, ist weithin nur als Orgelmeister bekannt. Mindestens so bedeutend ist aber sein Vokalwerk, das den krönenden Schlußstein der niederländischen Polyphonie darstellt. In vier umfangreichen Folgen hat Sweelinck sämtliche 150 Genfer Psalmen zu großen, fünf- bis achtstimmigen Motetten verarbeitet. Und diese vier Bücher Psalmen des großen Niederländers waren im Engadin nicht nur bekannt, sondern sie bildeten geradezu den Kern des Repertoires dieser Chöre. In kaum einer Handschrift fehlt der Name Sweelinck. Was Sererhard bei der Synode 1712 hörte, war ein Sweelinck-Psalm, und was er in seiner *Einfalten Delineation* dann beschreibt, ist offensichtlich – auch wenn der Name dort nicht genannt wird – der Vortrag dieser Musik.

Wie aber kommt diese niederländische Musik hundert Jahre nach ihrem Erscheinen ins ferne Hochtal hinauf? Selten glückliche Umstände helfen uns diese Frage beantworten: Im Gemeindearchiv von Zuoz liegen heute noch die originalen gedruckten Stimmbücher des gesamten Sweelinck'schen Psalmenwerks. Eine handschriftliche Eintragung darin besagt, daß ein Baltasar Planta sie 1707 in Amsterdam gekauft hat. Das Zuozer Patriziergeschlecht der Planta, deren Stammhaus dem großartigen Dorfplatz von Zuoz sein besonderes Gepräge gibt, hat also offenbar bei der Entwicklung des Engadiner Kirchengesangs die Hand entscheidend im Spiele gehabt. Ein Vetter des Baltasar von Planta war Oberst in holländischen Diensten. Er wird veranlaßt haben, daß der Zuozer Schulmeister, der den Kirchengesang leitete, zur weiteren Ausbildung nach Holland geschickt wurde ohne Zweifel auf Kosten dieser Kunstmäzene.

Abb. 3. Titelseite von Ms. A 30 im Churer Staatsarchiv.
Übersetzung der Titelseite: Eine kurze Anleitung zum Singen (und zur
Beachtung) der Pausen, zu zwei und drei Stimmen beschrieben. In
Gebrauch der ehrbaren und besonnenen Tochter Jungfrau Maritta [=
Marietta] von Planta ab AC [?] am 23. Januar des Jahres 1745.

1741 schreibt Baltasar Planta seinen Namen nochmals in eines
der gedruckten Sweelinck-Chorbücher und setzt dazu: "Seit
langem schwacher Sänger im Zuozer Chore". Um diese Zeit
muß die Sweelinck-Pflege einen neuen Aufschwung genommen
haben. Im Jahre 1744 wurde von den Gemeindeoberhäuptern zu
Zuoz die "Regula del chaunt" bestätigt. Der Kirchenchor war
eine feste Einrichtung geworden. Seit 1756 hören wir davon, daß
die Kirchensänger besoldet wurden; sie erhielten jährlich 30
Kreuzer aus der Gemeindekasse, seit 1768 36 Kreuzer. Dabei
wird den Säumigen mit Entzug der Besoldung gedroht. Während
bis dahin nur "ils signuors chantaduors" die Besoldung bekamen, erhalten nun auch die Sängerinnen ihren Lohn. Wer von
den Herren zwei Jahre ununterbrochen mitmacht, erhält nun 48
Kreuzer, die Damen der ersten Bank 12 Kreuzer, die auf den
beiden andern Bänken 20. Diese Differenzierung scheint daher
zu rühren, daß in der ersten Bank die schwächeren Sängerinnen
sitzen, die der "forsinger" (so heißt er auch im romanischen
Text der "Regula" immer) möglichst nahe bei sich haben will.

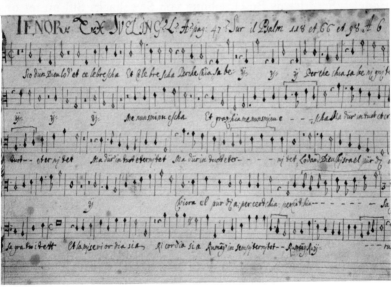

Abb. 4a und 4b. Zwei Seiten aus dem Innern des Ms. A 30, wo man in der Titelzeile das "Ex Sweling" erkennt.

Wenn Sererhard die Sänger in sieben Chöre aufgeteilt sah, so hat er offenbar die Aufführung eines siebenstimmigen Psalms erlebt, bei der die Sänger stimmenweise getrennt aufgestellt wurden. Wie das bei der bezeugten durchschnittlichen Mitgliederzahl von etwa 60 möglich war, bleibt uns allerdings verborgen. Nicht richtig informiert ist Sererhard offenbar, wenn er schreibt, der ganze Lobwasserpsalter sei in nur 24 besondere Melodeyen gebracht. Die Handschriften enthalten Abschriften von etwa doppelt so vielen Sweelinck-Psalmen. Ein Drittel dieses umfangreichen Werks war also in Gebrauch. Einzelne Stücke waren sogar in sehr starkem Gebrauch. "Magis in usu" heißt es in einer Handschrift bei einem Psalm. Der 108. Psalm, den wir zu Beginn wiedergegeben haben, gehört unter die sehr beliebten; er steht in 21 von den 26 Handschriften. Erstaunlich ist, daß zu den am stärksten verbreiteten ausgerechnet der dreistrophig durchkomponierte, achtstimmige 150. Psalm gehört; er steht in 15 der 26 Handschriften. Wenn dieser Psalm gelang, konnte man wahrhaftig den Hexameter skandieren: Omnia conandi docilis solertia vincit – Alles wagender Eifer zu lernen sieget am Ende! – Sererhards Beschreibung von Sweelincks Stil mutet uns merkwürdig an: "Jeder Chor [also: jede Stimme; M.J.] singt nur wenig Worte, der folgende empfacht dessen Stimm in der Eyl, da indessen der erstere pausirt, und allso circuliren sie und wechseln immer mit einandern ab auf die seltsammste Weiß, bis das Gesang vollendet ist."

Bei einem, der nur den Stil der Goudimel-Sätze kannte, bei dem stets alle Stimmen den Text gleichzeitig deklamieren und miteinander fortschreiten, mochte der polyphone Stil wohl tatsächlich zunächst diesen Eindruck erwecken. Auch für die Sänger selbst scheint das "pausieren" eine wichtige Rolle gespielt zu haben. Die Handschriften tragen zum Teil Titel. Da heißt es zum Beispiel:

Vna cuorta forma da cantaer per pausas à 4 et 5 vuschs. Descritta in üß da Sar Batrumieu I. Vedrosi. Anno 1742 die 6. Decembris.[6]
(Eine kurze Anleitung zum Singen (und zur Beachtung) der Pausen, zu vier und fünf Stimmen. Beschrieben in Gebrauch des Herrn Batrumieu I. Vedrosi. Im Jahre 1742, den 6. Dezember.)

Das ist die älteste erhaltene Handschrift mit Sweelinck-Psalmen.

---

6   Ms. A 30 (vgl. Abb. 3).

Später heißt es dann sogar:

Quaist Cudesch da Perpausas ais Scrit in Adöver Dalla Nobilissima et virtüusa Sig.ᵃ Margaritha G. De Perini. Schianf a 8. Aprile 1789.[7]
(Dieses Pausengesangbuch ist geschrieben zum Gebrauch der adligen und tugendhaften Frau Margaritha G. De Perini. S-chanf, den 8. April 1789.)

"Chiantar per pausas" – mit Pausen singen – bedeutet polyphon singen. Und so gibt es schließlich ein "Cudesch da Perpausas" – ein Pausengesangbuch. Jeder Musiker und Musikpädagoge weiß, daß Pausen auch Musik sind. Hier sind sie sogar zum Hauptmerkmal eines bestimmten Stiles geworden. Eine nette Illustration für jede Bemühung um ein rechtes Ernstnehmen der Pause in der Musik – und im Leben!

Man glaube nun aber nicht, die Oberengadiner im 17. und 18. Jahrhundert wären so verstiegen gewesen, daß sie nur noch komplizierte Polyphonie großer ausländischer Meister hätten singen wollen und können. In 22 dieser Handschriften finden wir beispielsweise das folgende schlichte Karfreitagslied, das sich also größter Beliebtheit erfreut haben muß und das unter Nummer 150 noch heute im deutschschweizerischen reformierten Kirchengesangbuch steht (siehe Abb. 5).

Das Lied findet sich nicht nur in den hier behandelten Handschriften, sondern es steht auch in einem gedruckten Engadiner Gesangbuch, der "Philomela" des Johannes Martinus ex Martinis, Pfarrer in Ramosch, in 2. Auflage 1702 in Zürich gedruckt. In der Mehrzahl der Handschriften steht bei diesem Stück: "Ex Seelenmusik". Damit ist ein Gesangbuch gemeint, das in St. Gallen 1684 zum ersten Mal erschienen war und das die Engadiner offenbar in der 6. Auflage von 1719 benützten. Auch die "Philomela" hat eifrig daraus geschöpft. In der deutschsprachigen Schweiz wurde es als Musizierstoff der Musikkollegien verwendet, niemals aber im Gottesdienst, wo man sich streng auf die Lobwasserschen Psalmlieder und einige wenige Festgesänge beschränkte. Die Engadiner scheinen hier freier gewesen zu sein. Sie haben nach Ausweis der Handschriften manche Sätze aus dieser und ähnlichen Quellen mit Texten aus dem Wietzel versehen und sie offensichtlich im Gottesdienst gebraucht. Damit kam neben dem polyphonen Stil der Sweelinck-Psalmen und anderer ähnlicher Sätze ein ganz neues

---

7 Ms. A 6418, Ms. A 339 und 3089 Ms. A 308.

Abb. 5: Nr. 159 im offiziellen Engadiner Kirchengesangbuch *IL CORAL* von 1987.

stilistisches Moment herein und sicherte dieser Kirchenmusikpfege eine Vielfalt, die sie anderswo in der Schweiz kaum hatte.

Immerhin: Wenn man in der 2. Hälfte des 18. Jahrhunderts "O Stramantur" sang, war man – zwar nicht 200 Jahre, wie bei Sweelinck, aber – doch 100 Jahre hinter der Zeit drein. Man müßte also von der Engadiner Kirchenmusikpflege ähnliches sagen wie von der heutigen: Sie lebt aussließlich von Werken und Stilen vergangener Zeiten und hat kaum den Anschluß an die Musik der Gegenwart.

Nun ist es allerdings erstaunlich, daß man im Engadin noch am Anfang des 19. Jahrhunderts Sweelinck gesungen hat. (Die jüngste der Churer Handschriften[8] ist zu Anfang des 19. Jahrhunderts geschrieben und wurde laut Besitzer-Einträgen 1815 und 1823 in Samedan immer noch benützt; und sie enthält noch

---

8 Ms. A 339 und 308.

zwei Sweelinck-Psalmen.) Wenn es schon erstaunlich ist, daß
man im Oberengadin Sweelinck gesungen hat, so ist es wohl
noch erstaunlicher, daß man dort noch 200 Jahre nach Sweelincks Tod seine Werke sang. Aber deswegen lebten die Engadiner des 18. Jahrhunderts oder um 1800 keineswegs etwa nur in
der Vergangenheit. Die eben genannte Handschrift enthält zum
Beispiel Lieder des 1810 verstorbenen Zürcher Komponisten
und Musikpädagogen Johann Heinrich Egli, also wenn auch
nicht gerade "moderne" so doch absolut zeitgenössische Musik!
Und so war es auch in den Jahrzehnten davor. Das sei an einem
letzten Beispiel gezeigt. Eine unserer Churer Handschriften[9]
trägt den Titel:

*Halleluja Musicale u Cudasch da musica Nel quael sun descrits
Alchüns Psalms et Canzuns spirituaelas, cun novas Melodias, a
2. 3 et püssas Vuschs. Descrit In Adoever della Honorata Casta
et Prudainta Juvna, Jungfrau Vintüra Celerer Da Bever. A°
MDCCLXIV.*

Dreierlei fällt an diesem Titel auf: Einmal "neue Melodien".
Zum andern: Nicht mehr fünf- bis achtstimmig, sondern: "für 2,
3 und mehr Stimmen". Und schließlich der blumige Wortlaut:
"Musikalisches Halleluja". Nun: da hat ein Werk der damals
neuen schweizerischen geistlichen Musik Pate gestanden, das
genau diesen Titel trägt: *Musikalisches Halleluja, oder schöne und
geistreiche Gesänge, mit neuen und anmuthigen Melodeyen beglei-
tet, und zur Aufmunterung zum Lob Gottes in Truck übergeben
von Johann Caspar Bachofen, V.D.M. et Cant. der Kirchen und
Schulen. Fünfte und privilegirte Auflage. Zürich, getruckt in Bürg-
klischer Truckerey. 1750.* Die erste Auflage war schon 1727 erschienen; 1755 war der Komponist gestorben. Die Lieder dieses
Buches sind für zwei hohe Stimmen und eine Männerstimme
mit Generalbaß geschrieben. Sie atmen einen ganz neuen Stil,
wie das Osterlied, das sehr beliebt gewesen sein muß (siehe
Abb. 6). Und das neben einem Sweelinck-Psalm! Wird da nicht
eine musikalische Beweglichkeit verlangt, die man heute bei
manchen Kirchenmusikern vergeblich sucht?
Eine letzte Frage mag offen sein: Hat denn das Engadin selbst
nichts beigetragen zu seiner Kirchenmusik? Musikalisch nicht.

---

9 Ms. A 308.

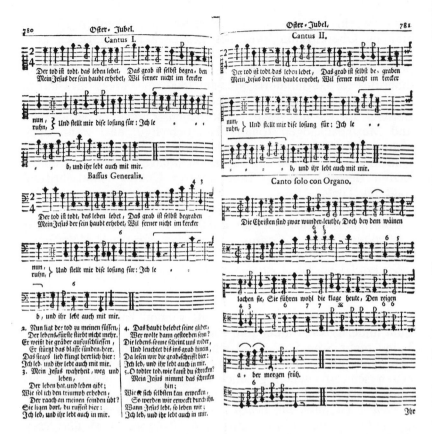

Abb. 6. Das Osterlied B. Schmolcks, in der Vertonung von J.C. Bachofen (1743), das sich in den Engadiner Handschriften in ladinischer Übersetzung findet (*La muort ais mort, La vita viva*).

Es gibt in den Handschriften zwar zwei oder drei Sätze, die offenbar von Engadinern geschaffen sind. Aber daran sind nun wirklich die Pausen das beste. Dennoch meine ich, daß hier unter dem Titel "Eigenleistung des Engadin" noch etwas zu sagen bleibt: Gerade bei den ins Ladinische übertragenen Bachofen-Liedern fällt es auf, daß verhältnismäßig viele nur je in einer einzigen Handschrift stehen, also offenbar von dem betreffenden Schreiber oder für ihn zu seinem Hausgebrauch hergestellt wurden. Wieviel einfacher wäre es gewesen, das Lied einfach deutsch zu singen; man wollte sich ja vor allem an der

80

neuen Musik erfreuen. Aber nein: Der Assimilationswille des Engadiners war stärker. Er wollte sich das Lied ganz aneignen, und das bedeutete, daß er die Musik abschrieb und den Text übersetzte. Nun erst konnte es als sein Lied gelten. Dieses Nebeneinander und Ineinander von unbefangener Weltoffenheit und selbstbewußter Assimilationskraft wird es auch heute sein, was der engadinischen Kultur eine Zukunft sichert. Die Kirchenmusik des 17. und 18. Jahrhunderts könnte hierin Modell sein. Wenn auch der Weg zum Ziel nicht immer ein so einfacher ist, wie hier, wo es mit dem Übersetzen und Unterlegen von Texten getan war, so dürfte doch der Eifer und Einsatz, der hinter dieser Kirchenmusikpflege steht, vorbildlich sein. Nochmals der von Sererhard zitierte Hexameter: Omnia conandi docilis solertia vincit – Der gelehrige Eifer, das Ganze zu wagen, wird siegen! Dann wird eine eigenständige Engadiner Kultur trotz Abhängigkeit von außen, trotz Infiltration durch den Fremdenverkehr, trotz der Nivellierungstendenz unseres Massenmedienzeitalters, möglich sein.

Summary

In the far south-east of Switzerland is the Engadin valley, through which the Inn river flows, where Rhaeto-Roman dialects are spoken. The church of the area, like that of neighbouring German-speaking Switzerland, is Reformed. As in the German areas of Switzerland, the congregational songs of worship in the churches are the psalms from the Genevan psalter. Since 1661 there has been an Engadin-Romansch, that is, Ladin, translation of the psalms for use with the Genevan melodies. For choral part-singing, which in a great many places replaced congregational unison, settings of the psalm-tunes were re-published in the Ladin edition issued in Basle. The single extant copy of the Ladin edition is found in the congregational archive of Zuoz. What is immediately noticeable is that a great number of the multi-voiced settings of the Genevan psalm melodies are the work of the Dutch composer Jan Pieterszoon Sweelinck. These settings, with their Ladin texts, were copied and became part of the repertoire of church choirs in the area of Engadin, as is witnessed by manuscripts in the Staatsarchiv, Chur. These Sweelinck psalm-settings were widely distributed and greatly loved in the area. This unicum therefore provides evidence for a significant dissemination of music.

Introit for Easter

Wim Kloppenburg

Texts: *Erschienen ist der herrlich Tag,* by Nikolaus Herman
(1560), stanzas 1, 2, 9, 13 and 14, translated into
Dutch by W.J. van der Molen; *Liedboek voor de Ker-*
ken (The Hague and Leeuwarden 1973), No. 200.
© 1973 Interkerkelijke Stichting voor het Kerklied,
The Hague.
Psalm 118, verses 23, 22, 17-18 and 15.
English translations © 1993 Robin A. Leaver.

Melody: *Erschienen ist der herrlich Tag,* by Nikolaus Herman
(1560), adapted from the medieval antiphon *Ad mon-*
umentum.

Setting: © 1992 Wim Kloppenburg.

1   Glorious has dawned this day of days,
in which we sing abundant praise.
For Christ is risen from the dead,
and all his foes has captive led. Alleluia.

    This is the day that the Lord has made,
let us rejoice, and let us sing with gladness.
Alleluia, alleluia, alleluia.

2   The source of evil, death and sin,
the depths of hell and all therein
have all been conquered by the Lord,
the risen Christ by all adored. Alleluia.

    The stone that the builders rejected
is now the head of the corner. Alleluia.
This the Lord Almighty has done;
it is wonderful for us who see it.
Alleluia, alleluia, alleluia.

3   The strength of death is now undone;
the stronger pow'r of life has won;
the claims of death are all in vain,
for Christ has brought us life again. Alleluia.

    I shall not die but I shall live,
and I shall proclaim
what the Lord has done for me. Alleluia.

82

The Lord has afflicted me,
bunt he did not surrender me to death.
Alleluia, alleluia, alleluia.

4   The whole creation far and near,
that in death's darkness lived in fear,
this day rejoices with renown
that this world's prince is overthrown. Alleluia.

Hear, songs of triumph and joy
in the tents of the righteous;
the right hand of the Lord is mighty and strong. Alleluia.

Glory to the Father and the Son and the Holy Spirit,
as it was in the beginning, is now,
and for ever shall be, world without end. Alleluia.
Alleluia, alleluia, alleluia. Amen.

5   So we should sing our joyful praise
and worthy Alleluias raise;
to Christ, our resurrected Lord,
all praise and glory be outpoured. Alleluia.

Introitus voor Pasen
Psalm 118 / Gezang 200

Wim Kloppenburg

koor unisono

Dit is de dag die de He- re ge- maakt heeft,
This is the day that the Lord has made,

orgel

la- ten wij jui- chen en ons daar- o- ver ver- heu- gen.
let us re- joice, and let us sing with glad- ness.

Hal- le- lu- ja, hal- le- lu- ja, hal- le- lu- ja.

allen

(begeleiding: zie str. 1)

2. De nacht, de zon- de en de dood, de hel, het leed, de angst, de nood, dit al- les
The source of e- vil, death and sin, the depths of hell and all there- in have all been

is te- niet ge- daan, nu on- ze Heer is op- ge- staan. Halle- lu- ja.
con- quered by the Lord, the ri- sen Christ, by all ad- ored.

85

allen

3. Die eens de buit was van de dood en weerloos lag in aar-de's schoot, Hij heeft het
The strength of death is now un- done; the stronger pow'r of life has won; the claims of

licht te-rug-ge-bracht, Hij schenkt het le-ven o- ver-macht. Hal-le- lu- ja.
death are all in vain, for Christ has brought us life a- gain.

koor

Ik zal niet ster-ven maar le- ven en ik zal de da- den des
I shall not die but I shall live, and I shall pro- claim what the

orgel

He- ren ver-kondi- gen. ST Hal- le- lu- ja
Lord has done for me. AB Hal- le-lu- ja

De Heer heeft mij zwaar ge-kastijd, maar aan de dood heeft Hij mij niet
The Lord has a- fflic- ted me, but he did not sur- ren-der

o- ver-ge-ge- ven.
me to death.

Hal- le lu- ja, hal- le- lu- ja, hal- le- lu- lja

4. Heel d'aarde, al het schepsel zal opstaan in 't zonlicht o-ver- al; voorbij is
The whole cre-a-tion, far and near, that in death's darkness lived in fear, this day re-

nu de droe-fe- nis, omdat de Heer ver-re-zen is. Hal-le- lu- ja.
joic-es with re- nown that this world's prince is o- ver-thrown.

Hoort, ju- bel-lied en ze- ge- zang in de ten-ten der recht
Hear, songs of tri- umph and joy in the tents of the

vaar-di-gen; de rech- ter- hand des He- ren doet krachti- ge
righ- teous; the right hand of the Lord is migh-ty and

Hal- le- lu- ja.
da- den. Hal- le-lu- ja.
strong.

E- re zij de Va- der en de Zoon en de hei- li- ge
Glo- ry to the Fa- ther and the Son and the Ho- ly

Geest, als het was in den be- gin- ne, nu en im- mer,
Spirit, as it was in the be- gin- ning, is now,

89

en van eeu- wig- heid tot eeuwig-heid. Hal- le- lu- ja.
and for ev- er shall be, world without end.

koor en orgel

S
A
Hal- le- lu- ja, hal- le- lu- ja, hal- le- lu- ja.
T
B

A- men

allen

5. Ook wij, wij zet-ten blij van zin een stralend hal-le-lu- ja in. O Christus
So we should sing our joy-ful praise and worthy Al- le- lu- jas raise; to Christ, our

die verre- zen zijt, wij prijzen uw aanwe- zig-heid. Halle- lu- ja.
re- surrec- ted Lord, all praise and glo-ry be out- poured.

voor Casper Honders
Pasen 1992

90

A Christmas Service in Dutch and English held in the Scottish Church in Rotterdam in 1801

Robin A. Leaver

While researching the background of a preaching lectionary, published in Rotterdam in 1782,[1] I came across the following octavo pamphlet:
GODSDIENSTIG | KERS-FEEST | OF | FEEST-GEZAN-GEN | IN DE | SCHOTSCHE KERK | TE | ROTTERDAM, | TER VIERING VAN HET KERS-FEEST | DES JAARS 1801. | (...) | DOOR | J. SCHARP, | (...) Te ROTTERDAM, | Bij J. P. VAN GINKEL, Boekverkooper, 1802.
(Devout Christmas-Festival or Festival-Songs in the Scottish Kirk in Rotterdam, for the Celebration of the Christmas-Festival of the Year 1801. By J. Scharp, Rotterdam: J. P. Van Ginkel, Bookseller, 1802.) xii and 68 pages.

The pamphlet contains a macaronic service of worship in Dutch and English, compiled and written by the Dutch Reformed pastor and poet of Rotterdam, Jan Scharp (1756-1828). Since Casper Honders encouraged his students to study the inter-relationships between Dutch and English hymnody,[2] and wrote on Scharp in the *Compendium (...) Liedboek voor de Kerken*,[3] an investigation of the contents of this booklet seemed particularly appropriate for this Honders Festschrift.

---

1 See Robin A. Leaver, *Lection, Sermon, and Congregational Song: A Preaching Lectionary of the Dutch Reformed Church (1782) and its Implications*, forthcoming in the Howard G. Hageman Festschrift (1993).

2 See, for example, the "doctoraalscriptie" by Piet Harinck, *De Engelse 'Hymn' in Nederland in de Negentiende Eeuw*, Rijksuniversiteit te Groningen, July 1982; and the doctoral dissertation by Robin A. Leaver, Rijksuniversiteit te Groningen, September 1987, later published in a revised form as *"Goostly Psalmes and Spiri-tuall Songes" English and Dutch Metrical Psalms from Coverdale to Utenhove 1535 - 1566* [Oxford Studies in British Church Music] (Oxford 1991).

3 *Een Compendium van achtergrondinformatie bij de 491 Gezangen uit het Liedboek voor de Kerken* (Amsterdam 1977), cols. 1027-28.

Following the constitution of the Republic of the United Netherlands in 1581, commercial relations between the Dutch and the British were intensified. The mercantile port of Rotterdam played a key role in this commerce and many English and Scots merchants and businessmen settled with their families in the city. Members of the Church of England were denied permission to conduct public services of worship in 1611, but were eventually granted authorization to use St. Sebastian's Chapel in 1627.[4]

This place of worship was shared with a French Reformed congregation, and, at a later stage, was also used by the Scottish Church in the city. Between 1703 and 1708 the Anglicans built their own church in Rotterdam. English Presbyterians formed a congregation in 1623 and subsequently, in 1716, moved into their own specially built church.[5] There also appears to have been an English Friends Meeting House, which had a chequered and uncertain history.

In the first half of the seventeenth century there was a small Church of Scotland congregation in Rotterdam, but it existed without a permanent minister. The first minister was appointed in 1643 and on 7 January 1644 the sacrament of the Lord's Supper was administered for the first time. The foundation stone of a new church building was laid on 13 November 1695, and two years later, on 20 October 1697, this Scottish Church in Rotterdam was dedicated.[6] The minister at the time was Robert Fleming, jun., the son of the previous minister of the church, and grandson of James Fleming, whose first wife had been a daughter of the Scottish Reformer John Knox. Robert Fleming, jun., was a also a poet of some note.[7]

At the time that the new church building came into use at the end of the seventeenth century, the Scottish Church in Rotter-

---

4 Information on the English churches in Rotterdam is derived principally from William Steven, *The History of the Scottish Church, Rotterdam: To which is subjoined Notices of the other British Churches in the Netherlands* (Edinburgh 1833).

5 It is this church in Rotterdam, rather than the Scottish church, that the Scotsman James Boswell, the great biographer of Dr. Samuel Johnson, attended on 15 January 1764; see Frederick A. Pottle (ed.), *Boswell in Holland 1763-1764* [The Yale Editions of the Private Papers of James Boswell] (New York 1952), 119.

6 For a description of the church, see Steven, op. cit., 127-28; see also an engraving of the church's exterior facing 127.

7 See the examples given in Steven, op. cit., 122 and 135.

dam served at least 800 people, but over the following century a significant decline occurred, so that in 1795 only 320 were counted.[8] Thus at the beginning of the nineteenth century the congregation could only support one minister, in place of two hitherto. Jan Scharp, the senior minister of the Dutch Reformed Church in Rotterdam ministered from time to time in the Scottish Church during these early years of the century. That the worship of this congregation should be led by a Dutch Reformed minister is not surprising since the basic Calvinist theology was common to both churches, and the congregation of the Scottish Church in Rotterdam was not exclusively made up of ex-patriot Scots. The lists of ministers, elders and deacons contain many Dutch names, such as De Vries, Hoog, Ho[o]rnbeek, Roos, Verbeek, etc,[9] and a good number of these Dutch families, including those of Scharp and Hoog, could claim Scottish ancestry.[10]

Following the custom of the Dutch Reformed Church, every seat in the Scottish Church was supplied with a quarto Bible and psalm book. The psalm books were later imprints of the 1650 Scottish Psalter: *The Psalms of David in Meeter: Newly translated and diligently compared with the Original Text and former (...) Allowed by the Authority of the General Assembly of the Kirk of Scotland, and appointed to be sung in Congregations and Families* (Edinburgh 1650). Customarily these psalm books were issued without tunes, although from the late 1660s a collection of just twelve tunes – all in Common Measure – was sometimes bound with the psalm book. By 1700 these melodies had assumed the status of the basic corpus of tunes for the worship of the Church

---

8 Steven, op. cit., 227.
9 Ibid., 336 and 368-69.
10 Jan Scharp's grandfather was born in London, and among his ancestors he claimed John Sharp (1572?-1648?), professor of divinity, Edinburgh University, and John Sharp (1645-1714), archbishop of York; see Steven, op. cit. 236. Thomas Hoog, who preached at Jan Scharp's funeral in 1828, was proud of his Scots ancestry; Steven (op. cit., 240-41) records: "The writer well remembers the animation which beamed in the good man's countenance when, adverting to this subject, he significantly pressed his hand to his heart, and exclaimed in the Dutch language, that he was a Scotchman through and through" ("door en door").

of Scotland.[11] In the mid-1750s a musical reform had begun, largely instigated by the Englishman Thomas Channon, who was almost certainly a Methodist. In Monymusk parish church near Aberdeen he established a choir and promoted the livelier tunes generated by the Evangelical Revival in England.[12] Channon took his singers to other parishes to promote his goals. For example, in January 1755 he is reported to have had a choir of seventy.[13] Six years later John Wesley heard the singing of Channon's choir in Monymusk Church on Thursday 7 May 1761, and recorded the following in his *Journal*: "Thirty or forty sang an anthem after [the] sermon, with such voices as well as judgment, that I doubt whether they could have been excelled at any cathedral in England."[14] The movement spread from Aberdeen to Edinburgh and Glasgow, and ultimately to many congregations of the Church of Scotland, including the Scottish Church in Rotterdam.

One of the ministers of the Rotterdam Scottish Church in the latter part of the eighteenth was Alexander Layel, who was minister of the Scottish Church in Dordrecht before moving to Rotterdam in 1770, where he remained until his death in 1796. It was during Layel's ministry that the Scottish Church in Rotterdam developed a significant reputation for church music. Steven writes of Layel's influence in this regard: "During his incumbency, and owing to his great partiality for sacred music, and by the pains which he took in improving this important, but much neglected branch of public worship, the Scottish Church became celebrated, and was much resorted to by amateurs during the weekly exhibitions."[15] Layel clearly promoted similar musical reforms to those that Channon had championed in Scotland by the formation of a choir to lead the worship of the church. To judge from the music of the Christmas service of

11 According to Millar Patrick, *Four Centuries of Scottish Psalmody* (London 1949), 111, the tunes are: COMMON TUNE, KING'S TUNE, DUKE'S TUNE, ENGLISH TUNE, FRENCH, LONDON (LONDON NEW), STILT (YORK), DUNFIRMLINE, DUNDEE, ABBEY, MARTYRS, and ELGIN; in Maurice Frost, *English & Scottish Psalm & Hymn Tunes c. 1543-1677* (London 1953) they are numbered respectively: 121, 202, 203, 19, 204, 42, 205, 206, 129, 207, 209, 210.

12 See Patrick, op. cit., chaps. 14 and 16.

13 Ibid., 153.

14 *The Works of the Reverend John Wesley* (New York 1831), Vol. 7, 97.

15 Steven, op. cit., 228.

1801, the musical reforms in the Scottish Church in Rotterdam, as in Scotland, were evangelical in character. Alexander Layel was encouraged in his attempts to improve the music of the church by the appointment of James Somerville as the senior minister in 1775. Around the time of Somerville's appointment, as Steven reports, "many pious and well disposed persons ardently wished that some additional Psalmody, more suited to the purposes of evangelical worship, were admitted to be sung in public."[16] No doubt Layel was one of the "pious and well disposed persons" desiring an expansion of the psalmody sung in the church.

Between 1742 and 1745 a committee of the General Assembly of the Church of Scotland worked on the preparation of scriptural paraphrases to be sung in addition to the metrical psalms. Eventually forty-five metrical paraphrases, many of them revisions of existing texts by Isaac Watts, Philip Doddridge and other English and Scottish writers, were published as *Translations and Paraphrases, in verse, of several Passages of Sacred Scripture* (Edinburgh 1745). But these "Paraphrases" were not officially sanctioned, principally because "the Moderates, then dominant in the Church, thought the collection too evangelical."[17] In 1749 the General Assembly of the Church of Scotland directed that a revised and corrected edition be prepared. This revision was published in 1751 but its authorization was for private rather than public use.[18] The *Paraphrases* may have been too evangelical for the Church of Scotland as a whole, but the Scottish Church in Rotterdam, some twenty years later, decided, after some discussion, to request permission from the General Assembly of the Church of Scotland to sing them in public worship. This was granted and the Rotterdam Scottish Church began singing the *Paraphrases* on 6 January 1779, the first Sunday of the new year. But at the beginning of the service, before the *Paraphrases* were sung, a paper written by James Somerville and approved by the Church Consistory was read from the pulpit. After giving something of the background of the *Paraphrases*, James Somerville stated that they had been drawn

16 Ibid., 208.
17 Patrick, op. cit., 212.
18 On the background, see John Julian, *A Dictionary of Hymnology*, 2nd. revised edition (London 1907), 1033-1034.

up "not from any spirit of innovation, but from a real desire more fully to promote the glory of God (...) the Consistory have agreed to admit these paraphrases as a part of their psalmody (...) and they pray that God may powerfully bless them for the advancement of his own praise and glory."[19]

A committee of the General Assembly, appointed in 1775, was then working on a substantial revision and expansion of the *Paraphrases*, which was eventually published and authorized for public worship: *Translations and Paraphrases, in Verse, of Several Passages of Sacred Scripture: Collected and Prepared by a Committee of the General Assembly of the Church of Scotland, in order to be Sung in Churches* (Edinburgh 1781). As soon as this newly published *Paraphrases* was available, it displaced the earlier version that had been in use in Rotterdam during the previous few years. Steven reports: "These Paraphrases, afterwards considerably altered and improved by a committee of the General Assembly, were introduced at Rotterdam, as soon as they had received the *imprimatur* of the mother Church."[20] At Christmas in 1801 these 1781 *Paraphrases* were still in use, but the musical aspects of the worship of the Scottish Church in Rotterdam appear to have been developed further.

At this period the Church of Scotland did not celebrate Christmas; in contrast, the Dutch Reformed Church had a long history of the observance of the principal festivals of the church year.[21] This Dutch practice clearly influenced the Scottish Church in Rotterdam, in which it was customary to observe Christmas with some form of "public worship accompanied with vocal music."[22] Towards the end of the year of 1801, the Church Consistory decided to ask Jan Scharp to preach a charity sermon on Christmas Day, Friday 25 December, for the benefit of the Scottish poor and a charity school in the city. Henricus Moens and P.M. Keller, respectively elder and deacon of the congregation, took the invitation to Scharp. Scharp, agreed and proposed that the whole service, including the sermon, prayers, introductions to the singing, and so forth, should be in poetic form. He

---

19 Consistory records, cited Steven, op. cit., 209.
20 Ibid., 209.
21 See the article by Leaver cited in note 1 above.
22 Steven, op. cit., 238.

also suggested that the event should be advertized beforehand in the city's newspapers, to ensure a good attendance.[23] In the event circumstances prevented the service from taking place on Christmas Day, and it was postponed to the following Wednesday, 30 December. Scharp reports that the service was a success and that the congregation included Christians from all denominations, including other poets of note.[24] The impact was such that this remarkable poetic exercise – reputed to have been written in eight days[25] – was published, sold-out, and reprinted.[26] The profits of the publication were added to the charitable aims of the offering taken at the service.

From the contents of the service it would seem that the congregation had access to copies of the 1781 *Paraphrases* and the Dutch psalter, *Het Boek der Psalmen, nevens de Gezangen bij de Hervormde Kerk van Nederland*, compiled in 1773 and authorized for use from January 1775. It is possible that the congregation also had access to copies of Watts's *Hymns and Spiritual Songs* (London 1707). The music for choir and soloists was presumably supplied in manuscript.

The *Godsdienstig Kers-Feest* gives the complete text of the service, that is, the sermon, prayers, introductions to the singing, the texts of the hymns, set-pieces and other items sung by the choir and soloists. In most cases the names of the British tunes are given, but before they can be investigated the order and textual content of the service needs first to be discussed. An outline of this poetico-musical service is given in sequence below:

[1]	Congregational Hymn	English
[2]	Sermon	Dutch
[3]	Choir	English
[4]	Congregational Psalm	Dutch
[5]	Trio [+ Choir ?]	Dutch
[6]	Congregational Hymn	English
[7]	Choir [?]	Dutch
[8]	Choir [?]	English
[9]	Charitable Appeal	Dutch
[10]	Choir	Dutch

---

23 *Godsdienstig Kers-Feest*, vii; see Steven, op. cit., 238.
24 *Godsdienstig Kers-feest*, vii.
25 Steven, op. cit., 238.
26 Scharp dedicated the pamphlet to the Consistory of the Scottish Congregation in Rotterdam and signed himself "Medebroeder in Christus"; *Godsdienstig Kers-Feest*, iii-iv.

97

[11]	Choir	Dutch
[12]	Duo	Dutch
[13]	Choir [?]	Dutch
[14]	Choir	Dutch
[15]	Choir [?]	English
[16]	Choir	Dutch
[17]	Congregational Hymn	English
[18]	Choir	Dutch
[20]	Congregational Hymn	Dutch
[21]	Benediction	Dutch

The service began with a hymn [1], No. 19 of the *Paraphrases* of 1781, *The race that long in darkness pin'd* (Isaiah 9.2-8). Scharp indicates that this was sung by the "Schotsche Zang-choor,"[27] however, since only the first stanza is given, perhaps this was sung by the choir and the remainder of the stanzas by the congregation.

The poetic sermon [2], on the Song of Simeon, followed and runs to no less than 34 pages of the pamphlet, and therefore must have taken at least an hour to deliver. The sermon was immediately followed by the choir singing stanzas 1-3 and 5 of Isaac Watts's hymn *Come let us join our chearful* [sic] *songs* based on Revelation 5.11-13 [3].[28] The choir and congregation then joined in singing a Dutch psalm [4]: *Hoe lieflijk, hoe vol heilgenot*, stanzas 1 and 2 of Psalm 84, from *Het Boek der Psalmen* (1773), set to the sturdy Genevan tune that first appeared in *Les Pseaumes mis en rime Françoise, Par Clément Marot, & Theodore de Bèze* (Geneva 1562).[29]

The remainder of the service comprised choral, vocal and congregational music, arranged before and after the central act of the charitable offering. A "Trio" was next [5], an irregular metrical text beginning "Zoo werdt vervuld der Vaderen verlangen," with a passage marked "solo", which was immediately followed by three stanzas of Common Metre, with a concluding "Alleluia" coda:

[1]   Een hemelsch heir vervong die stem.
        't Daalt neer bij Ephrata;
    Zij preezen en zij looven Hem,
        Hun zang was "Gods genaê."

---

27 *Godsdienstig Kers-Feest*, x-xi.

28 *Hymns and Spiritual Songs* (London 1707), Bk. I, No. 62.

29 See Pierre Pidoux, *Le Psautier Huguenot du XVIe siècle* (Basle 1962), No. 84.

[2]   Rechtvaardigheid hielt aan om straf,
        Genade dong "vergeef."
        Gods wijsheid, die zijn Zoon ons gaf,
        Roept "Zondaar! hoor en leef."

[3]   Genaê! gij opent 's Hemels poort, –
        Genaê! gij sluit de Hel. –
        Genaê! 't roll' bij de volk'ren voort! –
        Hij kwam! de Immanuël!
        Halelújah! enz.

The tune for this second section is given as SYDENHAM. All British tune books published before 1801 associate it with Isaac Watts's version of Psalm 150, *In God's own house pronounce his praise*. This Dutch text, however, owes nothing to Watts's psalm. The congregation then sang stanzas 1 and 6 of Paraphrase No. 37 [6]: *While humble Shepherds watched their flocks* (Luke 2.8-15), a revision of Tate and Brady's *While shepherds watched their flocks by night*. The tune to which it was set, ASHLEY, has a doxological refrain to be sung after each of the stanzas. The implication to be drawn from Scharp's pamphlet is that this addition was sung as a coda following the two stanzas, rather than as a refrain to each stanza (see further below).

"Nu volge weer een Neêrduitsch lied" (Now follows a Dutch song again) [7], a somewhat free paraphrase *From all that dwell below the skies*, Isaac Watts's version of Psalm 117:[30]

[1]   Nu onzen zang aan God gewijd!
        't Geloof is in zijn heil verbijd,
        Wij heffen blij Hosanna's aan
        Ter eere van Gods liefdedaên;

[2]   Zijn heerlijkheid blinkt in 't gezicht
        Van Jesus, met een straalend licht:
        Hij zendt voor ons zijn eigen Zoon,
        En spreidt in Hem zijn deugd ten toon.

It was presumably sung by the choir rather than the congregation.

"Nu (...) een Schotsch gezang" (Now a Scottish song) [8]: *Beyond, beyond the glitt'ring starry sky*. This was a variant cento of J. Fanch's *Beyond the glitt'ring starry globes* that first appeared in

---

30 *The Psalms of David Imitated in the Language of the New Testament* (London 1719).

99

the *Gospel Magazine*, June 1776,[31] but the form given by Scharp is identical with that found in Stephen Addington's *Collection of Psalm Tunes* (see further below). As with the previous item, it is described as a "song" but there is no indication who sang it. The presumption is that it was sung by the choir.

At this point the charitable appeal was made [9]: "Aanbeveeling der armen van de Schotsche gemeente" (Recommendation of the poor of the Scottish Congregation), which, like everything else in the service, was done in rhyme.[32]

The appeal was followed by a choral piece [10], introduced as follows:

> Het Choor hervatte nu den toon
> En sing *verlossing door Gods Zoon*
> Met *woorden* van een *Nêerduitsch* lied;
> Maar op der *Schotten maat*, die bij hen GREENWICH[33] hiet.[34]
> (The choir now enjoins in sound
> and sings of *redemption through God's Son*
> With *words* of a *Dutch* song;
> But to the *Scottish measure*, by GREENWICH is known.)

The text appears to be an abbreviated, somewhat loose, translation of *Plung'd in a gulf of deep despair*, by Isaac Watts[35] – with textual repetitions as required by the tune:

>   Gestort in 't allerdiepst verderf,
>   Vervreemd van God, van 's hemels erf,
> :||: Was voor ons in dien jammerstaat
>   Bij 't schepzel hulp noch raad. :||:
>   Wat uitzigt anders dan genaê?
>   Gods Zoon sloeg in dien staat ons gaê;
>   Hij was bewogen met ons lot,
>   Koomt tot ons nêer, brengt ons tot God.
>   Hij, God, bedekt zijn heerlijkheid,
>   In 't need'rig kleed der menschlijkheid,
>   Wordt vleesch, vervult de wet, en sterft,
>   Waar door Hij heil verwerft.
>   ô! Wat zondaars-min!

31 *The Gospel Magazine*, Vol. 3 (London 1776), 287; on the variants see Julian, *Dictionary of Hymnology*, 139-40.

32 *Godsdienstig Kers-Feest*, 43-44.

33 Following his custom elsewhere in *Godsdienstig Kers-Feest*, Scharp adds the phonetic pronunciation of the tune name in a footnote: "De uitspraak is *Krienwitsch*."

34 *Godsdienstig Kers-feest*, 45.

35 *Hymns and Spiritual Songs*, Bk. II, No. 79.

Looft, juicht en dankt, veréend in hart en zin.
Al 't menschdom juiche en 't Eng'len-heir stemme in!
:| |: Looft Jesus liefde in 't hemelhof,
Zijn lof rijst uit het stof. :| |:
Gij, Hemel-burgers! heft vrij aan
En leer ons hemel-toonen staan
Maar, schoon ge uw toon op 't hoogste stelt,
Zijn min wordt nooit naar eisch vermeld:
Wie is 't die haar verbreidt? –
Te kort is d'eeuwigheid.

This was followed by another piece for the choir [11], with a text based on the *Gloria in excelcis Deo*. It was sung in alternation in which each couplet of every stanza was successively sung by men, women, and chorus:

[1] [Men] *Eer zij God in 't hemelhof*
Eeuwig roem, en eeuwig lof!
[Women] Nu herstelt God *vreede op aarde,*
Vreê met God, zoo groot van waarde.
[Chorus] Ja, Hij koomt, der vad'ren wensch,
Welbehaagen in den mensch!

[2] *Eer* zij de onbeperkte magt!
't Licht verschijnt in deezen nacht!
Eer zij 't Gods-recht in 't vergeeven,
Nu verschijnt de Borg in 't leeven!
Eer zij Gods genade en trouw,
God wordt mensch uit eene vrouw.

[3] Met hem daalt de *Vrede* nêer,
Vrede door verzoenings-leer.
Vrede, door voldoen en sterven,
Vrede, door het heil-verwerven.
Vrêe met menschen, vreê met God,
Hij, hij schenkt het zaligst lot.

[4] God gaat Engelen voorbij,
Menschen, *Menschen,* zaligt Hij!
Waarom die? 't is *welbehaagen;*
God doet zelv' de heil-zon daagen.
't *Welbehaagen* stell' den toon.
Eer zij God in zijnen Zoon!

Next was a "Duo" [12], *'t Is dan waar, mijn Goël kwam,* which was followed by what appears to be a freely-written poetic meditation on the shepherds seeking the Saviour, presumably sung by the choir [13]:

Koomt, volgen wij der Herd'ren stoet
Van verre na in ons gemoed,
Om ook door ons geloof te zien,
Wat heil God aan den mensch zal biên.
Treed in, ziet hier het dierbaar kind,
In hemel en op aard' bemind,
Gods eevenbeeld, Gods eigen Zoon,
Met hem, den heerscher op zijn throon.
Zijn gantsche çieraad en zijn tooi
Zijn doeken, zijne sponde is hooi.
:||:   Hier op praalt gij :||: ô Heer! zoo schoon
:||:   Als ooit :||: een Koning op zijn throon. :||:
      ô! ô! <u>Jesus</u>! groot en wonderbaar!
      Dat nu ons hart :||: uw wooning waar'!
:||:   Dat niemand onzer ooit vergeet'
      Wat uwe liefde voor ons deedt. :||:

After this the choir sang what amounts to a Dutch equivalent of
the Scottish paraphrase sung at the beginning of the service, that
is, a metrical version of Isaiah 9.5-6 [14]. Scharp indicates that
only the first and the fifth stanzas were sung:

[1]   Ons is gebooren 't wonderkind,
       Ons is een Zoon gegeeven.
       De heerschappij ten leeven,
       Die op zijn schouder zich bevindt
       Is groot in 't hemelrijk.
       Zijn naam is *Wonderlijk.*

[5]   Gerichte met gerechtigheid
       Zal zijnen scepter sterken,
       God ijver zal 't bewerken
       Van nu aan tot in eeuwigheid,
       Jehovah zal dit doen,
       Looft Hem, der Zonden zoen!

It was sung to the tune of Psalm 21, that is, the Genevan tune
that first appeared in the *Pseaumes octante trois de David, mis en
rime Françoise* (Geneva 1551).[36]
"Nu volge 't Schotsche lied" (Now should follow the Scottish
song) [15] *O the delights, the heav'nly joys*, stanzas 1, 2 and 8 (in
a revised form) of the hymn by Isaac Watts.[37] As with *Beyond,
beyond the glitt'ring sky* [8], the form of the text is identical with
that found in Addington's *Collection of Psalm Tunes*. There is no

---

36 Pidoux, op. cit., 1: 21.
37 *Hymns and Spiritual Songs*, Bk. II. No. 91.

indication concerning whether it was sung by the choir or the congregation. The next item [16] was certainly sung by the choir, a somewhat free Dutch translation of James Allen's *Glory to God on high*, first found in the Appendix to the second edition of Allen's *A Collection of Hymns for the use of those who seek, and those that have redemption in the blood of Christ* (Kendal 1761). It appeared in a number of variants in later hymn books inspired by the Evangelical Revival, usually in an abbreviated form. Scharp indicates that the choir sang the second and last stanzas of this Dutch version:

[2]   Wij zingen staam'lend na,
       Tot roem van Gods genaê
         Der Eng'len zang,
       Waar meê ons lied zich paart.
       Hij is die hulde waard',
       Hij brengt de vreê op aard'
       De vreê op aard' *bis. bis. bis.*[38]
       Hij brengt de vrêe op aard'
       De vrêe op aard'.

[4?]   Nu rijze uit nietig stof
       De wêegalm van Gods lof,
         Ons ned'rig lied!
       Wat leeft geev' Jesus eer,
       Hij is de Vorst en Heer.
       Al't menschdom buig' zich nêer.
       Het buig' zich neer. *bis. bis. bis.*
       Al't menschdom buig' zich nêer.
       Het buig' zich nêer!

Next came a congregational hymn [17], *Hark, te* [sic] *glad sound, the saviour comes*, the 34th Paraphrase (Luke 4.18-19) – a revision of the hymn by Philip Doddridge – omitting the final stanza (st. 7).

The text of the final piece for the choir [18] was modelled on Alexander Pope's *The Dying Christian*, beginning "Vital spark of heavenly flame," written in 1712. However, the content of the Dutch version is quite different, a celebration of the birth of Christ rather than the death of a Christian (see further below):

---

38 *Bis* = repeat.

Largo.
Heiland Jesus gij Gods Zoon!
Nu gedaald van zijnen throon
Tot geluk van stervelingen!
U zij lof en roem! wij zingen,
Halelujah! u ter eer.
Ja, heerlijkheid zij onzen Heer!

    Affectuoso.
Eer zij God nu toegebragt .... *4 Maal.*
In den hemel zijner kracht! ... *2 Maal.*
Vrêe op aard' voor 't Adams-kind,
Voor 't volk van God bemind.
Zaligheid! oneindig groot!

    Andante.
:||:   Eeuwig leeven! bevrijd van dood! :||:
God schenkt ons zijn beminden Zoon:
Zijn gunst daalt tot ons van zijn throon.
Lof zij Hem toegebragt!

    Vivace for[te].
ô Jesus! u, u zij al de eer!
:||:   De Zoon van God is onze Heer :||:
Ja, Jesus u zij eer!
ô Jesus u, u zij al de eer!
:||:   De Zoon van God is onze Heer :||:
:||:   Ja Jesus! u zij de eer!
ô Heiland! u, u zij al de eer!
ô Zoon van God :||: gij zijt de Heer! :||:
Ja, Zoon van God! u zij al de eer. :||:

Following an extended prayer in verse [19],[39] the whole congregation joined in singing the "Nazang" (closing hymn) [20], *O Vader, dat uw liefde ons blijk'!* the last stanza (st. 7) of the "Avondsang" (Evening hymn) in the 1773 Dutch psalter, sung to the tune of Psalm 134, known in the English-speaking world as OLD HUNDREDTH. The rather lengthy service was finally concluded with a benediction in verse [21].

The Dutch texts for these congregational and choral pieces must have been written by Jan Scharp himself. The pamphlet *Godsdienstig Kers-Feest* carries only Scharp's name on the title page, and where he does quote the poetry of another – or even where he incorporates the substance of the work of others within his poetry – he is careful to credit or footnote the sources.[40]

---

39 *Godsdienstig Kers-Feest*, 60-67.
40 See, for example, *Godsdienstig Kers-Feest*, 2, 16, 22.

Scharp already had a reputation for writing poetry and hymnody and there is no reason to suppose the verse in this service was written by anyone else.
The Dutch texts of five of the items sung at this Christmas service appear to have been freely-composed:

[5a] *Zoo werdt vervuld der Vaderen verlangen*
[5b] *Een hemelsch heir vervong die stem*

[11] *Eer zij God in 't hemelhof*
[13] *Koomt, volgen wij der Herd'ren stoet*
[14] *Ons is gebooren 't wonderkind*
[18] *Heiland Jesus gij Gods Zoon!*

In content, however, these texts are similar to those that were popularized during the British Evangelical Revival of the later eighteenth century; indeed, one of them [18] is poetically structured after one of the most popular pieces of the period.
The remaining three are paraphrases of specific English hymn texts:

[7]   *Nu onzen zang aan God gewijd!* based on Watts's Psalm 117: *From all that dwell below the skies.*
[10]   *Gestort in 't allerdiepst verderf,* based on Watts's *Plung'd in a gulf of deep despair,* from his *Hymns and Spiritual Songs.*
[16]   *Wij zingen staam'lend na,* based on James Allen's *Glory to God on high.*

What is significant is that two of these texts were free translations of English originals by Isaac Watts. The hymnody and psalmody of Watts predominated in this Christmas service. In addition to these two Dutch versions, two of Watts's texts were sung in English, [3] and [15], and one of the Dutch texts, *Een hemelsch heir vervong die stem* [5b], was sung to a tune exclusively associated with a Watts psalm in the British tune books of the time.[41] Scharp was clearly inspired by the poetry of Watts, since at least two years earlier he had translated Watts's version of Psalm 96, *Sing to the Lord, ye distant lands,* as *Zingt den Heer, gij verre landen!,* published as No. 14 in the small collection issued under the title: *Eenige Gezangen van het Zendeling-Genootschap tot uitbreiding van het Evangelie* (Some Hymns of the

---

41 As will be demonstrated later, the tune book that Scharp probably used for this service, Stephen Addington's *Collection of Psalm Tunes,* was subtitled: *Adapted to Dr. Watts's Psalms and Hymns.*

Missionary Society on the Spread of the Gospel) (Amsterdam 1799).[42] But Scharp was not only interested in the hymns texts that had become popular through the British Evangelical Revival[43] but also in their associated tunes.

Throughout the service Scharp introduced each of the sung items in verse, and did so by almost always including the tune name of the music. Although frequently designated a "Schotschen toon," each tune name reveals a melody that has an English origin. The identification of each of these tunes is not altogether straightforward since different tunes share the same name. However, an examination of the metrical structures of the associated texts, together with an evaluation of the corpus of tunes current in later eighteenth-century British tune books, the identities of the tunes sung at this Christmas service in Rotterdam in 1801 can be determined with reasonably certainty: they turn out to be almost exclusively those that originated in or were

---

42 See A.W. Bronsveld, *De Evangelische Gezangen, verzameld in de Jaren 1803-1805, en in gebruik bij de Nederlandsche Hervormde Kerk* (Utrecht 1917), 403-405.

43 It is possible that a biblical image used by William Cowper influenced another hymn written by Scharp. Stanza 7 of Scharp's *Alle roem is uitgesloten!, [Evangelische Gezangen* (Amsterdam 1807), No. 38] begins:

Kan een vrouw haar kind vergeten,
Als haar zuigling schreit van pijn?
Zou z'een ware moeder heeten,
En zoo weinig moeder zijn?
Maar, al kon dit mooglijk wezen,
Vader! die mijn nooden ziet,
Vader! Gij vergeet mij niet;
Neen, dit heb ik nooit te vreezen.

This has direct echoes of stanza 3 of Cowper's *Hark, my soul! it is the Lord [Olney Hymns* (London 1779) Bk. I, No. 118]; God speaks:

Can a woman's tender care
Cease towards the child she bare?
Yes, she may forgetful be,
Yet will I remember thee.

The similarities could simply be explained by the authors' use of the same biblical source, Isaiah 49.15. On the other hand, since both hymns centre on God's love for sinful humankind, the English hymn could well have influenced the writing of the Dutch stanza, especially as it is known that Scharp had a particular interest in the hymnody of the British Evangelical Revival.

fostered by the Evangelical Revival of the second half of the eighteenth century (see Table below).

No	Tune name
[1]	Unspecified
[2]	EPSOM
[5a]	Unspecified (Trio)
[5b]	SYDENHAM
[6]	ASHLEY
[7]	DENBIGH
[8]	POLAND
[10]	GREENWICH
[11]	MAIDSTONE
[12]	Unspecified (Duo)
[13]	DENMARK
[15]	BROOMSGROVE
[16]	BERMONDSEY
[17]	BRABROOK
[18]	THE DYING CHRISTIAN

Scharp does not record the tune that the opening hymn, *The race that long in darkness pin'd* [1], was sung to. Since he refers to it at the end of his preface,[44] it was, presumably, not introduced in suitable verse as were the other items. This is unfortunate because these verses usually include the names of the tunes to which the texts were sung. It is possible that this Common Measure text was sung to one of the old Scottish psalm tunes that formed the basic corpus of tunes associated with the Scottish psalter.[45] But, given the nature of the music used elsewhere in the service, it is more likely that it was sung to a more recently-composed tune.

Come let us join our chearful songs [3] was sung to the tune EPSOM [3]. Although there were a number of tunes with this name in current use at that time, the most likely one would appear to be the set-piece[46] composed by Martin Madan and included in his *A Collection of Psalm and Hymn Tunes* (London 1769), commonly known as the *Lock Hospital Collection*. This through-com-

---

44 *Godsdienstig Kers-Feest*, xi.

45 The tunes are listed in note 11.

46 The term "set-piece" designates an extended composition on a poetic text, often, though not exclusively, a hymn or metrical psalm, in contradistinction to "anthem", which designates a work with a prose text. HTI (see following note) specifically excludes set-pieces.

posed piece, with its melodic phrase and textual repetitions and florid passages, attained some popularity, appearing in a number of tune books published in the late eighteenth, for example, John Rippon's *A Selection of Psalm and Hymn Tunes* (London [ca. 1792], and later editions), and Stephen Addington's *A Collection of Psalm Tunes* (London 1792, and later editions).

The next item [5] remains somewhat problematic from a musical point of view. The Dutch text is clearly in two sections, the first beginning "Zoo werdt vervuld der Vaderen verlangen", and the second with "Een hemelsch heir vervong die stem." Only one tune name is given: SYDENHAM. The first section [5a] is described as a "Trio" and contains a "solo" passage. The text is cast in an irregular metre and could not have been sung to the tune SYDENHAM. Considering the nature of other music sung at the service, it would seem highly likely that the Dutch text was assigned to the music of another British set-piece. Further research might reveal some of the possible musical settings.

The second section [5b] was obviously sung to SYDENHAM, since, unusually, the tune name is given a second time, in parenthesis before the text, and the metrical form is clearly Common Measure. The tune was composed by Isaac Smith and first appeared in the composer's *A Collection of Psalm Tunes* (London [ca. 1780]), with the name SYDENHAM. It is a through-composed tune in an ABA form (A = st. 1 & 3; B = st. 2), with concluding Alleluia, a form that is clearly followed by Scharp's Dutch text. The Hymn Tune Index [HTI][47] records 15 reprints of the tune before 1801. These include later editions of Smith's *Collection* (ca. 1782, ca. 1784 and ca. 1790); the ninth and tenth editions of *Sacred Melody. A General Collection of Psalm & Hymn Tunes* (London [ca. 1797 and ca. 1800]); two editions of Rippon's *Selection* (ca. 1792 and 1795); and five editions of Stephen Addington's *Collection* (1786, 1788, 1792, 1797, 1799).

ASHLEY, assigned to the text *While humble Shepherds watched their flocks* [6] is a Common Measure tune that first appeared in

---

47 HTI = Hymn Tune Index. This is a computerized index of all hymn tunes associated with English-language texts found in printed sources published from the earliest times until the year 1820, a continuing project of the University of Illinois. It is to be published in book form, edited by Nicholas Temperley, by Oxford University Press. I am particularly grateful to Professor Temperley and Charles G. Manns for access to the information.

the April issue of *The Gospel Magazine*, Vol. 1, published in London in 1774. The first tune book to include it was *Musica Sacra, being a Choice Collection of Psalm and Hymn Tunes, and Chants (...) as they are used in (...) the Countess of Huntingdon's Chapels, in Bath, Bristol, &c.* (Bath [ca. 1775]), in which it was given the name DUBLIN. A few years later it was included in the second edition of Aaron Williams's *Psalmody in Miniature, in III Books* (London 1778), with the new name ASHLEY. It was clearly a popular tune, since HTI records 34 reprints before 1801, including two editions of Rippon's *Selection* (ca. 1792 and 1795) and six editions of Addison's *Collection* (1780, 1786, 1788, 1792, 1797, and 1799). The tune has a concluding coda, designated "Addition" by Scharp,[48] thus the following text appears after the two stanzas of the 37th Paraphrase:

Glory, honour, praise and power
Be unto the Lamb for ever
Jesus Christ is our Redeemer
Hallelujah, Hallelujah,
Hallelujah, Praise the Lord.

The tune ASHLEY appears to have had some currency among the English congregations in Rotterdam, since it is also found in G. van Rooyen, *A Selection of Hymns for the Use of the English Presbyterian Church in Rotterdam* (Rotterdam [ca. 1810]).
The Dutch text "Nu onzen zang aan God gewijd!" [7] was sung to the tune DENBIGH, a Double Long Measure tune, with three-fold repetition of the last line. It made its first appearance ano-nymously with the name DENBIGH in Thomas Knibb's *The Psalm Singer's Help* (London [ca. 1767]), and later in *The Lock Hospital Collection* of 1769, where it was attributed to Martin Madan, the editor of the Lock tune book, and assigned to Watts's *From all that dwell below the skies.* It was another popu-lar tune; HTI records 55 reprints before 1801, including one edition of Rippon's *Selection* and six editions of Addison's *Collection* (1780, 1786, 1788, 1792, 1797, and 1799), in which the tune is associated with Watts's *From all that dwell below the skies.*
POLAND, the designated tune for *Beyond, beyond the glitt'ring starry sky* [8], is in Common Measure (with repetitions) and was

---

48 *Godsdienstig Kers-Feest*, 41.

composed by J. Husband. According to HTI there were only three appearances of the tune before 1801 – each with the name POLAND – all editions of Addington's *Collection* (1792, 1797 and 1799), in which it is given the additional description: "an Ode". The tune GREENWICH, assigned to the Dutch text *Gestort in 't allerdiepst verderf* [10], is a set-piece composed by Martin Madan and found in the *Lock Hospital Collection* of 1769. A through-composed piece with both textual and musical repetitions, GREENWICH appeared in a number of tune books published in the late eighteenth century, for example, Thomas Williams's *Psalmodia Evangelica* (London 1789), Rippon's *Selection* (ca. 1792, and later editions), and Addington's *Collection*,[49] where it appears with Watts's text *Plung'd in a gulf of deep despair.*

Eer zij God in 't hemelhof [11] was sung to the tune MAIDSTONE, composed by Benjamin Milgrove as HYMN 10 in his *Twelve Hymns (...) Dedicated to (...) the Countess of Huntington: Book III* (Bath 1781). Its next appearance was in the first edition of John Rippon's *Selection* of ca. 1792, where it was given the name BATH ABBEY. The name MAIDSTONE was apparently assigned to the tune by Isaac Smith, in the eighth edition of his *A General Collection of Psalm & Hymn Tunes* (London [ca. 1795]), though it might possibly have appeared in the earlier, no longer extant, sixth or seventh edition of the collection. Smith's collection formed the basis of the ninth and tenth editions of *Sacred Melody: A General Collection of Psalm & Hymn Tunes* (London [ca. 1797 and ca. 1800]), the only two appearances of the tune before 1801 recorded by HTI. The original form of the tune was in the metre 7.7.7.7 Doubled, which implies that the final couplet of each stanza, sung by the "Chorus" in the Rotterdam Christmas service, was repeated. A variant form of MAIDSTONE, modified into Long Measure Doubled, appeared in the eleventh edition of Addington's *Collection* in 1792. HTI records that there were only three appearances of the tune in this form and all of them were editions of Addington's *Collection* (1792, 1797 and 1799).

The Duo *'t Is dan waar, mijn Goël kwam* [12], like the Trio [5a], is not given a tune association. One presumes that, as with the

49 Since some editions are no longer extant, it is unclear exactly when the tune was first included in the *Collection*; it is found in the 1788 and later editions.

Trio, it was sung to the music of another British set-piece. Again, further research might reveal some pieces that match the metre of the text and that could therefore have been sung on this occasion in Rotterdam.

The tune DENMARK is assigned to the text *Koomt, volgen wij der Herd'ren stoet* [13]. This Long Measure tune was composed by Martin Madan, appearing in *The Lock Hospital Collection* of 1769. It was an extremely popular tune of its time; HTI records 55 appearances of the tune and its variant before 1801, six of them being editions of Addington's *Collection* (1780, 1786, 1788, 1792, 1797 and 1799). The tune is not found in pre-1801 editions of Rippon's *Selection*. Watts's *O the delights, the heav'nly joys* [15] was sung to the tune BROOMSGROVE. This is the Common Measure tune, with a repeated last line, that first appeared anonymously with the name UFFINGHAM in William Dixon's *Psalmodia Christiana* (Guildford [1789]). Later the same year the tune appeared in Thomas Williams's *Psalmodia Evangelica* (London 1789), with the name changed to BROOMSGROVE. Of the four subsequent reprints of BROOMSGROVE recorded by HTI that were issued before 1801, three are found in editions of Addington's *Collection* (1792, 1797 and 1799); no edition of Rippon's *Selection* of this period contains the tune.

The tune BERMONDSEY, assigned to the text *Wij zingen staam'-lend na* [16] is another composed by Benjamin Milgrove (see MAIDSTONE [10] above), and first appeared as HYMN 4 in the composer's *Twelve Hymns (...) Book III* (Bath 1781). Its next appearance was in the eighth edition of Addington's *Collection* of 1788, where it was given the name BERMONDSEY. According to HTI, of the subsequent 16 reprints of the tune, three appear in later edition's of Addington's *Collection* (1792, 1797 and 1799), and in two editions of Rippon's *Selection* (ca. 1792, and 1795).

The Paraphrase *Hark, the glad sound, the Saviour comes* [17] was sung to the fuging tune BRABROOK [17].[50] This three-voice fuging tune first appeared in the June issue[51] of *The Gospel*

---

50 See Nicholas Temperley and Charles G. Manns, *Fuging Tunes in the Eighteenth Century* (Detroit 1983), No. 974.

51 The HTI indicates that it appeared in the June issue. The additional engraved plates of the tunes issued during that year bear no date and are usually found at the end of the monthly issue. However, when the monthly issues came to be

Magazine, or Treasury of Divine Knowledge, Vol. 1 (London 1774), ascribed to "H.E.," but without a specific tune name. The first collection to include the tune with the name BRABROOK was apparently the third edition (the earliest extant) of Addington's *Collection* (1780). Of the 15 subsequent imprints recorded by HTI, five were various editions of Addington's *Collection* (1786, 1788, 1792, 1797 and 1799); no edition of Rippon's *Selection* includes the tune.

The final choral piece of the service was the Dutch text *Heiland Jesus gij Gods Zoon!* [18], sung to the tune THE DYING CHRISTIAN. This set-piece was composed by Edward Harwood and first published in the composer's *A Set of Hymns and Psalm Tunes* (London [ca. 1776]), a musical setting of Alexander Pope's famous poem beginning *Vital spark of heav'nly flame*. THE DYING CHRISTIAN, with Pope's text, was enormously popular in the late eighteenth and early nineteenth century in English-speaking areas on both sides of the Atlantic.[52] It was included in Addington's *Collection*, with Pope's poetry and the name THE DYING CHRISTIAN, until the twelfth edition of 1797. For the thirteenth edition, issued two years later, Pope's original text was replaced by a re-written version, beginning *Holy Spirit, heav'nly flame*. The brief "Advertisement" prefacing the Third Supplement of the thirteenth edition explains that Pope's words were exchanged for "more Evangelical ones, to suit other parts of the Book"; Harwood's music, however, was retained unchanged, but given the name THE CHRISTIAN'S SONG.

In 1822 the American composer Thomas Hastings commented: "The musick of the 'Dying Christian' consists wholly of the common-place ideas (...) From some fortunate circumstances in designing, the piece has found to produce a good effect on the

---

bound, there was nothing on the engraved pages of music to associate them with a particular monthly issue of the journal and could therefore be misplaced in the binding process. Thus in the British Library copy of the first volume of *The Gospel Magazine*, used by the editors of HTI, BRABROOK appears at the end of the June 1774 issue; in the copy in Speer Library, Princeton Theological Seminary, the tune is found at the end of the May issue.

52 On the popularity of setting in England, see Nicholas Temperley, *The Music of the English Parish Church* (Cambridge 1979), Vol. 1, 213-14 (the complete setting with Pope's text is given in Vol. 2, No. 47); for its American popularity, see Richard Crawford, (ed.), *The Core Repertory of Early American Psalmody* (Madison 1984), xxxiv-xxxv, and No. 28.

generality of listeners, though as a musical composition it falls in other respects below mediocrity."[53] The music expounds in sound the narrative of Pope's somewhat sentimental text. Crawford describes it thus: "THE DYING CHRISTIAN dramatizes a believer's thoughts as his earthly body dies and he is reborn in heaven. Musical contrasts support the miracle: stately, half-note motion as death approaches (...); an abrupt stir of bustling excitement as angel voices beckon (...); and a long, fast, repetitive paean of celebration of the Christian's new state of being."[54] But in Rotterdam at Christmas 1801 the music was employed for a quite different text on the Incarnation: the opening *Largo*, instead of being a meditation on death, becomes a celebration of the Son of God, Jesus, who comes to mortals (*stervelingen*) with salvation; in the *Affectuoso*, the "whispering angels" of death are displaced by a statement of praise to God who brings salvation to his people; the English and Dutch texts for the *Andante* are similar in that, whereas Pope speaks of the "receding world" as heaven opens at death, Scharp dwells on the thought of eternal life that conquers death; and in the concluding *Vivace* the English meditation on the words of St. Paul, *O death, where is thy sting?*, is replaced by somewhat repetitive Dutch lines expressing praise to the Saviour Jesus. It is clear that the popularity of THE DYING CHRISTIAN in the English-speaking world was the primary motive for including it in the 1801 Christmas service, since the Dutch text, while being functional, does not approximate to the competence of Pope's poetry.

All the identifiable tunes sung at the 1801 Christmas service in Rotterdam were popular and appeared in many British tune books published in the latter part of the eighteenth century, as the above discussion demonstrates. Two of the most popular tune books of the period were Rippon's *Selection* and Addington's *Collection* in their various editions. Rippon's *Selection* cannot have been the main tune book used for the 1801 Christmas service, since the editions of ca. 1792 and 1795 do not include, for example, the tunes POLAND [8], DENMARK [13], and BROOMSGROVE [15]. On the other hand, all the tunes can be found in editions of Addington's *Collection* published after 1791.

---

53 Thomas Hastings, *A Dissertation on Musical Taste* (Albany 1822), 210-11; cited Crawford, op. cit., xxxiv-xxxv.
54 Crawford, op. cit., xxxiv.

No earlier edition than the eleventh of 1792 could have been used, since this was the earliest to include the tunes EPSOM [3], POLAND [8] and BROOMSGROVE [15]. Significantly, the variant texts given by Scharp in *Godsdienstig Kers-Feest* for POLAND and BROOMSGROVE are identical with those associated with these tunes in Addington's *Collection*. But Scharp could not have used the thirteenth edition of Addington's *Collection*, issued in 1799, because he employs the tune name THE DYING CHRISTIAN, which was changed in that edition to THE CHRISTIAN'S SONG. Therefore, the probable primary musical source for this Christmas service in Rotterdam was either the eleventh or twelfth edition of *A Collection of Psalm Tunes for Publick Worship. Adapted to Dr. Watt's Psalms and Hymns. To which are added several other Tunes (with words to them) in Peculiar Metres. With a Short Introduction to Singing. By Stephen Addington*, published in London by J. Murgatroyd in 1792 and 1797 respectively. But Addington's *Collection* was probably not the only source, because the tune MAIDSTONE [11] only appears in this tune book in the modified metre Long Measure Doubled. In *Godsdienstig Kers-Feest* the associated text is clearly in the original metre of the tune, 7.7.7.7 Doubled. This implies that Scharp and his colleagues in the Scottish Church in Rotterdam had access to at least one other tune book, either printed or in manuscript.

Whatever the immediate origins of the music sung at this Christmas service, its general character conformed to the basically secularized style of the musical reforms introduced by the Evangelical Revival of the second half of the eighteenth century. It is a style that is in strong contrast to either the English or Dutch psalm tune tradition and instead approximates to the popular music of the day, being characterized by textual and musical repetitions, florid passages, with a propensity for ornamentation. The popularity of such music had probably passed its peak at the turn of the century, but some of the tunes continued to be sung well into the nineteenth century. The Church of Scotland as a whole was perhaps more conservative musically than the congregation of the Scottish Church in Rotterdam. For example, the tune books of James Steven[55] were somewhat popular in

---

55 On James Steven, see James Love, *Scottish Church Music. Its Composers and Sources* (Edinburgh 1891), 336. Steven (as opposed to Stevens) is a relatively uncommon family name. It is possible that James Steven was an elder relative of Wil-

Scotland in the early years of the nineteenth century. Steven's earliest tune book, *A Selection of Psalm and Hymn Tunes in Miniature* (Glasgow [ca. 1800]), went through at least five editions before 1817 but included none of the tunes sung in Rotterdam in 1801. In later supplementary collections issued by Steven three of the tunes are found: DENBIGH and BROOMSGROVE in *A Selection of Sacred Music. Vol. 2* (Glasgow [ca. 1803]), and the original form of MAIDSTONE in *A Selection of Sacred Music. Vol. 3* (Glasgow [ca. 1806]). This witnesses to a continuing Scottish use of at least some of these tunes sung in the Christmas service in the Scottish Church in Rotterdam in 1801.

The *Godsdienstig Kers-Feest* is not only an important document that reveals something of the musical traditions of the Scottish Church in Rotterdam, it also has an importance with regard to the development of hymnody, as opposed to psalmody, in the Dutch Reformed Church. In the latter part of the eighteenth century there were moves to expand congregational song considerably beyond the confines of metrical psalmody. There were a few hymnic items in the appendix to the official metrical psalter, *Het Boek der Psalmen*, compiled in 1773, and there was a long tradition of collections of hymns being officially approved by individual synods of the Dutch Reformed Church. But there was no single hymnal approved for use in all the synods of the church. An early campaigner for such a hymnal was Petrus Hofstede, senior Dominee of Rotterdam,[56] and his successor in Rotterdam, Jan Scharp, the author of *Godsdienstig Kers-Feest*, effectively became the primary figure in the editorial process that eventually produced the hymnal. The possibility for such an intersynodical hymnal was first discussed at the synod of Noord-Holland, meeting in Amsterdam in 1796. The *Godsdienstig Kers-Feest*, therefore, dates from the period of gestation when the possibility of a Dutch hymnal was actively being considered. A commission was formed with two or three representatives drawn from each of the nine synods of the Dutch Reformed Church.

---

liam Steven, who wrote the history of the Scottish Church in Rotterdam (see note 4 above). Such a relationship would perhaps partially explain why William Steven felt constrained to include references to music in his history of the Scottish Church in Rotterdam.

56 Cornelis P. van Andel, *Tussen de Regels: De samenhang van kerkgeschiedenis en kerklied* (Den Haag 1982), 172.

Jan Scharp was one of the three representatives of the Synod of Zuid-Holland and was appointed the primary secretary to the commission. Work on the proposed hymnal began in 1803 and was completed at the beginning of September 1805. It was published as: *Evangelische Gezangen om nevens het Boek der Psalmen bij den openbaren Godsdienst in de Nederlandsche Hervormde Gemeenten gebruikt te worden; op uitdrukkelijken Last van alle de Synoden der voornoemde Gemeenten, bijeen verzameld en in orde gebracht in de jaren 1803, 1804, en 1805* (Amsterdam 1806). The prefatory material comprised two documents, both dated 6 September 1805, marking the end of the commission's work. Jan Scharp's name is the last of three at the end of the first document, addressed "Aan de Nederduitsche Hervormde Gemeenten in ons Vaderland" (To the Dutch Reformed Congregations in our Fatherland), and his is the only name appended to the second, essentially a listing of the commission members. The hymnal contained 192 hymns; eight of these texts wholly, and three partially, were authored by Scharp.[57]

Some twenty-five years after its publication an unnamed Scottish reviewer wrote of the *Evangelische Gezangen*: "An immense majority of the pieces [in this hymnal] (...) directly relate to Jesus Christ and Him crucified; and in so far as we have been able to examine the remainder, they, too, seem to be decidedly evangelical both in spirit and matter."[58] Although the tunes found in the Dutch *Evangelische Gezangen* were more conservative than the music heard in the Scottish Church in Rotterdam in 1801, both were nevertheless united in a common evangelicalism that was encouraged and promoted by Jan Scharp.

---

57 None of the texts in the *Evangelische Gezangen* have ascriptions of authorship. Some twenty years after the publication of the hymnal Scharp identified his contributions in his *Afscheid van den openbaren Evangeliedienst* (Rotterdam 1826), 106: Nos. 5, 38, 39, 52, 61, 78, 123, and 155 are wholly his work; Nos. 72, 125, and 163 are partially his; see Bronsveld, op. cit., 28.

58 Anon., "Dutch Presbyterian Churches", in: *The Presbyterian Review* Vol. 1 (Edinburgh 1832), 598-99.

The Liturgical Use of the Organ in English Worship

Alan Luff

A familiar experience in an English liturgical setting is to hear being played a Chorale Prelude by J.S. Bach, perhaps from the *Orgelbüchlein*. It may well be that the mood of the music contributes to the worship. There will, however, be few present who are getting considerably more from the performance than the mood. It is being played, perhaps after the reading of the Gospel, as the preacher moves to the pulpit. The "cognoscenti" know that at the top of the most commonly used English edition[1] is the heading "Before the Sermon". Their meditative thoughts are thus made more precise, both here and when other chorale preludes are played.

It is unlikely however that even they are actually thinking words. The Chorale is rarely one used in an English translation even if one exists. There are a number of fine translations of German hymns used regularly in English churches, but by a strange accident their tunes do not have well known preludes by German composers (for example, INNSBRUCK, PASSION CHORALE, LOBET DEN HERREN). The exceptions are likely either to be sung to words other than those associated with them in German, for example *Valet will ich dir geben* (known in English hymn books as THEODOLPH, which is commonly sung in English as a fine Palm Sunday processional hymn) or to have a Chorale Prelude where the melody is difficult to follow (for example, J.S. Bach's *Komm heiliger Geist*, or Karg-Elert's *Nun danket alle Gott*).

Compare this with another experience. The occasion was a concert by the Salvation Army International Staff Band, a highly skilled ensemble. There were prayers and a hymn at the beginning, but the atmosphere was that of a concert with applause

---

1 Ivor Atkins (ed.), *The Organ Works of Bach* XV: *Orgelbüchlein* (London [ca. 1935]); see *Herr Jesu Christ, dich zu uns wend*. Ironically the other Prelude under the same heading is *Liebster Jesu, wir sind hier* whose melody is known in Britain, but is usually sung to words of devotion at communion.

after each item, even though, following the strict rule of the Army, every item was based on a hymn or song from the Salvation Army tradition. Then there was a solo item on the euphonium, played with great feeling. A quite different atmosphere pervaded the hall and at the end there was a prayerful silence. Quite clearly the words of this piece had been in the minds of all the Salvationists present and they were not words to be followed with applause. It was an experience closed to anyone who did not know the words, however much they enjoyed the playing as such.

The case that I wish to advance is that, although devotional nonvocal music may have value in setting a mood, it comes truly into its own only when it evokes a text, and that there is quite clearly a very large gap here between the experience of most English worshippers and those in the European continental Reformation tradition.

This first became clear to me in reading *Protestant Church Music* by Friedrich Blume and others.[2] It was astonishing to find such an emphasis on the chorales, particularly in the section "Renewal and Rejuvenation" by Adam Adrio. It became clear that the use of the melodies of chorales in instrumental works invoked not simply a general devotional mood but a precise one because the words of the chorales were being brought to mind. This meant, as work by Casper Honders has revealed, that there can be in this tradition a huge enrichment of the devotional content of both vocal and instrumental music.

For the English, the hymn has a much more recent history in worship than in the European churches of the Reformation. Although the Reformation in the 16th century gave us the metrical psalm in English this had no official position in the worship of the Christian body that had a musical tradition and resources, that is the Church of England.

There was domestic instrumental music of a devotional kind, for voices, keyboard and other instruments, but it was not based on the psalm tunes. There were only a few organ pieces based on psalm tunes, such as Henry Purcell's *Fantasia on the OLD*

---

2 Friedrich Blume et al., *Protestant Church Music* (London 1975), a translation enlarged and revised of *Geschichte der evangelischen Kirchenmusik* (Kassel 1964).

HUNDREDTH, but they were not common.[3]
It was not until the early years of the 18th century that freely composed hymns became accepted. This development was confined for something like a century to the dissenting churches, which had little musical tradition beyond the singing of metrical psalms, often without instrumental accompaniment. The Evangelical Revival of the second half of the 18th century produced a great flood of hymns, especially among the Methodists, Charles Wesley being the most productive writer and the finest. Some fine tunes were produced, but the musical resources of the movement were meagre. It was not until the 19th century that hymns gained acceptance in the established Church of England alongside the prose psalms and canticles of the *Book of Common Prayer* and the metrical psalms which were used in the parish churches in conjunction with the liturgy though not strictly part of it. Even then the hymns were not sung to any great extent in the cathedrals, where the professional musicians and large organs were to be found. It must also be said that the musical content of the hymns, even when the tunes were of a good musical quality and well fitted for congregational singing, had not the same monumental quality as those of Luther and the Lutheran tradition, nor did the tunes receive the elaborate musical settings that they were given by the musicians of the German churches and court chapels. Further, there were no hymn versions of the Eucharistic Canticles – the Kyries, Gloria, Creed, Sanctus, Agnus Dei – such as might have encouraged musical treatment of the melodies.
There was a school of organ composition in England but it was of a quite different nature from that of the European mainland. This is naturally intimately related, as both cause and effect, to the kind of organs that were built for English churches. The organs were mostly either without pedals or with a limited pedal board well into the 19th century and even the largest were small instruments by continental standards, and voiced in a much lighter manner. The standard form in which compositions were cast was the "voluntary." The origin of this, as the name implies (though it now refers to the music before and after the service, and is often taken to mean "non-essential music"), was in an

---

3 See further Nicholas Temperly, "Organ Settings of English Psalm Tunes". In: *The Musical Times* 122 (1981), 123-128.

improvisation at certain points in the service. There was a custom, possibly going back to the 16th century, that the organ played at the offices of Morning and Evening Prayer after the psalms.[4] It may even have been a survival from pre-Reformation times when in place of a sung responsory after the lessons, there was an organ solo. The custom continued well into the last quarter of the 19th century. The form was not fixed but the voluntary tended to have a slow introduction followed by a quicker movement, which would sometimes display a trumpet stop, hence the many entitled "Trumpet Voluntary." By the 18th century, although the custom of improvisation continued, there were a growing number of publications of voluntaries, some quite fine. While these often have a full texture in the slow first section, the faster section is usually in the form of a melody with figured bass. These were republished in the later years of the 19th century and the first half of the 20th with pedal parts and with the manual parts often worked out with very full texture. Many more have been rediscovered in recent years and published in editions which retain the original texture.[5] They have been found particularly useful by the many pianists pressed into service in parish churches in recent years who either are unable to play the pedals or who have little confidence in that department. When Mendelssohn made his first visits to London (the first was in 1829) he could not find a single organ on which J.S. Bach's organ works could be properly played. The situation was remedied by the time of his later visits and his advocacy was one of the reasons why the music of J.S. Bach was taken up by English musicians. Increasingly through the 19th century organs in the British Isles had pedal departments added. Unlike their North European counterparts these pedal departments were almost always quite inadequate in size and indistinct in tone. Nevertheless this change in organ building brought about the development of a school of organ playing and of native organ composition. This in

4 Nicholas Temperley, *The Music of the English Parish Church* (Cambridge 1979), Vol. 1, 135.

5 For example, the several volumes of C.H. Trevor (ed.), *Old English Organ Music for Manuals* (Oxford 1966) and of *Early Organ Music* (for manuals) by various editors (Novello, London). An important composer in this tradition was the blind contemporary of Handel, John Stanley (1713-1786). His thirty Voluntaries for Organ and Harpsichords (Op. 5, 6 and 7) have been published in a number of modern editions.

part coincided at the end of the 19th century and the beginning of the 20th with the appearance in Great Britain of a number of composers of a stature not seen since Henry Purcell in the 17th century.[6] Some of these contributed to the choral repertoire of church music and wrote organ music.

They did not however write much music based on hymn tunes. This was largely left to the minor figures, the kind of composer whose work is always important in the continuing work of providing music for the ordinary local churches, and indeed for the daily worship of the larger choral foundations, but whose work often dates quickly and in any case is not of a stature to be compared with the music of the great composers who have written for the organ. In addition to this, what was written was developed for a significantly different purpose from that which gave birth to the German Organ Chorale Prelude, and for which it was later developed.

The Prelude was as the name indicates, in the first place the introduction to the singing of the hymn. Such compositions were also used to take the place of specific stanzas of the hymn in an alternatim praxis in which the congregation and organ respond to one another. This has been demonstrated by the researches

---

6   See Frank Howes, *The English Musical Renaissance* (London 1966); Michael Trend, *The Music Makers* (London 1985). The greatest of the early figures in the revival of English music, Edward Elgar (1857-1934), was a Roman Catholic but wrote some music for English cathedral choirs and a small amount of organ music. Frederick Delius (1862-1934) wrote nothing for the church. C.H.H. Parry (1848-1918) and C.V. Stanford (1852-1924) were highly regarded in their days as composers and were influential as teachers; both wrote choral music for cathedral use which remains in constant use. See below for their organ music. R. Vaughan Williams (1872-1958) is possibly unique among major composers in that he was the music editor of an epoch making hymn book, *English Hymnal* (London 1906): he also shared the editing of *Songs of Praise* (London 1926; enlarged edition 1931). In his autobiographical writings, collected as *National Music and other Essays* (Oxford ²1987) he emphasizes how influential that work with hymns was on his whole outlook on music. Although advowedly an agnostic he wrote church music both for cathedral and parish choirs. Apart from his Hymn Preludes discussed below, he wrote a massive *Prelude and Fugue in C minor* for organ. In the next generation Arthur Bliss (1891-1975), William Walton (1902-1983), Benjamin Britten (1913-1976) and Michael Tippett (b. 1905) all contributed to the cathedral repertoire but wrote little for organ.

of Casper Honders in his articles about the Choral Preludes.[7] In Europe and Scandinavia today, the organist is expected to introduce the melody with a short movement on the organ, sometimes a variation on the melody, sometimes fugal. For those not able to improvise such introductions, there are published collections in the style. The custom in Great Britain is for the melody or part of it to be played over in plain fashion, using the harmonies of the hymn book. Organists are taught that the purpose of this is to set the pitch, the speed and the mood for the singing of the hymn. This therefore is a quite functional matter; efficiency rates above art in its execution. Since there is no place for a hymn-tune prelude in the worship, when a composer writes a work based on a hymn tune it is seen as a "voluntary" in the modern sense, that is a piece to be played before or after the service, or indeed at a recital. There is no custom in English services of the whole congregation sitting and listening to the music before and after the liturgy. In most churches the voluntary is music to cover the arrival of the congregation and

---

7 - Bachs Fughetta over "Dies sind die heilgen zehn Gebot". In: *Kerk en Theologie* 20 (1969), 192-198.
- Bachs grote voorspel voor orgel over "Vater unser im Himmelreich". In: *Vox theologica* 39 (1969), 35-41.
- Bachs großes Vorspiel für Orgel über "Christ, unser Herr, zum Jordan kam". In: *Musik und Kirche* 44 (1974), 124-129.
- "Allein Gott in der Höh sei Ehr" BWV 663: van dank naar troost. In: A.C. Honders, R. Steensma, J. Wit (ed.), *Gratias agimus. Opstellen over Danken en Loven, aangeboden aan Prof. Dr. W.F. Dankbaar* [Studies van het Instituut voor Liturgiewetenschap nr. 2] (Groningen 1975), 149-155. Also published in German, in: *Musik und Gottesdienst* 29 (1975), 106-110, entitled: "Allein Gott in der Höh' sei Ehr" BWV 663: Vom Dank zum Trost.
- "Het oude jaar is nu voorbij", BWV 614. In: W.H. Morel van Mourik (ed.), *Feestbundel aangeboden aan Adriaan Cornelis Schuurman ter gelegenheid van zijn 80e verjaardag* (Den Haag [1984]), 53-57.
- Vergleich von BWV 79² mit BWV 234⁵. In: R. Steiger (ed.), *Parodie und Vorlage. Zum Bachschen Parodieverfahren und seiner Bedeutung für die Hermeneutik: Bericht über die Tagung Heidelberg 1988* [Internationale Arbeitsgemeinschaft für theologische Bachforschung Bulletin 2] (Heidelberg 1988), 146-149.
- Super flumina Babylonis ... Bemerkungen zu BWV 653b. In: *Bulletin Internationale Arbeitsgemeinschaft für Hymnologie* 17 (June 1989), 53-60.
- Der Choralkantatenjahrgang (1724-25). Einige Überlegungen und Bemerkungen. In: R. Steiger (ed.), *Johann Sebastian Bachs Choralkantaten als Choral-bearbeitungen: Bericht über die Tagung Leipzig 1990* [Internationale Arbeitsgemeinschaft für theologische Bachforschung Bulletin 3] (Heidelberg 1991), 101-108.

their settling for worship and for their, sometimes noisy, conversation after it and their departure. The piece played is expected to reflect the mood of the season, but it has no precise devotional function. There are pieces in the English organ repertoire, particularly by more recent composers which show, by their titles, that there is an attempt to illustrate some aspect of the faith,[8] and movements from the great devotional organ works of Messiaen are played. But, since it is rare in church services to advertize the title of the voluntary, few in the congregation will be challenged to find the devotional theme in the music, and it is notorious that programme music cannot be "read off" easily. This ignoring of the purpose and inspiration of the music can go to strange lengths. For example, among the works of Herbert Howells,[9] who wrote eloquently for the organ, are two sets of "Psalm Preludes" each with a quotation from a psalm at its head. These are often announced, even in recital programmes, simply as, for example, "Psalm Prelude Set 2, number 2", with no reference to the biblical text that evoked the music, and which, presumably, it is intended to call to mind in the hearer. There is lacking in the English tradition the whole concept of instrumental music as an aid to devotion, in particular by its evoking the words that inspired it.

The most important exception to the failure of major English composers to get to grips with our hymn repertoire are the fourteen pieces in *Seven Chorale Preludes: Set One* (1912) and *Set Two* (1916) by C.H.H. Parry (1848-1918), together with the larger pieces by him based on hymn tunes, such as the *Chorale Fantasias* on THE OLD HUNDREDTH, O GOD OUR HELP and AN OLD ENGLISH TUNE. He was one of the leading figures in the revival of standards in English music, and these are substantial pieces of romantic music. Each of the preludes is headed by a quotation from the words most usually sung to the tune, showing what aspect of the text is being illustrated or illuminated by the music. Yet these are not often played. The same is true of the small handful of slighter hymn tune preludes by Parry's contem-

---

8   For example, Kenneth Leighton's *Et resurrexit. Theme, Fantasy and Fugue* (London 1967), and Olivier Messiaen's organ works from *L'Ascension* onwards.

9   Herbert Howells (1892-1983), a prolific composer in many fields, but throughout his life particularly active in writing for the cathedral tradition, both liturgical music and anthems. One of his hymn tunes, MICHAEL, is very widely used, but none of his considerable output of organ music was based on hymn melodies.

porary C.V. Stanford, who was equally important in the revival of English music composition, to be found among his two sets of *Six Short Preludes and Postludes* (1908). It is as though English organists are quite prepared to play Chorale Preludes from other traditions on tunes that mean little to their congregation, but are not happy to play pieces that introduce tunes that everyone will know.

It is interesting to analyse the position of the one other set of Preludes by a composer of international stature, the *Three Preludes (founded on Welsh Hymn Tunes)* (1920) by Ralph Vaughan Williams dating from the period after his work on *English Hymnal* (1906) in which he introduced a number of Welsh hymn tunes to English congregations. They are on three classical melodies of that tradition, BRYN CALFARIA, RHOSYMEDRE and HYFRYDOL. They are not often played as a set, although the composer directs on the title page, "These three Preludes are intended to be played as a Series; but they can also be performed separately." The first, on BRYN CALFARIA (Hill of Calvary) is a dramatic, bravura piece, very little played, on a tune very little used to English words. The second is an exquisite piece, pastoral in mood, played by almost every organist in the land: RHOSYMEDRE (also known as LOVELY), a tune that has been little used until the last few years when it has gained some circulation with an American text on the family.[10] This particular Vaughan Williams' Prelude is recognized by many church goers as a favourite organ piece rather than for its presentation, clear though it is, of a hymn melody. The Prelude on HYFRYDOL (Delightful) is a grindingly discordant treatment of one of the most widely used of the Welsh hymn tunes, yet it is again hardly ever played, this time because most congregations cannot get to grips with its musical style. Thus the contribution of one of the finest English composers to this genre can be said to be musically distinguished but devotionally barren, since the only one of the preludes to be frequently played so rarely evokes a text in the mind of the hearers.

In all this I discern a mixture of snobbery and embarrassment on the part of English church musicians. The most skilled of them have for the most part been those who have served in the

---

10 "Our Father, by whose name all fatherhood is known" by F. Bland Tucker (1895-1984).

Cathedrals and Collegiate Chapels with their professional choirs and a repertoire of liturgical music that had little place for hymns. They looked upon hymns as music for the parish churches and their choirs and for the nonconformist places of worship, bodies who were not to be compared in musical achievement with the great choral foundations. This is the snobbery. The embarrassment is with the popular and emotional appeal of the hymn with which musicians deeply nurtured in Anglican reserve and formality could not cope. This has much to do with the fact that the hymn came into Anglican worship in the 19th century when the greatest hymn tunes were romantic in their idiom and appeal, the worst sentimental and maudlin. The one musician of stature of that period who might have turned the tide was S.S. Wesley (1810-1876), whose *European Psalmist* (1872) was a fine collection of sturdy tunes, published as a counter to the prevailing softness of the time. He was the leading church composer of his generation, but did not go on to compose preludes on the tunes that he composed or so skillfully edited and arranged. On the whole however the musicians who might have been capable of laying the foundations of a repertoire of devotionally useful organ music were totally out of sympathy with the material which they would have had to handle. It is however true to say that the present generation of English cathedral organists show much greater sympathy for and understanding of the hymn. A lead in this was given by Benjamin Britten when he included three congregational hymns in his children's opera *Noye's Fludde* (first performance 1958). The opera is introduced by the singing of a hymn to the old psalm tune SOUTHWELL, and ends with the singing of the tune TALLIS CANON. The most moving point of the whole opera, and the most striking break with musical tradition is the singing at the height of the storm of the 19th century hymn *Eternal Father, strong to save*, with its refrain:

O hear us when we cry to Thee
For those in peril on the sea.

It is sung here as always to the tune MELITA, by John Bacchus Dykes (1823-1876), one of the finest of the 19th century composers of hymn tunes, but much maligned by serious musicians in the earlier years of this century. The majority of cathedral musicians no longer profess disdain at the humble hymn. They

125

are prepared to issue recordings of their choirs singing hymns. They have yet to make the move to see that hymns and therefore their tunes, given sensitive musical treatment, can be a powerful means of devotion in a service. One must add in this that those in charge of the liturgy themselves have not always freed themselves of the history of near contempt for the hymn. All too often it is seen as a mere "filler" in the service, instead of the potent force – be it for good or ill – that in fact it is.

The answer to our failure to put hymn material to best musical and devotional use may well lie in the cultivation once again of the art of improvisation. In English churches hymn tunes often provide the material for two kinds of improvisation: the first is the improvising of varied harmonies, often of an attention seeking kind, usually for a loud final verse; the second is the extension of music after the end of the hymn itself until all is ready for the beginning of the next stage of the service, a practice that encourages a rather bombastic rhapsodising on the tune, following as it does so often after a loud final verse. Thoughtful preluding and interpreting of the words of the hymn is a different matter. The formal fugato prelude that is so often heard in Scandinavia is not the answer: it is stereotyped and conveys little sense of the meaning of what is to follow. Many American organists cultivate the prelude to a higher art, and use it with discretion to prepare the heart and mind as well as the ear and voice for what is to follow. The particular home of this approach is in the Hymn Festival, where the organist has a key part not only in energizing the singing but in preluding upon the tunes in such a manner as to make the reason for the inclusion of the hymn at that particular place in the service apparent to those taking part, and in providing varied accompaniment to selected stanzas of the hymn.[11] Here is a good model and one that

---

11 There is a danger in this tradition that the event becomes centred upon the organist and his/her virtuosity, but this is a danger inherent in any church music. My own experience includes introducing Charles Wesley's *O for a thousand tongues to sing my great Redeemer's praise*. I had spoken briefly, at an American United Methodist service, of an informal gathering at the Wesley memorial in Westminster Abbey at which an international congregation had sung the hymn, and how indeed those words have provoked praise from many thousands of tongues. After proclaiming the first lines the organist, Sue Mitchell Wallace (of Atlanta, Georgia), burst in with a cascade of notes around the tune AZMON, in fitting response to both my words and those of the hymn. Her volume *Hymn Prisms: New*

might lead to the composition of a repertoire of preludes on English hymns that would stand up to use within the service and which congregations would learn not only to follow with pleasure as they recognize the tune but to use as a guide to prayer as the tune brings the words to mind.

---

colors and *Variations for Favourite Hymns* (Carol Stream 1985) gives some impression of the possibilities within this tradition.

Some Data concerning Organ-accompaniment and Organ-registration in Germany during the Nineteenth Century

Jan R. Luth

It is a known fact that, since the eighteenth century, Germany has significantly influenced church music in the Netherlands. In the eighteenth century most of the outstanding organists in the Netherlands were German. In the nineteenth century, although the organists were Dutch, many had received their training in Germany, among them J.G. Bastiaans, organist of the St. Bavo-kerk in Haarlem, J.A. van Eijken, organist in Rotterdam and Elberfeld, and D.H. Dijkhuizen, organist in Elburg.[1] In this article I will analyze some important German sources, chorale books and organ-methods, with regard to data relating to aspects of organ-accompaniment.

Accompaniment

First to be considered is the *Allgemeine Choral-Melodienbuch* by Johann Adam Hiller (1793). Hiller's *Choralbuch* was extremely influential throughout Germany, especially in Saxony, where until 1869 chorale books were published according to this model and that of Hiller's successor Schicht (1819).
Hiller contributed a detailed preface in which much information is to be found concerning congregational singing and its accompaniment. The tunes are written in an allabreve (3/2) metre and in modern keys. The harmonizations are constructed so that they can be played on an organ without pedal, but in which case

---

1 J.R. Luth, *"Daer wert om 't seerste uytgekreten..." Bijdragen tot een geschiedenis van de gemeentezang in het Nederlandse Gereformeerde protestantisme ca. 1550 - ca. 1852* (Kampen ²1986), 331-332; F.C. Kist, *De toestand van het protestantsche Kerkgezang in Nederland* (Utrecht 1840), 116.

the bass has to be played an octave higher. Hiller directs that accomplished players may treat the notation with some freedom, but amateurs should follow it accurately. Concerning harmony Hiller expresses the opinion that sparing use of dissonance is an enrichment; parallel fifths in the middle voices are permissible, but in the outer voices (soprano and bass) care should be taken to avoid them; the third can be added, but not greater intervals. The 4/3-chord (second inversion of the seventh-chord) is very useful in accompanying chorales, because it creates a suspension and makes the singing more smooth and pleasant.

In congregational singing there is "an keine durchaus einförmige und feste Melodie, an keine richtige und verständliche Harmonie zu denken. Wie gut wäre es, wenn alle die Melodie im Einklange sängen, und sich auf keine Harmonie einließen!" ("by no means a consistent or fixed melody, comprehended with a correct and understandable harmony. How good it were when everyone sang in unison and should not give harmony any consideration!").[2] This relates not only to the fact that there were many variants of melodies, but also to the undisciplined manner in which congregations used to sing, which probably made it very difficult for the organist to accompany.

Another source is the manual of C.C. Güntersberg. Since there is no preface, one must interpret the notation. From this it is clear that he encouraged the playing of short interludes between the lines of hymn tunes. The way in which harmonizations are printed makes it very likely that playing the melody on another manual other than the one used for the accompaniment was exceptional. Example 1 is Güntersberg's harmonization of *Vater unser im Himmelreich* (the harmonic outline appears to be very close that of Felix Mendelssohn's Sonate VI).[3]

Franz Schneider expresses the view that a chorale book should be published in which harmonizations are in four parts, so that four-part, rather than unison, singing should be the norm. But because a four-part setting becomes monotonous with repetition, the organist should sometimes play expansive chords, being guided by the content of the text and the size of the congrega-

2   Johann Adam Hiller, *Allgemeines Choral-Melodienbuch für Kirchen und Schulen* (Leipzig 1793), xiv.
3   C.C. Güntersberg, *Der fertige Orgelspieler* (Meissen [1823-1827]), 141.

Example 1

tion. Doubling the intervals is the preferred way of ac-
complishing this, which should be done without being over-scru-
pulous about parallel octaves. Further, Schneider argues, it is
possible to decorate the middle voices and the bass, but this
must be based on the setting in the chorale book, since the choir

130

Example 2

will be singing that setting.[4] When there is no choir, the organist is free to vary the bass line and the harmony.[5] Schneider
illustrates this with three examples of *Nun danket alle Gott* (see
Ex. 2).[6] Schneider gives several possibilities for the way in which
the accompaniment can be done. First is when the organist
holds the first chord of each line for as long as it takes the
congregation to begin singing. This will present no problems
when the interludes between the lines are given the same duration. The clarity of the first chord following the interlude, when
the congregation is to begin singing again, is obvious because
during the interludes the pedal is not used. The first note of the

---

4 Franz Schneider, *Handbuch des Organisten*, II. *Orgelschule* (Halberstadt 1830), 98,
   § 6-8.
5 Ibid., 100, § 12.
6 Ibid., 98-99.

131

pedal signals the beginning of the following line to the congregation. A second possibility is when the congregation begins and the organist joins in during the first line, but the entry must only occur at an important word, and never on its last syllable.[7] A third possibility is when the congregation sings the first line of a well-known hymn entirely without accompaniment.

Schneider indicates that a special approach is required to accompany new melodies, or to unlearn errors: the organist should play in plenum unison on the manual alone, or only the melody on the manual with staccato bass in the pedal (see Ex. 3).[8]

Example 3

In the second half of the nineteenth century August Gottfried Ritter criticized recent trends in accompanying the congregation: It is "einer vagen, hinüber und herüberschweifenden Harmonisierung, kein unwichtiger Grund hiervon ist dem Mangel einer klaren Einsicht unserer Orgelspieler in die harmonischen Verhältnisse der mit dem Zwischenspiel in Verbindung stehenden

---

7   Ibid., 102, § 18.
8   Ibid., 99-100, § 11.

Example 4

Accorde zu suchen" ("a vague, perambulating harmonization, the basis for which lies in no insignificant part in the dearth of a clear insight by our organists in discovering the harmonic relationship of the interlude to the existing setting").[9] Ritter illustrates his criticism with examples taken from existing chorale books. One is a setting of "Ach Gott vom Himmel sieh darein" (see Ex. 4). At 1. the chromatic passage e - d-sharp - d conflicts with the phrygian mode. At 2. the c-sharp is the third of the dominant A minor, but here the subdominant A is better. Further, the seventh-chord clashes with the following melodic line in A minor. The next melodic line following 3 is in C major, but the interlude forces one to consider G major as the tonic.
In the accompaniment chords which contradict wrong notes can be very useful, for example, when the melody rises half a step, the 2-chord (third inversion of the seventh-chord) is used in the

---

9 August Gottfried Ritter, *Die Kunst des Orgelspiels*, 7th ed. bound with: August Gottfried Ritter, *Praktischer Lehr-Cursus im Orgelspiel* (Leipzig [9]1872), 104.

Herzliebster Jesu, was

Example 5

accompaniment; when the melody is falling, a dissonance is useful.[10] In the melody *Herzliebster Jesu* it was customary in Ritter's time to sing the fourth note as f-sharp. Ritter, however, suggests an harmonization in which the triad foundation forces the congregation to sing f-natural (see Ex. 5). Ritter also recommends this approach when new melodies are introduced, and one can further promote the acquaintance with a new melody by playing such a harmonization of it as a prelude before the service and as a postlude at the close of the service.

Ritter demands that the accompaniment expresses the content of the hymn text. Therefore the organist should read line by line, and in this way follow all nuances and contrasts in the text. The better he penetrates the text, the better his accompaniment will be.[11] As an example he gave the melody *Herr Jesu Christ, dich zu uns wend*. The first two stanzas are, according to Ritter, a prayer; the third speaks of the joy of singing together with the heavenly hosts; and the fourth of respect for the Trinity. Therefore, argues Ritter, the accompaniment should reflect the differing content of these stanzas (see Ex. 6). But the organist goes too far when he tries to picture a single word, like natural phenomenons. Finally we read that the last note of every stanza, but especially the last note of the last stanza, is sung lengthened. The final cadence is I-IV-I, but can be extended, except for modal melodies.[12]

---

10 Ritter, op. cit., 97, § 96. Ritter, however, makes a mistake: there is no such chord in the example he cites.

11 Ibid., 98.

12 Ibid., 107-108, § 98.

Example 6

Interludes

During the nineteenth century there was much discussion of interludes. For example, Hiller writes, that their execution is strongly connected with the question of whether a hymn is to be sung "nach dem Tacte, oder ohne Tact" ("according to the metre, or without metre"). For Hiller a hymn is to be sung "nach dem Tacte," because it is the most natural, and the time to play an interlude is appointed by the rests between the lines.

135

Hiller illustrates the slow tempo of congregational singing (see Ex. 7: 1 = one syllable held for one beat; 2 = the syllable is held for two beats; 1 over a dash = a breathing-space).

1   1   1   1 2   1   1   1   1   1 2   1   1   1
Ach | Gott und | Herr | — wie | groß und | schwer | — find | mein
1   1   1   1 2   1 2   1   1   1 1   1 2   1   1
be | gangne | Sün | den | — da | ist nie | mand | — der | u. f. w.

Example 7

This custom appoints the duration which the organist has for the interlude: just one part of a measure, although extension is possible by taking the second half of the last note into the interlude.[13]
Hiller finds good examples of interludes in Johann Gottfried Vierling's *Orgelstücke* and in several compositions of Daniel Gottlob Türk.[14] He says that interludes should comprise but few notes, be in one to three voices, can simply consist of broken chords, and normally be played without pedals. When a melodic line begins with the same note as the previous line, it is better not to play an interlude, because the congregation already has the note.[15] Hiller does not notate interludes in his *Choral-Melodienbuch* but expects that they will be played, since he gives a number of examples (see Ex. 8). They must always lead to the first note of the next melodic line and should not in any way attempt to portray the meaning of the text.[16]
Congregational singing is commonly chaotic: therefore organists should not lag behind the congregations – not remain in their harmonies, nor go up to heaven and then fall down to the abyss till the congregation calls the organist to follow – but always lead.[17]

---

13 Hiller, op. cit., 18.
14 Ibid., 19, 24; see, for example, Johann Gottfried Vierling, *Sammlung leichter Orgelstücke nebst einer Anleitung zu Zwischen-spielen beym Choral*, 4 pts. (Leipzig 1790), and Daniel Gottlob Türk, *Von den wichtigsten Pflichten eines Organisten* (Halle 1787).
15 Ibid., 21.
16 Ibid., 27.
17 Hiller, op. cit., *Nachtrag*, 9.

Example 8

Another remarkable source is an article by Friedrich Kühmstedt, published in Eisenach in 1844, which was translated and published in a Dutch journal the following year.[18] He defends the use of interludes, although concedes that they are often at variance with the character of a hymn text. According to Kühmstedt interludes arose from the introduction of harmony which demanded variation from stanza to stanza. To express the varying affects of a hymn several harmonizations were required, and such harmonizations demand varying interludes. Without interludes there is no natural connection between the melodic lines. Further, according to Kühmstedt, it is a sin against aesthetics if the organist should simply cease at the end of every line, because a held chord cannot satisfy aesthetic sensibilities. Interludes therefore have a threefold purpose: to make the singing of the next line easier; to establish the "affect"; and to emphasize the punctuation.

Kühmstedt developed the following rules for interludes:

1. They must be a natural continuation of the melody; therefore one should avoid all extended passages, trills, and imitations.
2. The length of the interlude depends on the construction and punctuation of the hymn.
3. Harmonies should be "simple and natural" and consist of as few diminished seventh-chords as possible.
4. Interludes must not divert attention away from the hymn text.
5. Interludes should be played without pedal, which means that the pedal begins with the first note of each new melodic line.

---

18 Luth, op. cit., 335-336.

137

These rules of Kühmstedt imply that an organist should have a very good understanding of the text of a hymn.

The hymnologist Christian Palmer also belongs to the defenders of interludes. He writes that interludes in his time (1865) are condemned, but only when congregational singing is rhythmic, since in this case the fermatas disappear, leaving no opportunity for interludes. But Palmer's opinion is that congregational singing cannot do without interludes:

Man hält da entweder den letzten Ton der Melodie mit der Orgel etwas länger aus, als die Gemeinde, um von diesem Ton aus klar und bestimmt den ersten Ton der nächsten Zeile zu intoniren; oder man zieht die Hand ganz von der Orgel zurück und macht im Spiel, wie die Gemeinde im Gesang, eine Pause. Dies letztere, das dermalen vielfach geübt und anempfolen wird, ist das Häßlichste, eine wahre Zersetzung des Chorals; so oft die Pause eintritt, fehlt dem Ohre etwas und der neue Anfangsaccord platzt dann so plump herein, wie es gerade der Charakter der Orgel schlechthin nicht gestattet. Wie das bindende, vermittelnde Element im Gottesdienst ist, so hat sie auch hier zu vermitteln; die Gemeinde muß Athem holen, die Orgel nicht; vielmehr ist es eine der Schönheiten, die sie zieren, daß ihre vollen, unversiegbaren Töne immer wieder aus der Masse der Menschenstimmen auftauchen und dadurch den letztern immer neu die richtige Intonirung geben zur folgenden Zeile. (One either holds out the last note of the melody on the organ, as does the congregation, so that from this note, the pitch for the next phrase may be clear and understood; or one lifts the hands completely from the manuals and makes, just like the congregation, a pause in the playing. This last option (pausing), still widely experienced and recommended, is the ugliest – a true subversion of the chorale; whenever the pause appears, the ear lacks something, and the new entrance bursts in so clumsily, that the complete character of the organ is simply undermined. As a cohesive, meditating element in the service, one has to consider that the congregation must take a breath – not so with the organ. It is of much more beauty that interludes adorn the voice of the congregation with the organ's inexhaustible tones, thereby always through the preceding phrase they may give perfect intonation to the following lines.)

Simply holding a note at the end of a line sounds "empty"; the ear asks for a connecting chord and passing notes that lead to the next phrase. Although the interludes that were commonly found in contemporary chorale books were usually too long and too difficult, Palmer argues, they should not on principle be rejected, since they establish cadences and determine rests.[19]

In the seventh edition of the work by A.G. Ritter already mentioned,[20] there is a section devoted to interludes. Ritter defends

---

19 Christian Palmer, *Evangelische Hymnologie* (Stuttgart 1865; reprint: Leipzig 1978), 380-383.
20 See note 9.

them against opponents, because there is no rhythm in congregational singing. Lines which end with a hold are to be filled-in with interludes: whoever leaves them out will experience how long and tiresome the open rest is. The animation which is lacking in congregational singing is compensated for by the harmony of the accompaniment and the interludes played in between each of the melodic lines sung by the congregation. Interludes in chorale preludes and motets are good examples of high art. But interludes should be kept short; the pedal keeps silence throughout and the chord for the beginning of the next line has to be prepared very carefully, that is, in the right harmonic way.

Schneider belongs to those who would abolish interludes, on the grounds that they are usually abused. If they must be used then the only purpose they could have is in an harmonic and melodic connection between the lines of the chorale melody. The simpler and the less contrasting with the hymn, the better the interlude is. Schneider rejects word-painting of such concepts as joy, sadness, "thunder", etc; instead the organist should clearly establish the "Hauptempfindung" ("primary feeling"). The length of the interlude should be limited to three or four syllables of the hymn. Strange harmonies and extended passages should be avoided, because they conflict with the lines of the melody:

Das beste Zwischenspiel (vorausgesetzt, daß der Choral auf einer guten vierstimmigen Harmonie beruhe) ist dasjenige, wenn sich die drei obern Stimmen nach Endigung der Zeile, aus ihrer Lage, einfach (ohne gesuchte kontrapunktische Künstelei, die hier übel angebracht wäre) fortbewegen, bis der erste Ton jeder Stimme im Anfangsaccorde der folgenden Zeile auf eine natürliche Weise in der dazu hinreichenden Zeit folgen kann; vorzüglich muß der Anfangston der Melodie auf eine natürliche Weise dem letzten Tone des Zwischenspiels folgen. (The best interlude (provided that the chorale is set in a good four-part harmonization) is that which, if one moves on in a simple manner (without far-fetched contrapuntal contrivance, which at this point would only be properly mischievous) with the upper three voices following the ending of the line, from its original position to the first note of every voice in the beginning chord of the following line, with a natural melody filling the time between; there must be an excellent, free-flowing transition to the first note of the melody which follows the ending of the interlude).[21]

The organist should hold the first chord of a line till the congregation starts singing. If the interludes are of similar length the

---

21 Schneider, op. cit., 101, § 14.

congregation will have no problems, and the beginning of each line is marked by the fact that the pedal keeps silent during the interlude and only starts to sound with the first note of the next line.[22] As with Kühmstedt, who reflects German practice, Schneider reveals that the convention of signalling to the congregation to begin the next line by entry of the pedal was also common in the Netherlands.[23] Unlike English and American practice of the time, Schneider considers interludes between the stanzas as undesirable, since the break gives time for the organist to alter the registration. Examples of Schneider's lineal interludes are given in Example 9.

Example 9

In the second half of the nineteenth century the number of opponents of the practice of interludes continued to grow, notably Eduard Emil Koch and Christian Karl Gottlieb von Tucher among them.

Koch's view was that interludes became a necessity in a time of decay and they were designed to lead the congregation to the first note of a new line, and, with unknown hymns, to give time to read. According to Koch interludes were taken over from the cantata and motet, but he does not present any evidence to

---

22 Ibid., 102, § 17.
23 Luth, op. cit., 336.

support his view. Then, around 1840, they became simpler and better connected with the character of the melody, and the length was limited to four bars. Koch maintains that already by 1835 interludes were prohibited in some regions of Germany, for instance, in Baden.[24] This indicates that there must have been great diversity of practice, for, as we have seen, as late as 1857 Ritter was still maintaining that lineal interludes were necessary.[25]

Von Tucher speaks only of tasteless interludes: their use proves that every imagination of a melody as an organic unity is missing. He agrees with Ritter that the introduction of interludes is to be connected with the disappearance of singing the chorale melodies in their original rhythmic forms. For Von Tucher there are no harmonic or melodic reasons to defend them, and they are not required to give expression to the "affect" of the text, or – what Ritter also rejects – word-painting or any other musical exposition of the lines of the text. According to Von Tucher others are also of the opinion that the improvement of congregational singing begins with the abolition of interludes. He states that they were proscribed in Baden about 1850 and that nobody regretted the action.[26]

Registration

The same starting point concerning registration is sometimes found as in the eighteenth century. Von Tucher, for instance, directs the organist to play the melody on the Great and the other voices on another manual.[27]

---

24 The primary influence was A.F.J. Thibaut (1772-1840), founder and leader of the Heidelberger Singverein, who was also a leader in the renewal movement of the early nineteenth century: see *Die Musik in Geschichte und Gegenwart* (Kassel 1949-1986), Vol. 13, col. 333-334.

25 Eduard Emil Koch, *Geschichte des Kirchenlieds und Kirchengesangs der christlichen, insbesondere der deutschen evangelischen Kirche* (Stuttgart ³1872; reprint Hildesheim 1973), 457-459.

26 Christian Karl Gottlieb von Tucher, *Über den Gemeindegesang der evangelischen Kirche* (Leipzig 1867), reprinted as an appendix in: *Schatz des evangelischen Kirchengesangs im ersten Jahrhundert der Reformation* (Leipzig 1848-1867; reprint Hildesheim 1972), 33-35, 53.

27 Von Tucher, op. cit., 53.

In Güntersberg's manual we find some interesting data about registration. The following were common combinations:

Manual: Prinzipal 8', Gedackt 8', Flöte 4', Nasat 3', Gedackt 4'
Pedal: Subbass 16', Violonbass 16', Oktavbass 8', sometimes also Bourdon 16'

One can add:

Manual: Oktav 4', Oktav 2', Quint 3', Mixtur
Pedal: Prinzipal 16', Posaune 16'

Another popular combination was:

Prinzipal 8', Gedackt 8', Viola di Gamba 8', Flöte 4'

Güntersberg also gives the following cantus firmus registration:

Manual I (right hand):
    Prinzipal 8', Gedackt 8', Hohlflöte 8', Cornet 4 f. or Trompet 8'
Manual II (left hand):
    Viola di Gamba 8', Prinzipal 4', Flöte 4'

The frequent use of doubling the diapason and flute stops at the same pitch is remarkable, but this was the usual practice of the time. Ritter writes, as do many others in the nineteenth century, that registration depends on the size of the congregation and the difficulty of the melody. When there is a large congregation Ritter uses Viola di Gamba 8', coupled to Salicional 8' and Lieblich Gedackt 8', in the manual, and Subbass 16', or Violon 16' coupled to the manual, in the pedal. He recommends this registration for accompanying hymns which express "Demuth und Ergebung" ("humility and resignation"). As with Güntersberg, Ritter will often use a combination of stops of the same pitch. The organist can eradicate faulty congregational singing of the melody by playing the cantus firmus on a strongly registered manual of which the pipes are close to the congregation, that is, the Rückpositiv.[28] We find a similar approach in Schneider: he also states that the registration will depend on the size of the congregation, but for accompanying unknown melodies one should use the full resources of the organ.[29]

---

28 Ritter, op. cit., 97, § 96.
29 Schneider, op. cit., 99, § 10.

Conclusions

The established eighteenth-century practice of soloing-out the melody on one manual, and accompanying it on another, continued into the nineteenth century and is discussed in most sources. It was a common practice, not only for learning new melodies but also for clearly establishing known melodies in the ears of the congregation. The most important matter was to encourage the congregation to sing, and rules concerning harmony, such as forbidden parallels, were of lesser consequence.

Harmonizations found in the chorale books were ornamented and expanded for accompanying the congregation. Some authors, such as Ritter, go much further and explicitly demand that the organist should alter the harmonization from stanza to stanza expounding the content of the text. Harmony was also used as a means of enabling the congregation to sing more accurately. Interlineal interludes were generally played on manuals alone so that the entry of the pedal signaled to the congregation the beginning of the next melodic line. In some sources, such as Kühmstedt, the interlude is based on the contents of the text; in other sources, such as Palmer and Ritter, the interlude is played purely for aesthetic reasons. Notable is the doubling of 8' stops in the manual and of 16' stops in the pedal.

The influence of these German practices on Dutch usage is found, for example, in the introductions to the important chorale books of Johannes Gijsbertus Bastiaans[30] and J.A. van Eijken.[31] Emphasis on the church modes (cf. Ritter) is found in both chorale books; in Van Eijken's book, specially with reference to Thibaut. The preference for simple harmonizations in an attempt to emulate the seventeenth century is found in Bastiaans and Van Eijken, for example, and also with Koch, C.F. Becker and Thibaut.

---

30 Johannes Gijsbertus Bastiaans, *Vierstemmig Koraalboek voor koor (sopraan, alt, tenor en bas) en Orgel of Piano-Forte; bevattende al de melodieën der Evangelische Gezangen, bij de Nederlandsche Hervormde Gemeente in gebruik; ten dienste van kerk, zangvereeniging, school en huisgezin* (Arnhem 1852).

31 J.A. van Eijken, *De Melodieën der Psalmen en Lofzangen in gebruik bij de hervormde, waalsche, remonstrantsche en doopsgezinde gemeenten, vierstemmig bewerkt voor orgel of koor met Voor- Tusschen- en Naspelen* (Amsterdam [1853]), and *De melodieën der Evangelische Gezangen in gebruik bij de Nederduitsche Hervormde Gemeenten* (Amsterdam [1863]).

Proposals for registration from Van Eijken correspond closely to those found in German sources. Further, the Dutch historian Kist takes Schneider and his church music school in Dessau as an example worthy of imitation.[32] German examples of registration and preludes and interludes are also very important for Kist.[33]

Finally, the discussions about interludes in both German and Dutch are strikingly similar, and the roots of the practice in both Germany and the Netherlands are to be found in the eighteenth century.[34]

---

32 Kist, op. cit., 116.
33 Ibid., 100-101.
34 Luth, op. cit., passim.

Heil oder Gericht?

Das Blut Christi
in zwei Werken von Heinrich Schütz

Andreas Marti

Wenn Johann Sebastian Bach in den Turba-Chören seiner Passionen die Juden sprechen läßt, entsteht vor unseren Augen unweigerlich das Bild einer schreienden Volksmenge, eines tobenden Mob. Eine solche geradezu erbarmungslos negative Darstellung des jüdischen Volkes hat in der Kirche eine lange Tradition, und häufig datiert man diesen christlichen Antijudaismus zurück bis ins Neue Testament und hier vor allem ins Matthäusevangelium, das sich immer wieder kritisch auf die alttestamentlich-jüdische Tradition bezieht. Wenn auch bei vielen Autoren wenigstens betont wurde, es sei nicht Aufgabe der Kirche, den göttlichen Zorn am alten Bundesvolk auf Erden zu vollziehen, gab es doch – schmerzliche und schändliche Erinnerung – nur allzuviele, die diese Vorsicht nicht walten ließen. Dabei spielte der Satz "Sein Blut komme über uns und unsere Kinder" (Mt. 27,25) eine verhängnisvolle Schlüsselrolle. Rainer Kampling[1] hat auf diesem Hintergrund der genannten Stelle eine auslegungsgeschichtliche Studie gewidmet und dabei für die Alte Kirche eine durchgehende und sich verfestigende antijudaistische Auslegung konstatieren müssen. Daß auch Luther[2] schlimme Sätze gegen die Juden anzulasten sind, ist bekannt. Erstaunlich ist eigentlich, daß mit dem "Blut" nicht häufiger dessen Heilsbedeutung assoziiert wurde, wie sie ja von sehr vielen neutestamentlichen Stellen her naheliegen würde. Diese Spur findet sich etwa im Kommentar von Eduard Schweizer:[3]

---

1 Rainer Kampling, *Das Blut Christi und die Juden: Mt. 27,25 bei den lateinischsprachigen christlichen Autoren bis zu Leo dem Großen* [Neutestamentliche Abhandlungen Neue Folge Bd. 16] (Münster i.W. 1984).

2 Luthers Antijudaismus wird in seiner Auswirkung auf die Judenverfolgung der Hitler-Zeit beispielsweise dargestellt bei Eberhard Röhm / Jörg Thierfelder, *Juden – Christen – Deutsche* Bd. 2/I (Stuttgart 1992), 49 f. und öfter.

3 Eduard Schweizer, *Das Matthäusevangelium 2. Teil* [NTD] (Göttingen 1986), 333.

"Hebr 12,24 spricht anders vom Blute Jesu. Vielleicht hofft sogar Matthäus auf eine Erfüllung im Sinne von 26,28 [dem Kelchwort beim Abendmahl, A.M.]: daß Jesu Blut, nicht das von 23,35, versöhnend über sie komme." Hört man sich die Stelle in der Vertonung bei Heinrich Schütz, in seiner Matthäuspassion aus dem Jahre 1666 (SWV 479) an, ist der Eindruck von dem bei Bach gewonnenen sehr verschieden. Alles wirkt ruhiger, scheinbar gedämpft, gemäßigt, ohne den Aufruhr, den Bach darstellt. Das liegt zunächst ganz einfach daran, daß Schütz in seinen Passionen mit äußerlich sehr viel bescheideneren Mitteln arbeitet und einen Tumult so kaum nachzeichnen kann. Vielleicht aber steckt doch mehr dahinter – auch Schütz hätte ja durch unruhige Rhythmen und Dissonanzenhäufungen das Bild negativer prägen können. So erhebt sich die Frage, ob ihm bei der Komposition dieser Stelle Assoziationen an andere Formulierungen, in denen das Blut Christi vorkommt, gegenwärtig waren, ob er, so wie Schweizer das in seinem Kommentar für Matthäus ganz vorsichtig vermutet, zumindest an diesen anderen Sinn gedacht haben mag. Schütz hätte dabei auch an ein eigenes früheres Werk denken können, nämlich an das geistliche Konzert *Das Blut Jesu Christi* aus dem Jahre 1636 (SWV 298) für zwei Soprane, Baß und Basso continuo über 1 Joh. 1,7. Nun liegen freilich 30 Jahre zwischen beiden Kompositionen, aber man wird doch wohl annehmen dürfen, daß Schütz sich seines älteren Werkes noch erinnern konnte. Immerhin war es ihm ja wichtig genug gewesen, daß er es drucken ließ, und möglicherweise hat er es selber später auch wieder aufführen lassen. Zum Vergleich seien hier die Vertonung von Mt. 27,25 und der Anfang der Baß- und der zweiten Sopranstimme (die erste pausiert zu Beginn) wiedergegeben (Beispiel 1 und 2).
Der Vergleich zeigt eine überraschende Ähnlichkeit der beiden Vertonungen. "Das Blut" und "sein Blut" sind durch dieselbe steigende kleine Terz g-b vertont, beide Male wird der anfängliche g-moll-Dreiklang anschließend nach Es ausgeweitet. Es entsprechen sich weiter die Tonwiederholungen auf "Machet uns rein" und auf "komme über uns", und die in SWV 298 daran anschließende fallende Quart erscheint in der Matthäuspassion in der Baßstimme. Schließlich gleichen sich auch die Kadenzformeln auf "(Sohnes) Gottes" in den Takten 12 ff. von SWV 298 und auf "Kinder" am Schluß der Passage in der Matthäuspassion.

146

Beispiel 1 – SWV 479.

Jede dieser Beziehungen für sich genommen könnte vielleicht dem Zufall oder einer stilbedingten Verwandtschaft zugeschrieben werden. Ihre Häufung aber und auch ihre übereinstimmende Reihenfolge scheint auf eine Absicht des Komponisten hinzudeuten. Was diese Absicht in Bezug auf die Textauslegung gewesen sein mag, läßt sich nicht eindeutig eruieren. Dem steht neben der ohenhin immer vorhandenen Mehrdeutigkeit musikalischer Aussagen auch die Tatsache entgegen, daß in der Matthäuspassion keinerlei interpretierende Zusätze zum Bibeltext einen Rückschluß auf die Auslegung ermöglichen. (Der Schlußchor "Ehre sei dir, Christe", zusammen mit der auskomponier-

147

Beispiel 2 – SWV 298.

ten Überschrift der einzige Textzusatz, trägt für unsere Stelle direkt nichts aus.)

Vermutlich ginge man zu weit, wollte man in der Komposition die Bedeutung versteckt sehen, daß die Juden letztlich gerade das Heil auf sich wünschen, indem sie vordergründig das Gericht auf sich beschwören. Es wäre fast zu schön, den Humanisten Schütz auf diese Weise (allerdings nur dem Kenner vernehmlich) aus der traditionellen antijudaistischen Front ausbrechen zu sehen.[4] Eher schon läßt sich eine Dialektik vermuten, wie sie Kampling[5] bei Origenes gefunden hat: "Dasselbe Blut Christi bringt den einen Heil, weil sie in der Kirche sind, den anderen Unheil, weil sie nicht zur Kirche finden wollen." Die musikalischen Entsprechungen sind auch so im Text sinnvoll verankert: die Identität des Blutes Jesu hier wie da, die beiden Wirkungen – einmal zum Heil ("machet uns rein") und einmal zum Gericht ("komme über uns"), der Anklang von "Kinder" an "Gottes Sohn". Damit ist die matthäische Kritik am Juden-

---

4 Es müßte in der exegetischen und homiletischen Literatur der lutherischen Orthodoxie untersucht worden, ob allenfalls sogar zeitgenössische Belege für eine solche (sozusagen "trendwidrige") Exegese zu finden sind. Diese Arbeit würde aber den Rahmen der vorliegenden Miszelle bei weitem sprengen und sei der zuständigen Wissenschaftsdisziplin als hängiges Problem weitergemeldet.

5 Op. cit., 58.

tum zwar voll aufgenommen; offen bleibt aber die Möglichkeit, ja die Aufgabe, die scheinbar so brutal eindeutige Stelle in Beziehung zu setzen zu anderen Glaubensaussagen. Nichts anderes kann ja die Aufgabe textbezogener Musik sein, als durch die Schaffung von mehrschichtig-gleichzeitigen Bezügen jede vorschnelle Eindeutigkeit und damit auch Ideologisierung zu verhindern. Oder allgemeiner gesagt: Die Kunst hat die Aufgabe, die Liturgie offen zu halten, daran zu erinnern, daß es auf dieser Welt keine abschließend formulierbaren Definitionen und Interpretationen gibt.

Summary

There is a remarkable compositional connection between Schütz's setting of "Sein Blut komme über uns" ("His blood be upon us") in his *Matthäuspassion*, and his setting of "Das Blut Jesu Christi" ("The blood of Jesus Christ") in his *Geistliche Konzerte*. It seems likely that the blood of Jesus had a double-meaning for Schütz – one of salvation and the other of judgment – when he composed the *Matthäuspassion*. Such a possibility is revealing, since it suggests that Schütz mitigated the anti-Jewish interpretation of Matthew 27.25 by reference to the salvific significance of the blood of Jesus.

149

Genevan Jigsaw: The Tunes of the New-York Psalmbook of 1767

Daniel Meeter

The Dutch Reformed Church in North America was founded in 1628, in what was originally the Dutch colony of New Netherland.[1] When the English annexed the colony in 1664, they permitted the Dutch to maintain their churches. For the next century a distinctive Dutch-American culture flourished in New York and New Jersey, and as late as the American Revolution, the hundred or so Reformed congregations worshipped exclusively in the Dutch language. The one exception was the church in New York City, which had introduced English services in 1764. Even with exclusive use of the Dutch language, it had long been the largest and wealthiest congregation in New York, with two pastors, two schoolmasters, and two houses of worship, the "Oude Kerk" and the "Nieuwe Kerk." But by 1748, in the words of Dominee Gualtherus Du Bois, it had "begun to languish on account of the fact that the Dutch language is gradually, more and more being neglected" by the younger generation of the city.[2] Du Bois foresaw the necessity of "calling a minister, after my death, to preach in the English language, but in accordance with our manner and doctrine."[3]

In spite of considerable opposition, in January, 1763, the New York Consistory (*Kerkeraad*) sent a "blank call" to the Netherlands requesting an English speaking preacher who would serve "according to the Constitution of the Reformed Protestant Dutch Churches in Holland."[4] The call was answered by Dominee Archibald Laidlie, pastor of the Scottish Church in Vlissingen, and he began regular English preaching in New York in

---

1 The Dutch Reformed Church is now the Reformed Church in America; the "Collegiate Church" is in New York City.
2 Hugh Hastings (ed.) *Ecclesiastical Records of the State of New York*, 7 vols. (Albany 1901-16), 4:3038. Hereafter cited as *ERNY*.
3 *ERNY* 4:3038.
4 *ERNY* 6:3853-56.

150

1764. He sparked such a revival of the congregation's fortunes that within three years the Consistory erected the North Church, its largest yet, and called a second English preacher in 1770. Dominee Du Bois had stated that English preaching would have to conform to "our manner and doctrine", and that meant the use of the Genevan metrical Psalter, that most characteristic mark of Dutch Reformed worship. Thus, even before Laidlie accepted the Call, the New York Consistory undertook the project of translating into English the Dutch Psalter of Petrus Dathenus. At the meeting of July 5, 1763, the following minute was recorded:

> Is aan de Kerker: voorgedragen een ontwerp van enige Psalmen op Engelse Rym na onse zangtonen gestelt, die zo verre van de E: Kerkeraad zyn geapprobeert, en voorts tot een Committee aan gestelt om die in het gevolg opgestelt zullen worden natezien.[5]

Other records indicate that the Consistory also began at this time the translation of the Catechism, the Confession, and the Liturgy, the non-musical portions of the Dutch Psalter.[6]

What the New York Consistory wanted was a psalmbook that would allow for simultaneous psalmsinging in two languages

---

5   Consistory Minutes (Dutch), Liber B, fol. 293, The Archives of the Collegiate Church, New York. Translation: "The draft of certain Psalms in English rhyme, according to our music, was laid before the consistory, and so far approved, and moreover referred to a Committee for the looking after of those produced hereafter." The translation in *ERNY* 6:3872 is defective.

6   For a detailed history of the 1767 New-York Psalmbook, especially its Liturgy, see Daniel Meeter, *The North American Liturgy: A Critical Edition of the Liturgy of the Reformed Dutch Church in North America, 1793.* (Ph.D. dissertation; Drew University, 1989), 122-161. See also "The First English Psalm Book", in: *Year Book of the [Collegiate] Reformed Protestant Dutch Church of the City of New York* 3 (1882), 72-77; Oscar G. T. Sonneck, *Francis Hopkinson, the First American Poet-Composer (1737-1791) and James Lyon, Patriot, Preacher, Psalmodist (1735-1791)* (Washington D.C. 1905; reprinted, with a new introduction by Richard A. Crawford, New York 1967), 93-95; Virginia Larkin Redway, "James Parker and the Dutch Church", in: *Musical Quarterly* 24 (1938), 481-500; Carleton Sprague Smith, "The 1774 Psalm Book of the Reformed Protestant Dutch Church in New York City", in: *Musical Quarterly* 34 (1948), 84-96. *American Sacred Music Imprints 1698-1810: A Bibliography*, by Allen Perdue Britton and Irving Lowens and completed by Richard Crawford [cited hereafter as C, followed by the respective number(s)] (Worcester MA 1990), 398.

without confusion, as Elder Theodorus Van Wyck wrote in his Journal:

> Om daar door in onse Godsdienst onder het Zingen alle verwarringe voor te komen, so dat de Nederduitse en Engelsche Psalmen op een in derselve Melody soude kunne gesongen worden."[7]

The Consistory wanted simultaneous bilingual singing to serve the unity of their congregation, especially since the introduction of English worship had proven a hot issue. They wanted their English worship so closely to conform to Dutch usage that those who liked to sing in Dutch could do so at an English service.[8] The desire to have Dutch and English psalms "sung to the same tune at the same time" accounts for the Consistory not taking the much easier course of simply importing the English-language psalmbook of the English Reformed Church in Amsterdam (in the "Begijnhof") with which it was in constant communication. Their metrical psalms, arranged by J.Z. Triemer, could not be sung to the same melody as the Dutch since their psalter was the Anglican "New Version" of Tate and Brady.[9] Indeed, this concern was expressed by members of the New York Consistory within a confidential letter which they wrote to Dominee Laidlie

---

7 Theodorus Van Wyck, *A Journal of the Consistory of the Reformed Dutch Church of the City of New York in Regard to the Petitions of their Congregation for Calling an English Preacher and the Disputes arising therefrom - 1762* (unpublished manuscript) New-York Historical Society, New York, 55. Translation: " (...) in order to prevent thereby all confusion in the singing during our worship, so that the Dutch and English Psalms could be sung to the same tune at the same time."

8 Undoubtedly, even those who preferred to worship in Dutch could understand an English sermon well enough.

9 *A New Version of the Psalms of David. By N. Tate & N. Brady. And set to Musick by J. Z. Triemer* (Amsterdam 1753) [together with] *Hymns Adapted to Christian Worship, And particularly to the Celebration of Baptism and the Lord's Supper, Collected from J. Stennet, Js. Watts, and S. Browne, And Set to Musick by J. Z. Triemer* (Amsterdam 1753). This "Triemer" Anglican Psalter was printed in Dutch style, each psalm having a tune, and the music printed above each line of verse. In 1765, Bruyn published another version of "Triemer", in which the number of psalm tunes was increased from 123 to 154, and this version appeared again in a reprint by Henry Gartman in 1772.

The "New Version," like most English psalters, relies almost exclusively a single metre, Common Metre, 8.6.8.6. The Dutch psalter, like all Genevan psalters, uses at least 110 different metres, "each of which demands a particular form of tune"; Waldo Selden Pratt, *The Music of the French Psalter of 1562* (New York 1966), 26.

while he was still in Vlissingen, encouraging him to accept the Call. They wrote:

> We must not therefore omitt to inform you that we are preparing a New Version of the Psalms of David in English, adapted to the Melody of those now used in the Dutch Churches in order to give the greatest harmony & unity to both the Dutch and English in performing divine worship (...) and whereas the English Brethren in Holland have adopted the Version of Tate & Brady and have caused the same to be set to musick by printing therewith those singing notes which do not harmonize with our Dutch tunes Except the 100 psalm only, the Consistory and others the leading members of our Congregation have therefore thought it more Edifying to have the English Psalms sung upon the same Tunes now used in our Churches, for which purpose we shall in due time be prepared with Types for Printing them here, and if it should be so happen that you arrive among us before these Psalms are Printed, the Dutch Psalms may in the Intermediate time by used, which Cant however be the Case long.[10]

The letter is dated August 12, 1763. As it turned out, "the Intermediate time" was long, and it took four years for the book to appear.

The Consistory engaged the well-known Philadelphia poet and musician Francis Hopkinson (1737-1791) as the editor of the psalmbook.[11] Hopkinson was a distinguished lawyer, statesman, and writer, a "signer" of the Declaration of Independence, and one of the earliest of America's composers.[12] Hopkinson, an Anglican, had no apparent connection with the Dutch Church and is not known to have spoken Dutch. Perhaps the Consistory chose him on the basis of the tune book he had issued that same year:

A Collection of Psalm Tunes, with a few anthems and hymns, some of them entirely new, for the use of the United Churches of Christ Church and St. Peter's Church Philadelphia (Philadelphia 1763).[13]

---

10 Transcribed in Van Wyck's Journal, 66-68.
11 On Hopkinson, see Sonneck, op. cit., passim.
12 Smith, op. cit., 86.
13 See C 272. Robin Leaver has supplied the following information: "There are signs that Hopkinson relied quite substantially on such earlier collections as John Tufts's *An Introduction to the Art of Singing Psalm Tunes*, published in Boston and which reached its tenth edition in 1738, and James Lyon's *Urania*, published in Philadelphia in 1761, that is, just two years before Hopkinson's collection."

Hopkinson's collection contained 37 tunes, 10 of which were also to be found in the 1753 "Triemer". It may be that Hopkinson was already familiar with "Triemer," or only that both drew their tunes from the common stock of English tunes, some of which were derived from Genevan psalm tunes.[14]
The official minutes of the Consistory make no mention of Hopkinson until May 22, 1764, a year after the work began. Yet we know from the same confidential letter to Laidlie that he had been engaged from the beginning:

> The work is already begun and a considerable Progress made therein by Mr. Francis Hopkinson of Philadelphia, a gentleman in Every respect Qualified for the Laborious and Difficult task, and from the aprobation that his Version hitherto has met with by our Consistory and other members of our Church we flatter ourselves it will not fail of meeting your Concurrence, should we be so happy as to see you here as our Minister (...) [letter dated August 12, 1763].[15]

Also, Theodorus Van Wyck's notes on the aforementioned Consistory meeting (although he dates it July 4, 1763) state as follows:

> In tot bewys van de bequaamheyt in gaven van Voorzyde Hopkinson, wierd de KR voorgelegt de seven eerste achtereenvolgende Psalmen Davids neffens de 15. 23 en 24 alrede van dier heer voltrocken. Dewelke de K.Raad voor goed keurde.[16]

The clear implication of Van Wyck's statement is that when the Consistory's minutes state that "the draft of certain Psalms in English rhyme, according to our music, was laid before the consistory," this draft comprised the ten psalms (1-7, 15, 23, 24) by Hopkinson.
The project evidently did not go as quickly or as smoothly as

---

14 The ten tunes held in common by the two collections are: OLD 81ST, OLD HUNDREDTH*, OLD 119TH, BEDFORD*, CANTERBURY, LONDON NEW, ST. DAVID'S, ST. JAMES, ST. MARY'S, and YORK; those marked with an asterisk also appeared in the 1767 psalter.

15 Van Wyck's Journal, 67. Redway must have been ignorant of Van Wyck's Journal in order to make the suggestion that, "Meanwhile one of their own number had been trying his hand at versifying the psalms in English, in order to sing them with the old Dutch tunes"; op. cit., 492.

16 Van Wyck's Journal, 55. Translation: "To testify to the capability in gifts of the aforementioned Hopkinson, there were laid before the Consistory the first seven sequential psalms of David plus the 15th, 23rd, and 24th already finished by this man."

expected. The original supervisor of Hopkinson's work, named Evert Byvank, requested on May 22, 1764, "to be released from his engagement to versify the Psalms in English in the same manner as they are versified in Dutch."[17] The reason for Byvank's request is unstated, although it is tempting to speculate that he found Hopkinson's work not close enough to the Dutch. Indeed, the same Consistory action that released Byvank also stated:

(...) that the committee, with Mr. Hopkins [sic], inquire in reference to the best method of doing this according to the genius of the English tongue, and that the versifying be done accordingly.[18]

Does the phrase, "the genius of the English tongue" indicate that the Consistory was rethinking the priority of keeping it close to the Dutch? Had Hopkinson and the Consistory discovered for themselves how uncongenial the English language is to the Genevan metres?

Two months later, on June 29, 1764, upon receiving a letter from Hopkinson proposing a new plan of versification, the Consistory agreed to maintain his engagement "volgens de wyzen daar uytgeknipt" (according to the manner he chose there). Also:

De Kerkeraad accordeert om hem nu te betalen voor het veranderen van de reedsgedaane, viertig pistolen, en daar, nog te boven, voor het voltrekken van het geheel, honderd pistolen meer, waarvan fyftig zullen betaalt woorden als het werk op de nieuwe plan half zal gedaan zyn, indien Hopkinson het eischt.[19]

Apparently, Hopkinson had not yet finished the half of the job. He was to finish it now on "the new plan", and what had already been done, "de reedsgedaane", he was to begin to "veranderen", (either "change" or "revise") also according to the new plan.

Hopkinson's own correspondence records that he finished his

---

17 *ERNY* 6:3922.
18 *ERNY* 6:3922
19 Consistory Minutes Liber B, sub dat. 29 Juni, 1764. Translation: "The Consistory agreed to pay him forty pistoles now for the changing of that already done, and above that, for the execution of the whole, one hundred pistoles more, of which fifty shall be paid once half the work is done according to the new plan, should Hopkinson request it."

part of the project by December 13, 1765.[20] The publication of the book was held up for almost two years, however, although the Consistory records are silent on what the reasons might have been. Finally, on December 17, 1767, the book's printing was completed. The full title is:

> *The Psalms of David, with the Ten Commandments, Creed, Lord's Prayer, &c. in Metre: Also the Catechism, Confession of Faith, Liturgy, &c. Translated from the Dutch: For the Use of the Reformed Protestant Dutch Church of the City of New-York. New-York. Printed by James Parker, at the New Printing Office in Beaver-Street. MDCCLXVII.*[21]

The New-York Psalmbook was made to look very much like a traditional Dutch Reformed "psalmboekje". Every stanza of every psalm was given with its appropriate musical notation, following the Dutch custom. The typical introductory page of "musical instruction", with two sample scales, was included.[22] The musical type was imported from Amsterdam at some expense.[23] Although in 1765 the Consistory planned to print 2000 copies, by 1766 it had reduced the number to 1800.[24] Theodorus Van Wyck reported that when the Psalmbook was introduced on January 1, 1768, it was accepted with "General Satisfaction".[25] About five hundred copies were sold over the next

---

20 Redway, James Parker and the Dutch Church, 495.
21 C 398. Older bibliographies state that it was "the first book of music printed from type in America"; but see Richard J. Wolfe, *Early American Music Engraving and Printing A History of Music Publishing in American from 1787 to 1825 with Commentary on Earlier and Later Practices* (Urbana 1980), 32.
22 Translation of *Musijcks-Onderwijs*: "As a great Part of Divine Worship consists in the harmonious Singing of the Psalms, it has been thought necessary for the Benefit of those who are desirous to learn to Sing, to add the two following Scales, which being perfectly understood, will enable any Person to sing all the Psalms in the Book with Ease." There follow two scales in tenor cleff, in whole notes, one with two flats, and the syllables beneath, "Ut re mi fa sol la ci ut: Ut ci la sol la mi re ut," and the second, with no flats, and the syllables, "So la ci ut re mi fa sol: Sol fa mi re ut ci la sol." *The Psalms of David* [fourth unnumbered page].
23 The type cost 557 Dutch guilders, and was bought from the Amsterdam importer Daniel Crommelin, who had many relatives in New York. *ERNY* 6:4010.
24 *ERNY* 6:4010, 4076.
25 Van Wyck's Journal, 215.

year.[26] Hopkinson's name appears nowhere in the Psalmbook. The book includes full versifications of all 150 psalms, together with six hymns, that is, metrical versions of the Ten Commandments, the Song of Zacharias, the Song of the Virgin Mary, the Song of Simeon, the [Apostles'] Creed, and the Lord's Prayer.[27] But the book included only a total of 51 tunes. It becomes apparent that the New-York Psalmbook is something other than a straight translation of the familiar Dutch Psalter. All true Genevan Psalters, the Dutch included, used the full complement of 125 Genevan tunes for the 150 Psalms, plus standard tunes for the Canticles of Zacharias, Mary, and Simeon, the tune of Psalm 140 for the Ten Commandments, and, by this time, the familiar German "Vater Unser" tune for the Lord's Prayer. Thus, the New-York Psalmbook should have had 129 tunes, not 51. Examination of the New-York Psalmbook reveals that only 25 of the psalms, plus the Song of Mary and the Lord's Prayer, are set to the same tune as the Dutch (see Table 1).

Table 1: Psalms Set to Their Proper Tunes
SoM = Song of Mary; LP = Lord's Prayer.

1	24	36	100	142
2	25	49	117	SoM
3	26	57	118	LP
10	32	62	131	
12	34	66	134	
16	35	98	136	Total: 27

Of these 27 psalms, Psalms 66/98/118 share a common tune, as do Psalms 100/131/142 and Psalms 24/62, which means that there are 22 tunes in this group. Another 23 of the psalms are set to tunes that are their proper ones, but which are not in their familiar state. They might be called "abbreviated." What Hopkinson did was shorten each line of music, wherever possible, down to either eight or six notes, the standard lines of English metre.

---

26 *ERNY* 6:4139.
27 Dutch Psalters of the time also often included metrical versions of the Morning and Evening Prayers, the Prayers Before and After Meat, and the Hymn Before Sermon.

Psalm 21, a typical case, was abbreviated from 8.7.7.8.6.6. to 8.6.6.8.6.6. A few tunes were condensed in other ways, such as Psalm 11, which went from a combination of 11s and 10s down to all 10s (see Table 2).

Table 2: **Psalms Set to Abbreviated Versions of the Proper Tunes**

11	45	65	84	130
21	46	72	86	148
28	52	73	97	150
30	54	77	105	
42	55	80	113	Total: 23

Of these 23 psalms, Psalms 65/72 share a common tune, as do 77/86. There are, therefore, 21 tunes in this group, making a sub-total of 43.

What accounts for these "abbreviated" versions of the Genevan tunes? One would have expected the very opposite, that the tunes would have been untouched and the words "expanded." Indeed, the "new plan" of versification, which the Consistory adopted on June 29, 1764, apparently was for Hopkinson to adapt the English "New Version" of Tate and Brady to the longer lines and stanzas of the Genevan tunes by stretching the lyrics and rewriting them where needed. This is precisely what the Psalmbook's preface indicates:

To the Reader.

The Consistory of the Reformed Protestant Dutch Church of the City of New-York, having, by Reason of the Declension of the Dutch Language, found it necessary to have Divine Service performed in their Church in English; Have adopted the following version of the Psalms of David, which is greatly indebted to that of Dr. Brady and Mr. Tate; Some of the Psalms being transcribed verbatim from their version, and others altered, so as to fit them to the Music used in the Dutch Churches.[28]

But the preface is misleading. It is not so much that Hopkinson altered "Brady and Tate" to fit the "Dutch Music" as the reverse, that he altered the "Dutch Music" to fit "Brady and Tate"

28 *The Psalms of David* [third unnumbered page].

by abbreviating the tunes. Now, if this is the result of the "new plan" which took into account "the genius of the English tongue," why does the preface suggest the "old plan" was still in force?

Further, what the preface completely fails to mention is that fully 104 of the psalms and 4 of the hymns (69%) do not at all "fit the Music used in the Dutch Churches." True, 36 of these are set to unaltered Genevan tunes, but to different ones, not their proper ones. This would not have been critical for English psalmody, which, with its metres both simpler and more standardized than the Dutch, has always been flexible in assigning various tunes to various psalms. But Genevan psalmody holds particular psalms and specific tunes in an unbreakable union. It is remarkable that so conservative a Dutch Reformed group as the New-York Consistory allowed these unions of text and tune to be broken. Perhaps they did not want to broadcast the fact, and therefore the preface does not draw attention to it. But the silence of the preface could hide the problem only for a limited time, because as soon as the psalms began to be sung the alterations to the traditional tunes and their reassignment to other psalms would become obvious.

It is curious that the preface states that "Some of the Psalms [are] transcribed verbatim from [Tate and Brady's] version," when there is actually hardly a one of their psalms left intact. There are many individual lines of straight Tate and Brady, but these are almost always interspersed with other newly-written lines. Perhaps this statement was designed to confuse as much as clarify and thus conceal what the Consistory did not want to be broadcast, that is, the many changes to the tunes that had been made to fit them to English metres.

Table 3 lists the psalms which are set to a tune other than the proper one found in the Dutch psalter, and identifies these other tunes.

Table 3: Psalms Set to Different Unaltered Tunes

4=3	50=117	81=100	110=136	138=100
7=134†	56=35	85=LP	112=128	141=LP
8=24	60=134	88=134	114=134	145=SoM
9=100	61=LP	89=100	115=SoM	146=SoM
20=134	63=LP	90=66	123=100	
23=134	67=100	91=3	127=134	
27=100	68=100	95=100	132=134	
33=100	75=LP	96=100	135=136	Total: 36

† Psalm 134 = OLD HUNDREDTH in English psalmody

There are eleven tunes used for this group of psalms, only one of which (Genevan 128, not in Table 1) was not used for its associated psalm in the Dutch psalter (only for Psalm 112). This group adds one tune to the sub-total, which now becomes 44.

The final group of psalms are at least two steps removed from their proper Genevan tunes. They are set to abbreviated versions of tunes, which are not the proper ones. Indeed, some of these tunes (those designated by letters) are not even in the Genevan psalter. Three of them are English in origin: "a" is a variant form of Orlando Gibbons's ANGELS HYMN, "d" a variant of BEDFORD, and "f" is the tune MEAR.[29] Tune "b", which has strong echoes of Genevan Psalm 124, is the tune for Psalm 34 in Triemer's 1753 psalter,[30] but is in fact an older adaptation in the English psalm tune tradition that had made its first appearance in John Playford, *The Whole Book of Psalms (...) Composed in Three Parts* (London 1677), with the name PETERBOROUGH. But the immediate source may have been Triemer's 1765 edition, since there are two tunes that Hopkinson appears to have taken directly from this collection: the adaptations of the tunes for Psalms 37 and 59 are identical with the forms for

---

29 I thank Robin Leaver for having identified these. Orlando Gibbon's ANGELS HYMN was first published in George Wither, *Hymns and Songs of the Church* (London 1623); BEDFORD was first published in Francis Timbrell, *The Divine Musick's Scholar's Guide* (London [ca. 1720]); and MEAR was first published in Charles Woodmason's *A Collection of Psalms* (London [ca. 1735]). All three tunes made their first American appearance in James Lyon's *Urania* (Philadelphia 1761); BEDFORD and MEAR were also included in Hopkinson's 1763 collection.

30 Smith, op. cit., 93.

Hymn 37 and Psalm 54, respectively, in the 1765 edition of Triemer's psalter. The remaining two tunes, "c" and "e" have yet to be identified (see Table 4).

Table 4: Psalms Set to Abbreviated Versions of Different Tunes

Law = the Ten Commandments; SoZ = the Song of Zachariah; SoS = the Song of Simeon; ApC = Apostles' Creed.

5=25*	41=130	78=113	107=65	137=73
6=77	43=42	79=130	108=a	139=a
13=130	44=113	82=73	109=65	140=a
14=80	47=150	83=73	111=55	143=25*
15=80	48=113	87=113	116=b	144=113
17=42	51=42	88=77	119=b	147=148
18=113	53=80	92=45	120=84	149=150
19=105*	58=737	93=28	121=25*	
22=77	59=84	94=65	122=84	Law=d
29=80	64=80	99=97	124=80	SoZ=e
31=80	69=77	101=65	125=113	SoS=65
37=73	70=25*	102=77	126=113	ApC=f.
38=77	71=80	103=73	128=c	
39=55	74=77	104=84	129=28	
40=21	76=113	106=105*	133=a	Total: 71

Note: "25*" indicates an abbreviated version of the Psalm 25 tune, which also appears in its original form with the text of Psalm 25 (see Table 1). "105*" is not only abbreviated but slightly altered in lines three and four. These altered lines are similar to the German tune *Nun lobt und dankt Gott allesamen* (Zahn 2995).

There are 23 tunes used in this group, seven of which are not used elsewhere, namely, 25*, a, b, c, d, e, and f. Thus, the total number of tunes in the book is 51 (see further Tables 6-11 in the Appendix).

The contents of this Psalmbook raise a number of questions. First of all, did the Consistory completely change its expectations for the Psalmbook in the midst of its preparations? The original goal, we recall, was "dat de Nederduitse en Engelsche Psalmen op een in derselve Melody soude kunne gesongen worden."[31] In spite of what the preface suggests, out of 156 psalms

---

31 Translation: "That the Dutch and English Psalms could be sung to the same tune at the same time."

and canticles, only the twenty-six (17%) in Table 1 would have allowed for such bilingual singing. It might have been possible to have simultaneous singing of the twenty-three (15%) in Table 2, but this would require the English singers to ignore the musical notation and to slur many syllables over two notes, an absolute rarity in Genevan psalmody.[32] But more to the point is that the 107 psalms and hymns in tables 3 and 4 would be totally unusable for simultaneous singing. Beyond that, there would have been problems even in the exclusively English services. Most of the English worshippers would have known the Dutch Psalter tunes by heart, and all these, now paired with different psalms and in altered versions, would have caused them immense frustration. We could say that four-fifths of the book would have increased the very "alle verwarringe" ("all sorts of confusion") which the Consistory had wanted to avoid.

One might think that this result was due to the "new plan" adopted half way through the project. Were there too many difficulties encountered in trying to get a true Genevan Psalter? Is this why Evert Byvank resigned from the project? But then one would expect that the very first psalms submitted at the beginning of the project, numbers 1 to 7, 15, 23, and 24, would have used the proper Genevan tunes unabbreviated. Only four of them do, Psalms 1, 2, 3, and 24. The other six, Psalms 4, 5, 6, 7, 15, and 23, do not, and are paired with different tunes. Did these six originally fit their proper tunes, but subsequently, in Hopkinson's "veranderen", get reworked according to the "new plan?" But if this is what happened, why did he allow the 26 psalms of Table 1 to remain with their proper tunes, according to what will have been regarded as the "old plan"? Such questions as these, unfortunately, cannot be answered on the basis of the available ecclesiastical documents and correspondence.

The result of Hopkinson's work is that fully two-thirds of the tunes of the Genevan Psalter were excluded from English-language worship in the Dutch Reformed Church (see Table 5).

---

32 The Genevan Psalter, thoroughly "one syllable-one tone," has only six slurs in its 125 tunes. Pratt, loc. cit.

Table 5: Excluded Genevan Tunes

4	33/67	75	103	132
5/64	37	78/90	104	133
6	38	79	106	135
7	39	81	107	137
8	40	83	110	138
9	41	85	112	140
13	43	87	114	141
14/53	44	88	115	143
15	47	89	119	145
17/63/70	48	91	120	146
18/144	50	92	121	147
19	51/69	93	122	
20	56	94	123	SoZ
22	58	95	124	SoS
23	59	96	125	ApC
27	60/108	99	126	
29	61	101	128	
31/71	74/116	102	129	Total=86

Anyone who is familiar with the Genevan Psalter will recognize that some of the finest and best-loved tunes were thus excluded. There is no denying that this was a substantial loss.

The New-York Psalmbook was introduced in January of 1768, and the Consistory sold 500 copies over the next year.[33] But by printing 1800 copies the Consistory had obviously expected to sell many more. In March of 1769 there were still 1300 copies unsold.[34] Evidently the "General Satisfaction" which Van Wyck had reported did not last long nor go very deep. After several price reductions, by 1774 the Consistory was giving copies away.[35] It continued in use, though, and in the same year one New York musician published a book of harmonies for it:

A Collection of the Psalm and Hymn Tunes, Used by the Reformed Protestant Dutch Church of the City of New-York: agreeable to their Psalm Book, published in English: In Four Parts, viz. Tenor, Bass, Treble, and Counter.[36]

---

33 *ERNY* 6:4139.
34 *ERNY* 6:4139.
35 *ERNY* 6:4283, 4286.
36 Published in New York by Hodge and Shober, 1774. The book is number B 3821 in Bristol's *Supplement to Charles Evans' American Bibliography*, Readex Microprint Edition no. 42679. See the article by Carleton Sprague Smith, op. cit.

The general disruption of the American Revolution makes it impossible to determine the fortunes of either book after 1774. After the Revolution, the Dutch Reformed congregations in North America organized themselves into a Synod. They contemplated a new common service book. The Catechism, Confession, and Liturgy from the New-York Psalmbook were adopted, but the Hopkinson Psalter was politely ignored. The Synod published its own new Psalter, which avoided Geneva altogether, and went for straight and simple English common metre psalmody. Unfortunately, this meant that the (Dutch) Reformed Church in North America would be forever after cut off from the tradition of the Genevan Psalter. This has resulted not only in the loss of its greatest heirloom, but also in the isolation of its worship experience from the larger Reformed world, the effects of which are still felt today. Might things have been different if the New York Consistory had been able to succeed with its original conception for the psalmbook?

In 1985, when Professor and Mrs. Honders were visiting New Jersey, I showed Casper a copy of the New-York Psalmbook. Our specific interest was the English translation of the Netherlands Liturgy in the back of the book, the topic of my dissertation, but I noticed that Casper, for whom theology is most compelling when "er zit muziek in", could not keep his eyes off the metrical psalms in the front of the book. He suggested that some valuable work was waiting to be done; I answered that my own interest was in the Liturgy. But maybe after I was done with that...
My assignment, only half-heartedly accepted, is now fulfilled. But a life-long and wholehearted obligation to the Psalter continues. I learned Dutch by singing psalms with my immigrant grandfather. We learn Christ by singing psalms after generations of the faithful. We learn love by joining in such sweet music as that of Cas and Nel.

Appendix: Supplementary Tables

Table 6: Unaltered Tunes Used Only Once

1	16	34	128
2	25	36	142
10	26	49	
12	32	57	Total: 14

Table 7: Abbreviated Tunes Used Only Once

11	30	46	52	54
				Total: 5

Table 8: Other Tunes Used Only Once

c=128	d=Law	e=SoZ	f=ApC
			Total: 4

c and e = unidentified; d = BEDFORD; f = MEAR

Table 9: Unaltered Tunes Used More than Once

g = a "proper" tune used more than once

3	(3x):	3, 4, 91
24g	(3x):	8, 24g, 62g (properly also 95 and 111)
35	(2x):	35, 56
66g	(4x):	66g, 90, 98g, 118g
100g	(14x):	9, 27, 33, 67, 68, 81, 89, 95, 96, 100g, 123, 131g, 138, 142g
117g	(2x):	50, 117g (properly also 127)
134	(7x):	7, 20, 23, 60, 114, 127, 132, 134
136	(3x):	110, 135, 136
SoM	(4x):	115, 145, 146, SoM
LP	(6x):	61, 63, 75, 85, 141, LP

Table 10: Abbreviated Tunes Used More than Once

21	(2x):	21, 40
25*	(4x):	5, 70, 121, 143
28g	(3x):	28g, 93, 129 (properly also 109)
42	(4x):	17, 42, 43, 51
45	(2x):	45, 92
55	(3x):	39, 55, 111
65g	(7x):	65g, 72g, 94, 101, 107, 109, SoZ
73	(7x):	37, 58, 73, 82, 83, 103, 137
77g	(9x):	6, 22, 38, 69, 74, 77g, 86g, 88, 102
80	(9x):	14, 15, 29, 31, 53, 64, 71, 80, 124
84	(5x):	59, 84, 104, 120, 122
97	(2x):	97, 99
105	(3x):	19, 105, 106
113	(10x):	18, 44, 48, 76, 78, 87, 113, 125, 126, 144
130	(3x):	13, 41, 79
148	(2x):	147, 148
150	(3x):	47, 149, 150

* Tune 25 also appears unabbreviated with its proper psalm.

Table 11: Other Tunes Used More than Once

a = ANGELS HYMN	(4x):	108, 133, 139, 140
b = PETERBOROUGH	(2x):	116, 119

Psalm 112,
gelezen, gezongen, gepraktizeerd
Hymnologische bespiegelingen
rond een vergeten psalm

Bernard Smilde

Van alle boeken van het Oude Testament is ongetwijfeld het Boek der Psalmen het meest bekend en geliefd. Deze populariteit wil nog niet zeggen, dat alle psalmen even goed gekend worden. Iedere christen zal binnen deze 150 liederen van Israël zijn of haar voorkeuren hebben. Waar men het hele Psalter aan één stuk doorleest of doorbreviert, passeren ze natuurlijk alle 150 de revue. Maar bij bepaalde gelegenheden worden sommige uit en te na geciteerd, terwijl andere op de achtergrond blijven. In de eredienst komen evenmin alle psalmen even vaak aan bod. In zijn laatste vormgeving kent het *Graduale Romanum* voor de zondagen van een heel jaar fragmenten uit 46 psalmen. De *Randstadbundel* (1979) heeft in diverse liedvormen 35 psalmen, *Gezangen voor Liturgie* (1984) heeft er 71. In de kerken van de calvinistische traditie werden aanvankelijk alle psalmen even vaak gezongen: men zong er een aantal vóór en een aantal na de predikatie; de nummers waren op borden aangegeven voor de zondagse en door-de-weekse diensten. Zo was het althans te Genève. Daarbij was er totaal geen samenhang met de lezingen of de tekstkeuze van die dienst. Psalm 83 kreeg dus dezelfde kans om "populair" te worden als psalm 84. Eerst geleidelijk veranderde dit.

Ook in Nederland is een paar eeuwen geleden die Geneefse methode in zwang gebleven, op sommige plaatsen zelfs tot in de 19e eeuw. Misschien gaat het psalmzingen van Hendrik de Cock in zijn Groninger gevangenschap, waarvan Ypma melding maakt,[1] nog op dit gebruik terug.

Het lijdt geen twijfel of het selectief gebruik door de predikan-

---

1 A. Ypma, "Het godsdienstig lied en de Afscheiding", in: A.C. Honders, R. Steensma, J. Wit (ed.), *Het lied en de kerk: Hymnologische opstellen* [Studies van het Instituut voor Liturgiewetenschap nr. 3] (Groningen 1977), 209-245.

ten, meer in aansluiting aan de rest van de liturgie, moest wel leiden tot het "voortrekken" van een bepaalde groep psalmen en verwaarlozing van een ander deel. Per predikant, plaats en tijd is dit natuurlijk heel verschillend geweest en voor een deel is dat het nog. Wat betreft het gebruik van de berijmde psalmen in Nederland, zou men kunnen komen tot een globale indeling in vier groepen:

a. psalmen die bij iedere kerkganger bekend en geliefd zijn, zoals 25, 42, 43, 65, 72, 84, 89, 98, 103, 116, 118, 119, 121, 122, 130, 138, 146.

b. psalmen die niet elke zondag worden aangeheven, maar die toch tot de algemeen bekende behoren en zonder problemen in iedere gemeente kunnen worden gezongen. Te denken is aan de psalmen 8, 19, 24, 56, 87, 91, 97, 105, 111, 145.

c. psalmen die weliswaar niet geheel vergeten zijn, maar die niet vaak op onze liederenborden prijken, bijvoorbeeld psalm 2, 3, 34, 38, 40, 48, 124, 126, 127.

d. psalmen die in de meeste gemeenten nooit of hoogst zelden worden gezongen, zoals psalm 7, 11, 13, 39, 41, 59, 83, 109, 112, 114, 129, 137.

Natuurlijk zullen er plaatsen zijn, waar men een bepaalde psalm in een andere categorie zou willen plaatsen. Verschillende van de nu niet genoemde liederen zouden eventueel in een randgebied tussen de vier categorieën moeten worden ondergebracht. Soms vinden in een gemeente verschuivingen plaats door de komst van een nieuwe predikant of cantor-organist.
Je vraagt je af: hoe komt het, dat een bepaalde psalm in de vergeten groep terechtkomt?
Soms zijn er duidelijk problemen met de tekst; het laat zich denken, dat menig predikant er niet over zal piekeren bepaalde wraakpsalmen als 109 of 137 de christelijke gemeente op de lippen te leggen. Soms is het de melodie die moeite geeft. Hoewel we over het algemeen kunnen zeggen dat de Geneefse melodieën door geboren pedagogen zijn geschreven, moeten we toegeven, dat er enkele zijn, die moeilijkheden bij de gemiddelde gemeente opleveren vanwege ritmische figuren of melodische wendingen. Dit geldt bijvoorbeeld voor psalm 41, 114 en 129.
Daar staat tegenover – en naar het mij voorkomt geldt dat in de meeste gevallen – dat er psalmen in de d-groep zijn terecht gekomen, waarbij noch de tekst noch de melodie aanleiding

geven tot die verwaarlozing. Zoals in het geval van psalm 112, de psalm die ik in dit artikel wat nader onder de aandacht zou willen brengen.

Psalm 112 noem ik een vergeten psalm. Niet alleen in Nederland, ook in calvinistische kerken in het buitenland wordt hij niet vaak gezongen. De jongste editie van de Frans-Zwitserse kerk heeft 71 psalmen, die van de protestantse kerken in Frankrijk 84, maar in geen van beide bundels wordt psalm 112 aangetroffen. Ook de Duitstalige kerken in Zwitserland met hun 40 psalmen laten het op dit punt afweten. De laatste redactie van het *Psalter Hymnal* van de Christian Reformed Churches in Amerika herstelde weliswaar een aantal Geneefse melodieën in ere, maar die van psalm 112 is er niet bij. We vinden haar in het hieronder nader te noemen *Book of Praise*, waarin de complete erfenis van Calvijn is overgenomen. Ook in de Romana is weinig aandacht voor deze psalm. In alle drie zoëven genoemde bundels schittert psalm 112 door afwezigheid.

Dat ik mij wat meer in het bijzonder beziggehouden heb met deze psalm, heeft te maken met het feit dat ik als "hymnologischer Berater" ben aangetrokken door de "Psalmenkommission" van de Evangelisch-reformierte en de Altreformierte Kirche in Duitsland. Deze kerken gebruiken merendeels nog de Psalmberijming van Matthias Jorissen uit 1793.

Jorissen was afkomstig uit Wesel, studeerde in Duisburg en Utrecht, en werd, na enige Nederlandse gemeenten te hebben gediend, predikant bij de Duitse "reformierte" gemeente te Den Haag. Daar was toen nog de Duitse berijming van Ambrosius Lobwasser uit 1572 in gebruik, die weinig beter was dan de Nederlandse van Petrus Datheen uit 1566. Jorissen, een neef van Gerhard Tersteegen, was ook dichterlijk begaafd. Hij ergerde zich aan het stuntelige werk van Lobwasser en schreef in een jaar tijd een complete nieuwe berijming, die hier en daar duidelijk geïnspireerd is door de Nederlandse "Staatsberijming" van 1773. Zijn werk is breed opgezet: halve strofen vulde hij steeds aan tot hele. Zijn berijming bevat zeker geïnspireerde regels en strofen. Een groot dichter kunnen we Jorissen echter niet noemen. Wel beschikte hij over een behoorlijke dosis taalvaardigheid. Al is zijn werk doorgaans hoger te taxeren dan dat van de dichters van onze Staatsberijming, toch krijgt men nu meer en meer oog voor de bezwaren die aan deze bundel kleven: breedsprakigheid, verouderde taal, piëtistische sfeer. Aanvankelijk kreeg ik de indruk, dat de "Psalmenkommission" geporteerd zou zijn voor geheel nieuw werk. Bij de voortgang van het werk bleek dat men toch te sterk aan de traditie was verknocht en, waar enigszins mogelijk, de teksten van Jorissen wilde handhaven of restaureren. Zo liepen ook bij psalm 112 de meningen uiteen.

Psalm 112 gelezen
Vorm en inhoud

Een blik in de Hebreeuwse bijbel is voldoende om te zien dat psalm 112 in de grondvorm een uiterst regelmatig model vertoont: afgezien van het opschrift "Halleluja", hebben we te maken met een zogenaamde alfabetische psalm, die bestaat uit 22 regeltjes, die steeds beginnen met een letter van het Hebreeuwse alfabet. Deze regels zijn ook allemaal ongeveer even lang; ze hebben drie heffingen, soms vier. De voorgaande psalm 111 heeft precies dezelfde structuur: ook hier een Hallelujaopschrift en 22 regeltjes volgens het Hebreeuwse alfabet, regels met meestal drie en een paar maal vier heffingen. Deze structuur is zo schematisch en overzichtelijk, dat zij zelfs in vele vertalingen typografisch nog herkenbaar is.

Deze alfabet-structuur wijst volgens de commentatoren² op een ontstaan in de kringen van na-exilische wijsheidsleraren. Tengevolge van deze kunstige vorm is een ander kenmerk van Hebreeuwse poëzie wat op de achtergrond geraakt, namelijk het "parallellismus membrorum": de gedachten van twee op elkaar volgende zinsdelen lopen inhoudelijk niet steeds streng evenwijdig. Soms lijkt het ook alsof bepaalde losse stereotype uitspraken in de psalmen zijn bijeengebracht. Toch zijn beide psalmen in zich een volstrekte eenheid; er is wat de gedachtengang betreft geen sprake van brokkeligheid.

Ook in woordgebruik is er overeenkomst aan te wijzen tussen beide psalmen. Zo vinden we:

חפץ (lust hebben, behagen scheppen) in 111:2b en 112:1b;
ישׁרים (oprechten) in 111:1b en 112:2b;
סמך (steunen, vaststellen) in 111:8a en 112:8a;
זכר (ל) עולם (eeuwig gedenken) in 111:5b en 112:6b.

Nog opvallender is het feit, dat 111:3b en 112:3b woordelijk gelijk zijn. De Statenvertalers vertaalden hier geheel concordant: "en zijn gerechtigheid bestaat in eeuwigheid." De vertalers van het Nederlands Bijbelgenootschap (1951) durfden deze consequentie niet aan en vertaalden in 111: "houdt eeuwig stand", en

---

2   Zie bijvoorbeeld H.J. Kraus in: *Biblischer Kommentar Altes Testament* XV/2 (Neukirchen 1961).

in 112: "houdt voor immer stand". Wat is namelijk het geval? Die nimmer aflatende gerechtigheid heeft in 111 betrekking op de houding van JHWH en in 112 op die van de vrome. Inhoudelijk is er tussen beide psalmen een groot verschil. Psalm 111 is een hymnisch leerdicht over de genadige toewending van God naar zijn verkoren volk. Die heilstrouw van God (verbond) wordt geïllustreerd met een aantal voorbeelden uit de geschiedenis van Israël. Hiermee wil de zanger zijn toehoorders opwekken in deze geloofshouding te delen en zo met deze lofprijzing in te stemmen. In psalm 112 hebben we te maken met de keerzijde van de medaille: het gaat over het geluk van de gelovige, die uit die verbondstrouw van JHWH leeft en wiens leven daarvan de sporen draagt: hij houdt zich aan Gods geboden en is daarom barmhartig en mededeelzaam jegens de arme. Hij houdt vol ondanks duisternis, vijandschap, spot en bedreiging. Deze rechtvaardige is niet alleen een gelukkig mens, maar hij heeft ook een grote toekomst. De tegenstanders kunnen zich wel ergeren aan zijn voorspoed, zij gaan tandenknarsend ten onder. In psalm 111 is het de Heer die gerechtigheid betoont en wiens gerechtigheid stand houdt; in psalm 112 is het de gelovige die de verbondstrouw van JHWH van zijn kant met verbondstrouw beantwoordt. Ook voor zijn houding kan het woord gerechtigheid worden gebruikt. Van die menselijke gerechtigheid wordt gezegd dat die bestendig is.
Een soortgelijke dubbelzijdigheid vinden we tenslotte in het gebruik van de woorden חַנּוּן וְרַחוּם (genadig en barmhartig) die de dichter van psalm 111:4 gebruikt als epitheta van JHWH en in psalm 112:4b als eigenschappen van de rechtvaardige mens.
Het kan niet anders of de onbekende dichter(s?) van deze psalmen heeft/hebben het besef gehad dat deze beide aspecten van de gerechtigheid zozeer bijeenhoren dat dit tot uitdrukking moest komen in formele gelijkheid. Gaan we te ver als we stellen dat het daarom in hoge mate waarschijnlijk is dat de psalmen 111 en 112 uit de pen van dezelfde dichter zijn gevloeid? Dogmatisch gesproken zouden we zeggen: in psalm 111 ligt het accent op de rechtvaardiging door het geloof en in psalm 112 op de heiliging. Onwillekeurig denken we aan antwoord 64 van de Heidelbergse Catechismus: "het is onmogelijk, dat, zo wie Christus door een waarachtig geloof ingeplant is, niet zou voortbrengen vruchten der dankbaarheid".
We noteren dat deze formele gelijkheid van twee psalmen in het

171

Hebreeuws binnen het kader van de 150 uniek is. Terecht hebben de verzamelaars ze ook onmiddellijk achter elkaar geplaatst. Dat zou er trouwens op kunnen wijzen dat ze die zo ook hebben aangetroffen in hun oorspronkelijk materiaal.

We merken nog op dat lezing en vertaling van de Hebreeuwse tekst weinig of geen problemen verschaffen. Enig verschil bestaat er ten aanzien van de interpretatie van vers 4a (psalm 112). De vertaling uit 1951 heeft hier, zoals de meeste andere vertalingen:

Voor de oprechten gaat het Licht in de duisternis op.

Lamparter[3] vertaalt:

Er (= de godvrezende; B.S.) leuchtet als Licht im Dunkel den Frommen.

In diezelfde geest ook König en *The New English Bible*:

(He is) a beacon in darkness for honest men.

Wat de tweede helft van dit vers betreft, willen sommigen met de Syrische vertaling de copula ‎ו‎ voor ‎צַדִּיק‎ schrappen om dan te vertalen:

genadig en barmhartig is de rechtvaardige.

Het voordeel van deze laatste lezing is, dat men nu een betere aansluiting bij vers 4b krijgt, maar inhoudelijk maakt het weinig verschil.

Deze psalm schijnt zich alleen te bewegen op het terrein van de persoonlijke ethiek. De Thora bevat natuurlijk tal van aanwijzingen en instellingen voor het maatschappelijk leven in groter verband. We denken aan wetten op de lossing van slaven en land, aan het leviraatshuwelijk, aan het verbod op het nemen van rente van een volksgenoot enzovoort. In hoeverre die wetten inderdaad zijn nagekomen, weten we niet. Maar ook dan viel er blijkbaar genoeg tussen wal en schip. Ook bij de beste wetgeving blijft een persoonlijke ethische levenshouding onontbeerlijk als inspiratie en als correctie.

De enige plaats in het Nieuwe Testament die aan psalm 112

---

3 In de serie *Die Botschaft des Alten Testaments* 15-II (Stuttgart 1959).

refereert, is 2 Cor. 9:9, waar psalm 112:9 naar de Septuaginta wordt aangehaald:

ἐσκόρπισεν, ἔδωκεν τοῖς πένησιν,
ἡ δικαιοσύνη αὐτοῦ μένει εἰς τὸν αἰῶνα.
(Hij heeft uitgedeeld, aan de armen gegeven,
zijn gerechtigheid blijft in eeuwigheid.)

Paulus formuleert in de hoofdstukken 8 en 9 van deze brief een uitgebreide aanbeveling van de collecte, die overal in de gemeenten gehouden zal worden ten bate van de verarmde gemeente te Jeruzalem. (Werelddiakonaat is dus niet pas iets van de 20e eeuw!) De christenen uit de heidenen kunnen daarmee hun verbondenheid aan de christenen uit de Joden tonen. Paulus zendt Titus met nog een andere broeder om een en ander voor te bereiden. Hij behandelt de zaak bijzonder serieus. Het is voor hem een testcase van geloof, liefde en dankbaarheid. Vergeleken met andere brieven van Paulus heeft deze opvallend weinig citaten uit het Oude Testament. Paulus had in dit verband ruime keuze gehad om andere teksten te kiezen, bijvoorbeeld uit het boek Spreuken of uit de Thora. Hij neemt een vers uit psalm 112. Deze psalm moet hem dus helder voor de geest hebben gestaan. Hij beseft dat milddadigheid in het geven geen luxe is, maar bij het "gewone" patroon van het christenzijn hoort. Dat de diepste wortels voor het betonen van gerechtigheid niet liggen in menselijke deugd of verdienste, blijkt uit het slot van dit hoofdstuk, waar hij eindigt met:

Gode zij dank voor zijn onuitsprekelijke gave! (2 Cor. 9:15)

Psalm 112, gezongen
De melodie van Genève 1562 en de berijmingen

De psalmen 111 en 112 behoren tot het laatst gereedgekomen deel van het rijmpsalter van Genève. De teksten zijn van de hand van Theodore de Bèze, die het werk van Clement Marot voltooide. Heeft hij oog gehad voor het tweelingkarakter van deze psalmen? Misschien. Hij berijmde beide psalmen in zes zesregelige strofen. Voor psalm 111 koos De Bèze echter het schema AAbCCb,[4] zodat de tekst gezongen kon worden op de melodie van psalm 24, die voor het eerst in Genève 1542 voorkomt en die pas in de zetting van Loys Bourgeois in 1547 de melodische en ritmische vorm kreeg, waarin wij haar nu kennen. Voor psalm 112 nam De Bèze een model dat we in het gehele Geneefse Psalter nergens anders tegenkomen, namelijk aabccb. Datheen en Marnix hielden zich aan dit schema. Joh. Eusebius Voet, wiens berijming als basis diende voor die van 1773, veranderde dit schema in aabbcc. Dat deed ook de berijming van het gezelschap "Laus Deo, salus populo", terwijl de compilatie die Hendrik Ghijsen in 1686 in zijn *Den HOONIG-RAAT der Psalmdichten (...)* had samengesteld uit 17 verschillende berijmingen, zich nog aan De Bèze's model had gehouden. De Interkerkelijke Berijming uit 1968 volgde het rijmschema van 1773. Men kan dit betreuren: het omarmend rijm van Genève is wat gevarieerder. Daar staat tegenover dat het schema van Voet c.s. beter bij de melodische structuur past. Tenslotte vermelden we nog dat de Duitse berijmer Lobwasser De Bèze correct volgde, terwijl Jorissen het schema van 1773 overnam.

Zo deed ook W. Helder (1972) in de jongste Engelse berijming *Book of Praise, Anglo-Genevan Psalter* van de Canadian Reformed Churches (Winnipeg 1984).

Ook de *melodie* van psalm 112 behoort in het Geneefse psalter tot de laatst gereedgekomen groep, een groep die op naam staat van Maistre Pierre. Nog altijd is het geen uitgemaakte zaak of deze daarvan de componist of slechts de copiïst/redactor is geweest. Na de jongste publikatie van Pierre Pidoux mag het welhaast zeker genoemd worden, dat hij niemand anders is dan Pierre Davantès, bijgenaamd Antesignanus, de classicus uit Rabasteins in Bigorre, die in 1559 burger van Genève was geworden. Hij moet een soort stenografische notatie van het solmisatie-systeem hebben uitgevonden, waarvoor hij in 1560 privilege ontving.

---

4 Bij deze schematisering wijzen hoofdletters op staand of mannelijk rijm, kleine letters op slepend of vrouwelijk rijm.

In voorbeeld 1 is de melodie van psalm 112 afgedrukt, zoals die sinds 1562 in alle edities ongewijzigd is te vinden.[5]

112 Beatus vir qui timet
O BIENHEUREUSE LA PERSONNE   BEZE

GE 62

1. O bienheureuse la personne   2. Qui craint l'Eter-nel et s'addonne

3. Du tout à sa Loy tresen-tiere.   4. Sa race en terre se-ra forte

5. Car Dieu benit en toute sorte   6. Des bons la race droiturie-re.

Voorbeeld 1

Deze melodie staat – evenals die van psalm 111 – in de dorische modus. Regel 1, 4 en 6 eindigen op de tonica, regel 2 en 5 op de dominant en regel 3 op de mediant. In regel 1 en 2 wordt als top de zevende trap bereikt, één van de primaire tonen in de dorische modus. Regel 3 en 4 bewegen zich in een wat bescheidener omvang. Opvallend is de inzet van regel 5 met het oktaaf van de finalis d. Dit zou een reden kunnen zijn om het rijmschema van 1773 verkieslijker te achten dan dat van Genève 1562. Regel 6 heeft nog een kleine opstuwing naar de septiem om dan dalend via de dominant weer terug te komen op de finalis. Bezien we echter regel 6 wat nader, dan blijkt allereerst dat de laatste zes noten melodisch precies gelijk zijn aan die van regel 1, alleen het ritme is anders. Bovendien bestaan de eerste drie noten uit hetzelfde melodisch materiaal als in regel 1: in regel 1 a, c, b, en in regel 6 a, b, c. Deze verwantschap van begin-en slotregel geeft deze psalm iets markants. We zijn hier bijna bij de inclusio van psalm 1, waar begin en slotregel volkomen identiek zijn. Zo vinden we enige waardevolle ingrediënten voor een karakteristieke melodie.

5   Hier overgenomen uit: Pierre Pidoux, *Le Psautier Huguenot* I (Bâle 1962). Deze notatie komt geheel overeen met die uit de facsimile-uitgave *Les Psaumes en vers français avec leurs mélodies* (Genève 1986).

Er is evenwel nog iets anders aan de hand, waardoor deze psalm zo'n hechte constructie heeft. We treffen namelijk in vier achtereenvolgende regels een stijgend tetrachord aan. Hier vinden we in regel 2: d, e, f, g (zelfs nog aangevuld met a); in regel 3: f, g, a, bes; in regel 4 weer: d, e, f, g; en in regel 5: a, b, c, d (zie voorbeeld 2).[6]

PSALM 112

Voorbeeld 2

Pidoux noemt als een van de karakteristieke eigenschappen van de melodieën uit 1562 het veelvuldig voorkomen van herhaalde tetrachorden, zowel stijgend als dalend of gecombineerd.[7] Als voorbeeld van stijgende tetrachorden noemt hij psalm 55, van dalende psalm 49, 54 en 56, en van gecombineerde psalm 94, 102 en 150.

Pidoux heeft ons hier op een kenmerkend spoor gezet, wat betreft de melodieën uit 1562, al roept zijn registratie wel enkele vragen op. Niet alle door Pidoux genoemde voorbeelden zijn namelijk even relevant. We gaan ze na en komen dan tot de volgende bevindingen:[8]

---

6 Naar de notatie van *Book of Praise* (Winnipeg 1984).
7 In zijn "Introduction" in de in noot 5 genoemde facsimile-editie, 23.
8 De noten in de volgende registratie corresponderen met die van de notatie uit het *Liedboek voor de Kerken* ('s-Gravenhage 1973).

Ps.55 Regel 5 heeft twee stijgende tetrachorden, maar Pidoux heeft niet vermeld dat regel 4 bestaat uit twee dalende tetrachorden. De componist heeft zich hier kennelijk laten inspireren door de tekst: "Entens à moy, exauce moy!"
Ps.49 Hier wordt in regel 8 het tetrachord d, c, b, a herhaald.
Ps.54 In regel 6 zien we de herhaling van het dalend tetrachord d, c, b, a. Pidoux vermeldt niet dat ook regel 8 weer met hetzelfde tetrachord inzet.
Ps.56 Hier vind ik geen letterlijke herhaling van hetzelfde tetrachord. Wel eindigt regel 3 met een tetrachord in het lage deel van de hypo-jonische modus en begint regel 4 met een tetrachord in het hoge gedeelte (zelfs een pentachord). Voorts vinden we hier nog een dalende reeks in de tweede helft van regel 7 (a, g, f, e), gevolgd door een eveneens dalende reeks in regel 8 (bes, a, g, f; zelfs een pentachord als men de beginnoot c meerekent).
Ps.94 Als voorbeeld van een combinatie stijgend/dalend noemt Pidoux psalm 94. Hier moet hij zich hebben vergist. Heeft hij psalm 84 bedoeld? Daar hebben we in elk geval een herhaling van een dalend tetrachord in regel 3 (a, g, fis, e) en diezelfde reeks kwam ook al voor in regel 1. In het hogere deel van de modus vinden we die nog eens als inzet van regel 6: d, cis, b, a. Maar van combinatie van stijgend en dalend is in psalm 94 geen sprake.
Ps.102 Hier vinden we geen herhalingen, maar wel een drietal losse tetrachorden, namelijk in regel 4: e, f, g, a; in regel 5: g, a, b, c; en in regel 7 dezelfde groep noten.
Ps.150 Ook in deze psalm kan ik niets vinden van de door Pidoux gesignaleerde combinatie. Alleen in de regels 5 en 8 vinden we het dalend tetrachord b, a, g, fis.

Het heeft mij erg verwonderd, dat Pidoux onder de psalmen met herhaald tetrachord geen melding maakt van psalm 75, waar we te maken hebben met een door de tekst gesuggereerde herhaling in regel 1 en 2 op de woorden "Loué sera" in het ritmisch gevarieerd dalend tetrachord d, c, bes, a (zie voorbeeld 3).

O Seig - neur, Lou - é se - ra, lou - é se - ra ton re - nom.

Voorbeeld 3

Bovendien vinden we in deze psalm nog het tetrachord c, bes, a, g in regel 5 en in de slotregel: bes, a, g, f.

Bij Pidoux' voorbeelden ontbreekt psalm 112, waar we in vier regels een stijgend tetrachord vinden, dat aan deze melodie een bijzonder karakter geeft. Pidoux vermeldt onze psalm wel in een ander verband, namelijk vanwege wisseling van grote en kleine sext; dit verschijnsel treedt op, waar een snelle mutatie van hexachordum naturale in hexachordum molle plaatsvindt. Pidoux ontdekte dit in niet minder dan zeven psalmmelodieën, waaronder de onze: regel 2 eindigt met c, b, a, terwijl regel 3 onmiddellijk inzet met a, bes, a, het zogenaamde fa-super-la-verschijnsel.

Alles met elkaar genoeg aanwijzingen om te concluderen, dat we in psalm 112 te maken hebben met een waardevolle, zelfs karakteristieke melodie, die mede door zijn groot aantal secundeschreden goed zingbaar is. Gelet op de melodie is er dan ook geen enkele reden waarom deze psalm tot de zelden of nooit gezongen liederen zou moeten behoren. Integendeel! We willen nog nader ingaan op een aantal *berijmingen* van deze psalm. Wat het strofental betreft: met De Bèze hielden Datheen en Marnix het op zes; zo deden ook de Nederlanders en Jorissen het in de 18e eeuw. In onze eeuw bleven ook Snijdelaar en de jongste Tsjechische berijming daarbij. Hasper berijmde deze psalm in zijn drie versies (1936, 1948 en 1949) in vijf strofen. Zo ook Muns,[9] Blok,[10] de Interkerkelijke Berijming,[11] Luijkenaar Francken[12] en Gerben Brouwer[13] in het Fries. De berijmers van het *Book of Praise* en van de jongste Duitse berijming konden met vier strofen toe. Zo deed ook H.A. van Dop in het Indonesisch.[14] Wat de kwaliteit van hun teksten betreft, lopen de berijmingen sterk uiteen.

Bij De Bèze treffen we geslaagde regels in strofe 2, regel 4-5:

Dieu de sa clairté belle et pure
Esclaire leur nuict plus obscure

Bij het zingen breekt de zon door op de hoge d (inzet 5e regel op het woord "Esclaire"). Sterk is ook de afsluitende 6e regel van strofe 6:

Periront, quoy qu' ils sachent faire

waar het woord "periront" proclamerend klinkt op de drie lange noten, waarmee de melodie hier inzet. Datheen laat in vers 6 de goddelozen "uitdrogen en sterven". Ook Marnix gebruikt daar het woord "verdroghen". In 1773 (J.E. Voet) treft ons de burgerlijke toon van de 18e eeuw in regels als:

---

9 L.W. Muns, *Psalmen en Lofzangen* (Groningen 1959).
10 A. Blok, *Het Bijbels Psalmboek* (Sondel 1971).
11 Opgenomen in het *Liedboek voor de Kerken* ('s-Gravenhage 1973).
12 In: *Psalter 1980* (Amsterdam 1981).
13 In: *Lieteboek foar de Tsjerken* (Ljouwert 1977).
14 In: *Mazmur* (Jakarta 1986).

Hij toont zich ieders liefde waardig
(strofe 2, regel 5)

en

Hij schikt naar 't recht zijn huisbelangen
(strofe 3 regel 3).

Bij Hasper is in exegetisch opzicht opmerkelijk verschil tussen zijn eerste versie uit 1936 en de revisies uit 1948 en 1949. In de eerste Proeve was namelijk de rechtvaardige in strofe 2 zelf het licht voor z'n omgeving:

Welzalig is op aard te noemen
hij, dien men als een licht kan roemen.

Maar bij de revisies werd dat:

God is het Licht voor alle oprechten,
voor wie zich niet aan rijkdom hechten

De duisternis wordt dan niet genoemd. Meer pastoraal dan poëtisch klinkt het aan het slot van strofe 3:

Een hart dat vrede heeft van binnen,
zal 't altijd van den vijand winnen

waarbij de eerste regel aan Jan Luyken[15] doet denken. Goed gevonden is in strofe 5 de vierde regel, waar van de goddelozen wordt gezegd:

dat zij door nijd zichzelf verteren

Muns, Blok en Luijkenaar Francken hebben zich over het algemeen weinig door deze psalm laten inspireren. Het licht in strofe 2 werd bij Muns "de dageraad van Gods genade". Bij Blok is weer de rechtvaardige zelf het licht. Een nieuw beeld vond hij in de slotregel:

omdat de Heer hun wens doet stranden

---

15 Vgl. *Liedboek voor de Kerken* (1973), gezang 433:2.

179

Bijzonder stroef verloopt de berijming van Luijkenaar Francken (in *Psalter 1980*) met regels als:

't Gaat hem goed, die, zo armen klagen
leent vol ontferming wat zij vragen

of:

met vreugd ziend op wie hem bestrijden

Meer kwaliteit heeft ongetwijfeld de Interkerkelijke Berijming 1968, die aldus luidt:

1 God zij geloofd en hoog geprezen.
Welzalig die de HERE vrezen.
Wie in zijn hart Gods wet bewaarde,
zijn nageslacht is groot op aarde.
Wie vrolijk voortgaat op Gods wegen,
beërft een overvloed van zegen.

2 Zijn goede naam wordt nooit te schande,
zijn recht is veilig in Gods handen.
Zelfs in de nacht ziet hij het dagen,
een glans van liefd' en welbehagen.
Gods waarheid zal voor al de zijnen
als zonlicht in het duister schijnen.

3 Wel hem, die geeft te allen tijde,
die zich door liefd' en recht laat leiden.
Hij is standvastig, wankelt nimmer,
zijn goede trouw bestaat voor immer.
Voor kwaad gerucht zal hij niet vrezen,
de HEER zal steeds zijn schuilplaats wezen.

4 Standvastig blijft hij bij zijn plannen,
nooit zal de vrees hem overmannen.
Hij slaat met vreugd de vijand gade,
geen haat, geen boosheid kan hem schaden.
Mild is zijn hart en vol erbarmen
schenkt hij zijn gaven aan de armen.

5 Zijn recht houdt stand, niets kan hem deren,
zijn goede naam is hoog in ere,
terwijl de vijand van het goede
vergaat van machteloze woede,
want al zijn boosheid is gebreideld
en al zijn plannen zijn verijdeld.

De coproductie van Jan Wit en J.W. Schulte Nordholt kwam
hier tot fraaie resultaten. Kort en krachtig klinkt het in vers 2:

Zelfs in de nacht ziet hij het dagen

Sterk is ook de slotstrofe met de regels:

terwijl de vijand van het goede
vergaat van machteloze woede,
want al zijn boosheid is gebreideld
en al zijn plannen zijn verijdeld.

Als geheel nog sterker geïnspireerd is de nieuwe Friese berijming van Gerben Brouwer, die we hier volledig afdrukken:

1 Oan God de lof, oan Him de eare!
   Heil, dy't yn freze foar de Heare
   har wolberet foar 't kweade wachten:
   Hja wurde sterk yn har geslachten.
   Wa't op 'e rjochte wegen rinne,
   oerfloed fan heil is om har hinne.

2 Har rjocht is by de Hear bewarre.
   Hja kinn' de wielde net fertarre;
   dy is te grut, want alle dagen
   rinne oer fan godlik wolbehagen
   en op 'e dage stiet Gods sinne
   oer dy't foar 't ljocht ornearre binne.

3 By goud en sulver oer de mjitte,
   hja sille de earmen net ferjitte;
   hja jouwe en liene 't út oan harren,
   dy't yn 'e earremoed bedarren.
   Hja wike net en bliuwe yn eare:
   har namme is feilich by de Heare.

4 Hja litte har net twinge of steure.
   Al is de fijân yn 't labeuren,
   hja sille 'm sûnder muoite of pine
   ferslaan en om 'e finger wine.
   Hja wolle libje en libje litte:
   hja sille de earmen net ferjitte.

5 Hja komme oerein mei macht en eare.
   Gjin kweade kin har opgong keare.
   Har rjocht en leafde gean tegearre.
   Wa't oan de hillgen komt, sil stjerre.
   Al brûst syn grime ek oer de râne,
   fan al syn dwaan komt neat te lâne.

In beeldende taal worden hier de contrasten weergegeven. Van de oprechten wordt gezegd:

Hja kinn' de wielde net fertarre

Zij zullen de vijand

sûnder muoite of pine
ferslaan en om 'e finger wine

En van die vijand zingen we aan het slot:

Al brûst syn grime ek oer de râne,
fan al syn dwaan komt neat te lâne

Het is mij niet bekend of tot nog toe ooit iemand op de gedachte is gekomen in een berijming iets weer te geven van de bijzonder kunstige vorm van de Hebreeuwse tekst. Wat het Duitse taalgebied betreft, is de berijming van Jorissen voor onze tijd bezwaarlijk te handhaven. Er is sprake van rijmarmoe (twee maal het rijmpaar: Segen/Wegen); te veel verouderde werkwoordsvormen (gibet, liebet, enz.), zodat vervanging wenselijk is. Ik schreef een nieuwe berijming in vier strofen. Toen die klaar was en ik me voorbereidde op een preek over deze psalm, zag ik dat men deze naar zijn inhoud kan samenvatten met het woord van Jezus dat in Handelingen 20:35 is overgeleverd: "Het is zaliger te geven dan te ontvangen." Deze tekst luidt in verschillende Duitse vertalingen: "Geben ist seliger als Nehmen." Die spreuk bestaat uit 24 letters. Mijn berijming telde 24 regels. Vers 1 begon met "Gelobt sei Gott", dus met de G van "geben". Er waren nog een paar regels waarvan de beginletters correspondeerden; de overige kon ik passend maken door omzetting of andere formulering. Zo ontstond het volgende acrostichon:[16]

Gelobt sei Gott, der Lust zum Leben
erweckt und Freude gibt am Geben.
Bei dem, der geht auf seinen Wegen
entspringt aus reiner Quelle Segen.
Neu wird ihm täglich Gottes Gabe
in Nachwuchs, Nahrung, Haus und Habe.

---

16 Ook opgenomen in mijn bundel *Eine andre Welt* (Franeker 1992).

Sein Licht strahlt auf in dunklen Stunden.
Trost hat er stets beim Herrn gefunden.
Sein Herz kennt Mitleid und Erbarmen;
er leiht aus Lieb und hilft den Armen.
Labsal bringt er, wo Not und Sorgen;
in Gottes Huld ist er geborgen.

Gerechtigkeit erblüht und Treue
erquickt ihn Tag für Tag aufs neue.
Rastlos mag ihn das Unheil quälen –
Angst kann nicht seine Ruhe stehlen.
Laßt die Verleumder ihn nur schmähen,
sie müssen machtlos untergehen.

Nie ist er andrer Leid verschlossen,
er bleibt im Wohltun unverdrossen.
Hat er nur Halt an Gottes Gnaden –
macht ihm die Mißgunst keinen Schaden.
Es ist die Zukunft ihm beschieden
nach Gottes Recht in Glück und Frieden.

(Bernard Smilde, 5.8.1992)

In deze herdichting zijn vooral twee elementen verwerkt waarop Kraus in zijn commentaar wijst.[17] Het eerste is het geluk van de mens die geeft, al halen anderen de schouders erover op. Het tweede is het feit, dat deze gever geen beklagenswaardig mens is, maar juist iemand die toekomst heeft.

Uiteraard ontmoeten we de Geneefse psalmmelodie in tal van bewerkingen bij componisten als Claude Goudimel, Paschal de l'Estocart, Claudin le Jeune en onze grote J.P. Sweelinck. Cornelius Becker (1602) berijmde deze psalm in zijn *Psalter Davids Gesangweis (...) zugerichtet*. Hij koos daarvoor de structuur van het bekende lied *Was mein Gott will, das g'scheh allzeit*. Later voorzag Heinrich Schütz deze tekst nog eens van een eigen melodie.

In Bachs cantates heb ik nergens een rechtstreekse relatie met psalm 112 kunnen vinden. Cantate 197 begint wel met de woorden: "Dem Gerechten muß das Licht immer wieder aufgehen", maar dit is een citaat uit psalm 97:11 en 12 en niet uit psalm 112. Inhoudelijk komt het slotkoraal van Cantate 39 nog dicht bij psalm 112, met de woorden

---

17 H.J. Kraus, op. cit.

Selig sind, die aus Erbarmen
sich anlehnen Fremder Not,
sind mitleidig mit den Armen,
bitten täglich für sie Gott.
Die behülflich sind mit Rat,
auch wo möglich mit der Tat,
werden wieder Hülf empfangen
und Barmherzigkeit erlangen.

Deze tekst is de zesde strofe van het lied *Kommt, laßt euch den Herren lehren* van David Denicke uit 1648. Hier is duidelijk inspiratie vanuit psalm 112 merkbaar, hoewel het slot refereert aan het woord van Jezus uit de Bergrede: "Zalig de barmhartigen, want hun zal barmhartigheid geschieden" (Mt. 5:7). In de negentiende eeuw zijn verzen uit psalm 112 verklankt door Felix Mendelssohn-Bartholdy in zijn oratorium *Elias.* In dat werk ("nach Worten der heiligen Schrift") wordt de episode van de opwekking van het zoontje van de weduwe te Zarfat besloten met een koor, waarvan de tekst luidt:

Wohl dem, der den Herrn fürchtet,
und auf seinen Wegen geht.
Dem Frommen geht ein Licht auf in der Finsternis
von dem Gnädigen, Barmherzigen und Gerechten.

Het eerste vers is een citaat uit psalm 128:1, maar de eerste helft daarvan is gelijk aan psalm 112:1a. Het tweede vers is letterlijk psalm 112:4. Mendelssohn, die goed thuis moet zijn geweest in de bijbel, heeft deze teksten met bijzonder veel liefde behandeld. Het eerste thema is lyrisch van karakter:

Wohl dem, der den Herrn — fürch-tet und — auf sei - - nen We-gen geht!

Het tweede klinkt meer markant met drieklankbreking:

Den From-men geht das Licht auf in der Fin-ster-nis.

De stemvoering in de koorpartijen is vloeiend, de orkestratie verzorgd, waarbij de cello-partij opvallend is, die met z'n voortstuwende zestienden als het ware het blijvend geluk van de rechtvaardige illustreert:

Psalm 112 gepraktizeerd

Er is – in de meeste gevallen gelukkig – een verband tussen liturgie en leven. Maar wanneer zo'n markante psalm in de liturgie wordt veronachtzaamd, kan het niet anders of dit is te merken in de levenspraxis van kerk en christenheid. In de bijbelse fundering van ons diakonaal christenzijn speelt psalm 112 vrijwel geen rol. Op zondag Werelddiakonaat wordt uit en te na gezongen uit psalm 72 en 146, maar psalm 112 komt er meestal niet aan te pas. Dit bleek mij bij informatie bij de redactie van het blad *Diakonia* en bij de diakonale bureaux van de Nederlandse Hervormde Kerk en de Gereformeerde Kerken in Nederland. Ds. H.A. Moolenaar meldde mij, dat hij allerlei uitgaven over het diakonaat heeft nagezocht, of er iets over deze psalm zou zijn gepubliceerd. Dit bleek niet het geval te zijn. Noch in het werk van W.A.Z. Tieman en H. Zunnenberg, *Bevrijd tot verbondenheid: Actueel diakonaat* ('s-Gravenhage 1990), noch in dat van A. Noordergraaf, *Oriëntatie in het diakonaat* (Zoetermeer 1991), wordt aandacht aan deze psalm besteed. Ook *De eerste dag*, de reeks *Postilles* en *Woord in Beweging* hebben geen verwijzing naar psalm 112. De psalm is evenmin gebruikt als uitgangspunt in de preekschetsen die de laatste jaren worden uitgegeven ter gelegenheid van de zondagen voor het Werelddiakonaat.
Dit negatieve resultaat brengt ons tot de vraag: zit daar iets achter? Is het een signaal? Is ons leven dan zo weinig een gevend leven? We zingen graag en veel van een gevende God van psalm 111 ("Aan wie Hem vrezen gaf Hij spijs"). Maar de God die ons naar zijn beeld herschept en leert geven, is ons vaak ver en vreemd. We maken deel uit van een consumptiemaatschappij en dat weerspiegelt zich tot in onze kerkelijke praxis en onze liturgische selectie. Een al te selectieve omgang met bijbel en kerklied is tot schade voor kerk en wereld.

We beseffen tegenwoordig meer dan ooit dat het met persoonlijke ethiek niet toe kan. De oproep tot gerechtigheid en bestrijding van armoe vraagt om politieke en economische vertaling. Maar dat mag geen uitvlucht zijn voor persoonlijke betrokkenheid en inzet. Die kunnen worden gevoed door bijbelse inspiratie; deze vinden we niet alleen bij wet en profeten, bij epistel of evangelie, maar ook in de kunstige lyriek van het onvergelijkelijke boek der Psalmen.

Summary

In the Netherlands most Reformed (Calvinist) churches sing metrical psalms to the melodies of the French Genevan psalter of 1562. Not all of these melodies are equally popular: about a quarter of them are regularly sung, whereas another quarter are either seldom or never sung. Psalm 112 is one such psalm. Following the discussion of the Hebrew structure of this psalm, a structure that is shared by the previous psalm, Psalm 111, together with a consideration of the content of Psalm 112, the author discusses the nature of the French Genevan melody that was composed for it. For him it is difficult to understand why this melody has been largely ignored in the Netherlands, since it is not difficult to sing and its overall form is clearly defined. Lines 1 and 6 share a basic melodic form. Lines 2, 3, 4 and 5 all contain the same rising tetrachord, respectively: d, e, f, g; f, g, a b-flat; d, e, f, g; and a, b, c, d. Pierre Pidoux has shown that this is a particular characteristic of the melodies of 1562, and the Psalm 112 melody is a good example of the craftsmanship of the Genevan composers. It is a matter for regret that this psalm is seldom used in the Dutch liturgy. In the light of the concept of Christian *diakonia* this psalm demands to be read, sung and lived by, especially since liturgical neglect leads to poor Christian practice.

"Fallt mit Dancken, fallt mit Loben Vor des Höchsten Gnaden=Thron."

Zum IV. Teil des Weihnachts-Oratoriums von Johann Sebastian Bach

Renate Steiger

Unter dem Titel "Tröstendes Echo: Zur theologischen Deutung der Echo-Arie im IV. Teil des Weihnachts-Oratoriums von Johann Sebastian Bach" hat Ernst Koch im *Bach-Jahrbuch* 1989[1] die "Fundierung der Interpretation der Echo-Arie in der Theologie und Frömmigkeit des 17. und 18. Jahrhunderts" in Angriff genommen. Koch hat zu diesem Zweck Zeugnisse aus dem näheren und weiteren theologischen Umfeld Bachs zusammengetragen, in denen verschiedene geistliche Deutungen des Echos belegt sind. So konnten Gebet, Lobgesang und Kirchenmusik als Echo auf die in der Heiligen Schrift vernommene Rede Gottes verstanden werden, andererseits, der Echo-Arie des Weihnachts-Oratoriums verwandter, das Echo als Gottes oder Jesu Antwort auf die Fragen und Klagen des angefochtenen Glaubens. Diese Antworten Gottes bzw. Jesu haben, wie Koch feststellt, immer freundlichen und tröstlichen Charakter.

Ernst Kochs Beobachtungen bringen die Forschung in dieser Frage ein gutes Stück voran, zeigen sie doch auf, daß das Echo oder der "Widerschall" als Sinnbild verstanden wurde und der ästhetischen Vermittlung bestimmter theologischer Aussagen und Topoi diente. Die Beobachtungen zum erbaulichen Schrifttum der Zeit stellen auch die Frage nach dem geistlichen Sinn der musikalischen Verwendung des Echos auf eine historisch gesichertere Grundlage.

Ich möchte Kochs Beitrag aufgreifend die Interpretation des Textes von Teil IV des Weihnachts-Oratoriums etwas weiterführen. Hierzu sei das folgende Emblem mitgeteilt, das Kochs resumierende Feststellung, die im Echo zu vernehmende "Antwort des angerufenen Christus ist in jedem Falle tröstlich",[2] weiter

---

1 *Bach-Jahrbuch* 75 (1989), 203-211.
2 Ebda, 210.

Abb. 1. Heinrich Müller, *Geistlicher Danck=Altar* (Rostock 1670), neben Seite 352 (Wiedergabe mit freundlicher Genehmigung der Herzog August Bibliothek Wolfenbüttel).

bestätigt (siehe Abb. 1). Das Sinnbild findet sich im *Geistlichen Danck=Altar* von Heinrich Müller[3] neben der Auslegung von Psalm 103,3 "(Lobe den Herrn, meine Seele, und vergiß nicht, was er dir Gutes getan hat!) Der dir alle deine Sünde vergibt und heilet alle deine Gebrechen" und trägt das Motto DULCE ASSONAT ECHO: "Süß tönend stimmt das Echo bei." (Assonanz ist der technische Ausdruck für "Reim". Reim ist der Gleichklang, der Echo-Reim. So läßt sich dieses Motto als identische Aussage verstehen: es bildet den Bildinhalt in sprachlicher Verdoppelung ab.) Der die Stimme nach oben richtende Beter spricht "Erbarm dich mein" – als Echo tönt Jesu Stimme zurück – die Spiegelung wird auch graphisch sinnfällig –: "Erbarm mich dein".

Welcher theologische Topos ist hier ins Bild gebracht, worauf bezieht sich diese Invention? Eine Antwort auf diese Frage finden wir in den zeitgenössischen Predigten über Heilungsgeschichten, z.B. in Predigten auf den 14. Sonntag nach Trinitatis, Evangelium: Lk 17,11-19 (Heilung der zehn Aussätzigen). Zehn aussätzige Männer begegneten Jesus, "die stunden von ferne / Und erhuben ihre Stimme und sprachen: Jesu / lieber Meister / erbarm dich unser." Zu diesem Vers schreibt Heinrich Müller in der Evangelischen Schluß=Kette:[4]

Kurtz / aber doch kräfftig. JESU. Dieser sein Tauffname zeichnet sein Hertz. Voll Heyls der Name / das Hertz voll Heyls. Ein Heyland heisst / ein Heyland ist er / und ist in keinem andern Heyl / als in ihm. Wann ich meinen Jesum nenne / so nenne ich das eintzige Heyl meiner Seelen. Jesu/ du heisst ein Heyland / wollen sie sagen / so heyle; ein Helffer heisst du / so hilff uns auch. Sein Name muß ihn zwingen / [. . .] Menschen heissen offt was sie nicht sind / und sind offt / was sie nicht heissen. Mancher heisst Friedlieb / und hasset doch den Frieden. Ein ander ist ein Unchrist / und heisst doch Christian. Bey Gott ist Nam und Ruhm / Werck und Wesen ein Ding. Gott heisst er und beweiset sich auch gütig / ein Nothhelffer

---

3   Heinrich Müller, *Geistlicher Danck=Altar* (Rostock 1670), neben 352; vorh.: Herzog August Bibliothek Wolfenbüttel (HAB). Ich habe dieses Sinnbild schon einmal vorgestellt im Reader zu meinem Vortrag "Sprachbilder und Bildersprache: Bachs Kantaten und die geistliche Emblematik seiner Zeit" im Rahmen des Symposions der Internationalen Arbeitsgemeinschaft für theologische Bachforschung beim 65. Bachfest der Neuen Bachgesellschaft vom 13. - 19. November 1990 in München, Seite 21 mit Text WO IV 38-40.

4   Heinrich Müller, *Evangelische Schluß=Kette / Und Krafft=Kern / Oder Gründliche Außlegung der gewöhnlichen Sonntags=Evangelien* (Frankfurt am Main 1672), 14. Sonntag n. Trin., 1002 b; vorh.: HAB. Dieser Titel befand sich auch in Bachs Bibliothek.

/ und hilfft in Nöthen / ein Heyland / und heylet alle unsere Gebrechen. Darffst an seiner Hülffe nicht zweiffeln. Weil er Helffer heisst / so muß er helffen / weil er Heyland heisst / so muß er Heyl bringen. Sein Name zwinget ihn.

Und zu dem Ruf "erbarm dich" führt Müller aus:[5]

[Es ist die] Barmhertzigkeit Gottes das einige Heylbrünnlein. Wer Heyl und Hülffe finden wil / der suche sie nirgend als bey der Barmhertzigkeit Gottes. ERBARME DICH. Indem sie umb Erbarmung flehen / erkennen sie ihr Elend / denn der Elenden pflegt man sich zu erbarmen. Wo die m i s e r i a vornan gehet / da folgt die m i s e r i c o r d i a auff dem Fusse nach. Wer elender als ein Aussätziger? noch elender ein armer Sünder. Die Sünde eine Quelle alles Elendes und der Sünder das Elend selbst. drumb wann die Sünde das Gewissen nagt / wie der Aussatz den Leib / alsdann geseufftzet: M i s e r e r e , Erbarm dich mein / o HErre Gott / nach deiner grossen Barmhertzigkeit! Aus lauter Barmhertzigkeit vergibt Gott die Sündē/ nit die kleine nur / sondern auch die grossen nach seiner grossen Barmhertzigkeit.

Auch hier klingt Psalm 103,3 an: der erste Halbvers ("Der dir alle deine Sünde vergibt") in dem Abschnitt über Gottes m i s e r i c o r d i a : "Aus lauter Barmhertzigkeit vergibt Gott die Sündē"; den zweiten Halbvers zitiert Müller bei der Erklärung des Namens J E S U S:

"du heisst ein Heyland / wollen sie sagen / so heyle; ein Helffer heisst du / so hilff uns auch." Bei Gott stimmen Name und Wesen überein. Er heißt "ein Nothhelffer / und hilfft in Nöthen / ein Heyland / und heylet alle unsere Gebrechen".

Übereinstimmend rekurrieren die Ausleger in diesem Zusammenhang auf die Bedeutung des Namens Jesus. Sein "Herz" ist an seinem Namen abzulesen, er ist mit Jes 63,1 "ein Meister zu helfen".[6] Stichwortartig bringen die Prediger in Erinnerung, was sie der Gemeinde am Neujahrstag ausführlich darzulegen pflegten.[7]

---

5 Ebda, 1003 b.
6 Werner Neumann hat in BWV 78 *Jesu, der du meine Seele* Arie (Duett) 2 die Anspielung auf diesen Vers nicht erkannt und interpungiert daher unsinnig "Wir eilen mit schwachen, doch emsigen Schritten, / O Jesu, o Meister, zu helfen zu dir"; vgl. NBA I 21 und *Sämtliche von Johann Sebastian Bach vertonte Texte* (Leipzig 1974).
7 Vgl. auch Johann Arnd, *POSTILLA, Oder Geistreiche Erklärung Der Gewöhnlichen Sonn= und Fest=Tags=Evangelien*, herausgegeben von Johann Jacob Rambach (Leipzig und Görlitz 1734), 14. S. n. Trin. 2. Pred., 219 ff.; Johann Gerhard, *Postilla: Das ist Auslegung und Erklärung der sontäglichen und fürnemsten Fest=Evangelien / über das gantze Jahr* (Jena 1663), 14. S. n. Trin., 445; Heinrich Müller, *Evan-*

Wenden wir uns also Predigten auf Neujahr, das Fest der Beschneidung und Namengebung Jesu, zu. Evangelium ist Lk 2,21:

"Vnd da acht Tage vmb waren / daß das Kind beschnitten würde / Da ward sein Name genennet I E S V S. Welcher genennet war von dem Engel / ehe denn er in Mutter Leibe empfangen ward."

Nach Martin Moller[8] ist an diesem Tag dreierlei zu betrachten:

Zum Ersten / Wie wir recht Christlich das Newe Jahr anheben sollen. [nämlich mit Lob, Preis und Dank für Gottes Wohltaten; vgl. Teil IV Eingangssatz, "Fällt mit Danken, fällt mit Loben"]
Zum Andern / Von der Beschneidung deß Herrn Christi.
Zum Dritten / Von dem hochtröstlichen Namē I E S V S.[9]

Zum dritten Stück führt Moller aus:[10]

Erkläre mir nun auch den Hochtröstlichen Namen I E S V S.

GErne wil ichs thun / liebe Seele / Aber es ist der Name Jesus so schöne / so süsse / so lieblich / so freundlich / vnd so trostreich / daß ich nicht weiß / wo ich anfangen sol. Je weiter ich nachdencke / Je mehr ich finde: Je besser Lust ich zu reden und zu schreiben gewinne: Je mehr ich aber rede oder schreibe / Je süsser vnd tröstlicher mir der thewre Name wird in meinem Hertzen.
Ja / meine Seele / I E S V S heist auff Deutsch ein Helffer / ein Heyland / ein Seligmacher. Denn so spricht der Engel: **Du solt seinen Namen Jesus heissen / denn er wird sein Volck Selig machen von allen jren Sünden.** (Mt 1[,21])
O Jesu / mein HErr vnd mein Gott / wie gar billich führest du diesen Namen / denn es ist ja sonst in keinem andern Heyl / vn̄ ist auch vns elenden Menschen kein ander Name gegeben / darinne wir sollen Selig werden. (Apg 4.[12]) [. . .]
Vnd ob es wol ist dein eigener Name / damit du deine Person wilt nennen lassen / so mahlet er vns doch dein gantzes Ampt so eigentlich vnd herrlich vor / daß so offt ich den Namen Jesus nenne oder höre / so offt sehe ich darinnen / wie in einem Spiegel / alle deine grosse vnaußsprechliche Wolthaten / die du / O Jesu / an mir gethan hast / vnd noch thust. [. . .]
Ja / mein HErr / du namest dich meiner an / ehe ich dich kandte: Vnd warest mein Vorsprecher / ehe ich dich suchte. Ja da ich in Sünden todt war vnter Gottes grim̄igen Zorn / vnd schüldig der ewigen Verdamniß / vnd keine Hülffe noch Rath war weder im Himel noch auff Erden / Tratestu ins Mittel / redetest mein Wort /

gelisches *PRAESERVATIV wider den Schaden Josephs [. . .] Herausgezogen Ausz den Sonn= und Fest=Tags Evangelien* (Frankfurt und Rostock 1681), 14. S. n. Trin., 1026 f.; alle Titel vorh.: HAB; der Titel von H. Müller war in Bachs Besitz.
8 Martin Moller, *PRAXIS Euangeliorum: Einfeltige erklerung vnd nützliche betrachtung der Euangelien / so auff alle Sontage vnd vornemesten Fest Jährlich zu predigen verordnet sind* (Görlitz 1601), Neujahr, 140 ff.; vorh.: HAB.
9 Ebda, 141.
10 Ebda, 150-152.

vnd sprachest: **Vater / ich wil sie erlösen aus der Hellen / vnd vom Tode erretten /
Todt / ich wil dir eine Gifft sein / Helle / ich wil dir eine Pestilentz sein.** (Hos
13.[14])
Ewiger Gott / mein HErr / wie gewaltig hastu solch dein Erbieten erfüllet/ wie
redlich hastu mir geholffen. Denn du sprungest mir zu vom hohen Himel herab /
vnd namest an dich meine Menschliche Natur / vnd wordest mir in allen Stücken
gleich / doch ohne Sünde. (Joh 1.[1 ff.]; Hebr 4.[15]) Vnd ob du wol Reich warest
/ bistu doch vmb meinet willen Arm worden / auff das ich durch deine Gnade
Reich und Selig werde. (2.Kor 8,9)

Im Namen Jesu ist nach Moller "wie in einem Spiegel" sein
Amt anzuschauen. Sein Name "zwingt" ihn, wie Heinrich Müller
sagt, unser Heiland und Seligmacher zu sein. So gewiß wie auf
den Ruf das Echo antwortet, so gewiß erlangt der Beter Jesu
Hilfe.[11] Die Echo-Arie im Neujahrs-Teil des Weihnachts-
Oratoriums greift also einen Auslegungstopos der Neujahrspredigt auf, sie setzt die Deutung des Jesus-Namens poetisch-musi-
kalisch um, sie bringt die Gewißheit unserer Rettung vom ewigen Tod der Verdammnis in einem Sinnbild zur Anschauung.
Die von der sprachlichen Bedeutung von יש ע ausgehende Erklärung des Jesus-Namens[12] ist aber nicht abzutrennen von den
Ausführungen darüber, wie und wodurch Jesus "sein Volk selig
gemacht hat von allen ihren Sünden" (Mt 1,21). Die Auslegung
des Namens wird von den Predigern inhaltlich gefüllt anhand
der Erklärung der Bedeutsamkeit von Jesu Beschneidung. Beschneidung und Namengebung gehören theologisch zusammen.
Heinrich Müller:

DAs heutige Evangelium / wie kurtz es immer ist / so ist es doch ein kleiner Biblischer Außzug und Begriff der gantzen H. Schrifft. Denn es hält uns vor das
Gesetz in der Beschneidung / das Evangelium in dem Namen Jesu.[13]

---

11 Vgl. den Titel von Johann Hecht, *Der Andächtigen Seelen An Sonn= Fest= und
   Bußtagen verlangte / auch durch ein himmlisches ECHO erlangte Jesus=Hülffe* [. . .]
   (Leipzig 1684); zitiert bei Koch a.a.O., 207.
12 Vgl. Johann Olearius, *Biblische Erklärung Darinnen / nechst dem allgemeinen
   Haupt=Schlüssel Der gantzen heiligen Schrifft* [. . .], Teil V (Leipzig 1681), 397 b
   über die derivatio des Namens (vorh.: HAB; der Titel war in Bachs Besitz); siehe
   auch die typologische Deutung der beiden Träger des Namens Josua im Alten
   Testament auf Jesus, hier Seite 397 a/b und bei Heinrich Müller, *Evangelischer
   Hertzens=Spiegel / In Offentlicher Kirchen=Versammlung / bey Erklärung der Son-
   ntäglichen und Fest=Evangelien* (Frankfurt am Main 1679), Neujahr, 780 f. (vorh.:
   HAB).
13 Heinrich Müller, *Evangelischer Hertzens=Spiegel*, a.a.O., 779.

Lassen wir noch einmal Martin Moller ausführlicher zu Wort kommen:[14]

Warvmb hat sich denn mein HErr Jesus beschneiden lassen?

Du bist ja wol / mein HErr Jesu / der rechte Zahlmeister / der für vns elende / beschüldigte / verkauffte Sünder bezahlet hat. Ja HErr/ gleich wie ein Kauffmann / so er zu Marckte komen wil / den Zoll schüldig ist zu geben / bey verlust aller seiner Wahren: Also bin ich auch schüldig deinem Gesetze den vollkomenen Gehorsam / so ich ins Ewige Leben eingehen wil / bey vermeidung ewiger Straff vnd Pein.
Was sol ich aber thun / mein HErr Jesu? Sihe / ich habe weder zu zollen noch zu zahlen / drumb trifft mich der Fluch deß Gesetzes / vnd versencket mich ins ewige Verderben. Du aber / mein HErr / steckest dich in meine Schuldt / niemest meine Vbertrettung auff dich / thust dich vnter das Gesetze / vnd zollest vnd zahlest für mich alles gantz reichlich / gantz vberflüssig / nicht nur für eine oder etliche Sünden / sondern für alle vnd jede / vnd machest mich gantz Zollfrey / daß weder Teuffel noch Todt / weder Gesetz noch Helle mich zuschätzen haben ewiglich.
Du zahlest aber / mein HErr Jesu / nicht mit Goldt oder Silber / sondern mit deinem heyligen thewren Blut (1.Petr 1.[18 f.]) / ja in deiner Beschneidung hastu dein erstes Blutßtröpfflin vergossen / dein schmertzliches Leyden angehaben / vnd deinem Vater hiemit das erste AnGelt für mich verrichtet. Denn durch dich / HErr Jesu / haben wir die Erlösung in deinem Blute / vnd dein Blut macht vns rein von aller Sünde. (1.Joh 1.[7])
Ich dancke dir / HErr Jesu Christe / daß du dich durch deine Beschneidung vnter das Gesetz gethan (Gal 4.[4]) / vnd den Fluch auff dich geladen. Ja ich dancke dir / mein Heyland / daß du durch deinen vollkomenen Gehorsam dem Gesetz genug gethan / vnd mit deinem Heyligen Blute für mich bezahlet / den Fluch deß Gesetzes von mir genomen / vnd mich deinem Vater versöhnet hast.

Jesu Beschneidung ist das Angeld, mit dem er angefangen hat, für unsere Sünde zu zahlen.[15] Mit seiner Beschneidung will der Heiland:

"dir gleichsam eine Versicherung geben / daß der völlige Abtrag / die völlige Bezahlung unserer Sünden / warhafftig solte folgen durch sein Blut am Creutz".[16]

Diese wenigen Zitate dürften deutlich belegen, daß die communis opinio der Bachforschung, Teil IV des Weihnachts-Oratoriums habe allein die Namensgebung zum Inhalt

---

14 Martin Moller, *PRAXIS Euangeliorum* a.a.O., 148, 149 f.
15 Martin Moller a.a.O., 141.
16 Heinrich Müller a.a.O. (Anm. 12), 779.

und lasse "jede Beziehung auf die Beschneidung Jesu weg"[17], nicht zutreffend ist. Vielmehr läßt sich beobachten, daß der Text von Teil IV alle wesentlichen Stichworte und Gedanken einer zeitgenössischen Neujahrspredigt enthält (außer der Bezugnahme auf den Beginn eines neuen Kalenderjahrs). Auf die Beschneidung und das heißt: auf "die Erlösung, so durch Christum Jesum geschehen ist" (Röm 3,24), "die Erlösung durch sein Blut, die Vergebung der Sünden" (Kol 1,14; Eph 1,7) deutet im Eingangssatz das Stichwort *Gnadenthron* (vgl. Röm 3,25), im Rezitativ und Choral Nr. 38 der zweite Stollen des Ristschen Liedes: "Der du dich vor mich gegeben / An des bittern Kreuzes Stamm". Zum Mittelteil des Eingangschors "Gottes Sohn / Will der Erden / Heiland und Erlöser werden" vergleiche man Johann Olearius:[18]

Es ist aber die Beschneidung Christi ein solcher A c t u s oder Handlung und ein denckwürdiges Stück seiner Erniedrigung / da unser Heyland warer Gott und Mensch in seinem angenommenen Fleisch bey der blutigen Verletzung desselben sich freywillig dem Göttlichen Gesetze unterworffen/ und durch Vergiessung seines theuren Blutes unser JEsus / Erlöser und Heyland worden ist / zu GOttes Ehre und unserm ewigen Heyl /, Trost und Seligkeit.

"Heiland und Erlöser", das, was sein Name bedeutet, wurde Gottes Sohn durch die Beschneidung, durch sein Treten unter das Gesetz und den Beginn seines Leidens. Hier schließt sich theologisch auch die Sterbensthematik an, die den Schluß von Rezitativ 38 und die Arie 39 bestimmt.[19]

---

17 Koch a.a.O., 205 mit Anm. 17; vgl. Alfred Dürr, *Die Kantaten von Johann Sebastian Bach: Mit ihren Texten* (München und Kassel ²1985), 192; Walter Blankenburg, *Das Weihnachts-Oratorium von Johann Sebastian Bach* (München und Kassel 1982), 93.

18 Johann Olearius a.a.O. (Anm. 12), 396 b.

19 Koch a.a.O., 210 stellt fest, daß "das Sterben [. . .] in den zeitgenössischen Predigten am Neujahrstag eine gewichtige Rolle spielte", geht aber auf die Frage, warum dies so ist, nicht weiter ein. - Vgl. Heinrich Müller, *Praeservativ* (Anm. 4), Neujahr, 169: "Sind wir im Tode? JEsus unser Leben. Schröckt uns die Finsternüß? JEsus unser Licht. Dräuet uns die Hölle? JEsus unser Himmel. O m n i a   n o - b i s   J e s u s   e s t, ja alles ist er uns in allem. Der Name JEsus unser Hertzens=Trost/ auch in der letzten Todes=Stunde/ dann wann ich nicht mehr reden kan/ so kommt JEsus und nimmt mein letztes Seufftzen an. Ach! mein Hertz/ dieser JEsus hat deinen Namen im Himmel angeschrieben/ schreibe du diesen seinen Namen dir zum Trost ins Hertz. Wo du gehest oder stehest/ da laß

Folgen wir dem Gedankengang, wie ihn Johann Gerhard entwickelt:[20] Im Alten Testament hat Gott etliche Freistädte verordnet, in denen Todschläger vor der Blutrache sicher waren (Num 35, 9 ff.). So ist Christus "das rechte r e f u g i u m ", ein sicherer Ort unserer Zuflucht.[21]

Wenn derowegen dein Gewissen bekümmert ist / daß du die Gebot Gottes überschrittē / so halte dich an Christum / derselbe hat sie alle erfüllet an unser statt. [. . .] Ferner / hat uns Christus von Sünden selig gemacht / so hat er uns auch erlöset vom Tode / denn der Tod ist der Sünden Sold. Rom. 6. und der Stachel des Todes ist die Sünde. wo demnach keine Sünde ist / da ist auch kein Tod.

Es folgt der Einwand, "das sey gesungen / ehe gewunnen", da die Erfahrung lehrt, daß wir alle sterben müssen, auch, die an Christum glauben. Antwort:

Die Zertrennung Leibes und der Seelen ist für Gottes Augen nicht der rechte Todt / sondern die Empfindung des Zorns und des göttlichen Gerichts. das mercke daher: Die Verdamnüß wird genennet der ewige Todt / Apoc. 20.

Daher unterscheide Christus Joh 8,51 f. sterben und den Tod sehen und schmecken. Hat Christus von Sünden selig gemacht (Mt 1,21), so hat er uns auch erlöst vom künftigen Gericht, Joh 5,24. Zweiter Einwand: Dies ist wider die Schrift, die bezeugt, wir müssen alle vor dem Richterstuhl Christi offenbar werden, Röm 14,10. Darauf antwortet Gerhard, das sei wohl wahr,

aber die Gläubigen kommen nicht in das schreckliche verdamliche Gericht/ sondern sie werden hören den Zuspruch des ewigen Lebens. Wer gewiß weiß / daß er eine gute Sache hat / und daß der Richter recht richtet / derselbige fürchtet sich nicht / für dessē Richterstuel zukomen. Der Gläubigen Sache ist durch Christum gut gemacht / denn sie sind durch ihn Gott versöhnet / auch wird Er selber Richter seyn / der für ihre Sünde bezahlet hat / drüm dürffen sie sich für diesem Richter nit fürchtē.

---

dir JEsus im Hertzen schweben. Der theureste Schatz im Hertzen/ das süsseste Honig auff der Zungen/ die lieblichste Music in den Ohren/ das schönste Bild in deinen Augen soll dir JEsus seyn." Die Sätze 38 - 40 des Weihnachtsoratoriums zeigen sprachliche Anklänge an diese Passage.
20 Johann Gerhard, *Postilla* (Anm. 7), Neujahr, 86-88.
21 Vgl. die Anspielung im Choral Nr. 22 der *Johannes-Passion*: "Durch dein Gefängnis, Gottes Sohn,/ Muß uns die Freiheit kommen;/ Dein Kerker ist der **Gnadenthron**,/ **Die Freistatt** aller Frommen [. . .]"

Vgl. hierzu den Schluß von Rez. 38:

Was jagte mir zuletzt der Tod für Grauen ein?
Mein Jesus! Wenn ich sterbe,
So weiß ich, daß ich nicht verderbe.
Dein Name steht in mir geschrieben,
Der hat des Todes Furcht vertrieben.

Und endlich:

Hat uns Christus von der Sünde erlöst, so hat er uns auch von der ewigen Verdammnis erlöst, denn wo keine Sünde ist, da ist auch keine Verdammnis, Röm
8,1.

Gerhard schließt:

Aus diesem allen mögen wir verstehen / was für eine grosse Wolthat es sey / daß
uns Christus von Sünden selig gemacht / und demnach/ was für ein heilwertiger
Name der Name Jesus sey / welcher dieses alles in sich begreifft.

So schließt sich im Namen Jesus die Auslegung wieder zusammen, in der Gerhard ausgebreitet hatte, was Mt 1,21 beinhaltet:
"er wird sein Volk selig machen von ihren Sünden." Und Gerhard krönt seine Neujahrspredigt mit dem Satz:

Der Hohepriester ging mit Blut in das Allerheiligste Gott zuversöhnen. [Hebr
9,1-7] Hie [h]aben wir den rechten Gnadenstul und Gottesblut beysammen.[22]

Mit diesem Resümee führt Johann Gerhards Predigt am Fest
der Beschneidung und Namengebung Jesu auf die Schriftstelle

---

22 Vgl. Ex 25,17-22, Lev 16,12-15, Röm 3,23-25, Hebr 4,16. Vgl. Heinrich Müller,
Praeservativ (Anm. 7), Neujahr, 176; vorh.: HAB: "Euch allen miteinander wil ich
schencken die heilige Bluts=Tröpfflein / und den süssen Namen JEsu. Darumb
hat er sein Blut vergossen/ daß er euer Schutz sey. Das Blut JEsu Christi / des
eingebohrnen Sohns Gottes/ wie Johannes redet. (1.Joh 1. v.7) Das theure Blut
wie Petrus saget. (1. Petr 1. v.19) Was könte theurer seyn zu unser Erlösung/ als
Gottes Blut? da haben wir die Reinigung von Sünden / denn das Blut JEsu macht
uns rein von allen unsern Sünden. Wann der Teuffel das Sünden=Register auff-
weiset/ thut JEsus einen Strich hindurch mit seinem Blute / und löschet aus alle
unsere Sünde." Hierzu BWV 78 *Jesu, der du meine Seele*, Arie 4: "Das Blut, so
meine Schuld durchstreicht,/ macht mir das Herze wieder leicht / und spricht mich
frei [...]". - Auch bei Müller finden wir wie bei Johann Gerhard die auffallende
Rede von "Gottes Blut"; sie ist aufgrund der communicatio idiomatum der beiden
Naturen möglich.

hin, die Martin Luther als Zusammenfassung des Evangeliums galt, als "der Mittelplatz [. . .] der gantzen Schrifft":[23]

> Vnd werden on verdienst gerecht aus seiner Gnade / durch die Erlösung / so durch Christo Jhesu geschehen ist / Welchen Gott hat furgestellet zu einem Gnadenstuel / durch den glauben in seinem Blut / Da mit er die Gerechtigkeit / die fur jm gilt / darbiete / in dem / das er SVNDE VERGJBT/ welche bis an her blieben war / vnter göttlicher gedult.[24]

---

23 Vgl. Luthers Randglosse zu Röm 3,23 ff.: D. Martin Luther, *Die gantze Heilige Schrifft Deudsch* (Wittenberg 1545). - Lucas Cranach d. Ä. hat die zentrale Bedeutung der Rede vom Gnadenstuhl für die Theologie des Reformators eindrücklich dargestellt auf dem Altar der Weimarer Stadtkirche von 1553. Das Hauptbild zeigt (neben einer Fülle von heilsgeschichtlichen Einzelszenen) im Vordergrund rechts drei Männer unter dem Kreuz: den Täufer, der auf den Gekreuzigten weist, den greisen Maler selbst, mit Gebetsgestus, und Martin Luther, der in der Linken eine aufgeschlagene Bibel hält. Ein Blutstrahl aus der Seitenwunde Jesu trifft auf das Haupt Cranachs, Martin Luther gibt die Deutung des Geschehens: mit der Rechten zeigt er in der Schrift auf den dem Betrachter zugewandten Text von Hebr 4,16 (der Parallelstelle zu Röm 3,25): "Darumb lasset vns hinzu tretten / mit freidigkeit zu dem Gnadenstuel / Auff das wir barmhertzigkeit empfahen / vnd gnade finden / auff die zeit / wenn vns Hülffe not sein wird." Darüber ist der Vers 1.Joh 1,7 zu lesen: "Das Blut Jesu Christi reiniget uns von allen Sünden." An den Hebräertext schließt auf der rechten Buchseite Joh 3,14 f. an. Vgl. Herbert von Hintzenstern, *Lucas Cranach d. Ä. Altarbilder aus der Reformationszeit* (Berlin ²1975), 106 ff. Das Altarbild dürfte Bach bekannt gewesen sein. Vgl. auch die Kantaten auf Mariä Reinigung BWV 83 *Erfreute Zeit im neuen Bunde*, Arie 3: "Eile, Herz, voll Freudigkeit / Vor den Gnadenstuhl zu treten. / Du sollst deinen Trost empfangen / Und Barmherzigkeit erlangen [...]"; BWV 125 *Mit Fried und Freud ich fahr dahin*, Rez. 5: "[. . .] es wird der Welt,/ So Zorn und Fluch auf sich geladen,/ ein Stuhl der Gnaden / Und Siegeszeichen aufgestellt [. . .]"
24 Röm 3,24 f.; Schreibweise nach der Ausgabe von 1545. Die Verse gehören zu den von Luther selbst ausgewählten, im Druck herausgehobenen "Kernstellen" der Bibel; vgl. Hartmut Hövelmann, *Kernstellen der Luther-Bibel: Eine Anleitung zum Schriftverständnis* [Texte und Arbeiten zur Bibel V] (Bielefeld 1989). Martin Schloemann hat, Hövelmann weiterführend, kürzlich darauf aufmerksam gemacht, daß innerhalb der durch Fraktur hervorgehobenen "Kernstelle" Röm 3,24-26 zwei Worte eine doppelte Auszeichnung erfahren: die von Luther schon 1533 in Majuskeln gesetzten Wörter "SVNDE VERGJBT". Vgl. M. Schloemann, "Die Mitte der Schrift: Luthers Notabene", in: Wolfgang Erich Müller und Hartmut H.R. Schulz (hrsg.), *Theologie und Aufklärung: Festschrift für Gottfried Hornig zum 65. Geburtstag* (Würzburg 1992), 29-40, hier 34 f. Die "plakative Markierung" der zwei Wörter über die *remissio peccatorum* weisen den locus de iustificatione als den Hauptartikel, als die "Mitte der Schrift" aus (vgl. a.a.O., 37 f.). Auch in Teil IV des Weihnachtsoratoriums ist die *remissio peccatorum* das zentrale Thema, abgehandelt unter dem Topos vom Namen Jesu, "welcher genennet war von dem Engel", nämlich in Mt 1,21, und dessen "Übersetzung" lautet "er wird sein Volk selig

197

Es kann kein Zweifel bestehen daran, daß der von Bach mit "Festo Circumcisionis Christi" überschriebene IV. Teil des Oratoriums mit dem Stichwort "Gnadenthron" im Eingangssatz auf Röm 3,25 (Hebr 4,16) weist[25] und damit die Blutthematik angesprochen ist. Dieses auch an der Komposition zu zeigen, sei einem weiteren Beitrag vorbehalten.[26]

Ich fasse zusammen: Die von Ernst Koch aus zeitgenössischen Quellen belegte Deutung des Echos als Sinnbild für die tröstliche Antwort Gottes oder Jesu auf das Gebet der Gläubigen ist zutreffend und ein ergiebiger Ansatz für die Interpretation von Teil IV des Weihnachts-Oratoriums. Die strukturelle Analogie von Echo und Gottesantwort ist inbezug auf ihren speziellen Gebrauch im Detempore wie folgt zu begründen und inhaltlich zu füllen: Das Echo bot sich für die Auslegung des Neujahrsevangeliums als sinnfälliges poetisch-musikalisches Mittel an, da der "Hochtröstliche Name IESVS" seinerseits das Amt des Heilands und Erlösers "spiegelt",[27] der Name seinen Träger zur Barmherzigkeit "zwingt".[28] Denn bei Gott ist "Name und Wesen *ein* Ding".[29] Die identische Struktur von Name und Bedeutung (Mt 1,21: Jesus = Seligmacher) spiegelt sich akustisch im Echo. Die Gewißheit und Verläßlichkeit des Echos stärkt den angefochtenen Glauben als "süßes Wort":[30] DULCE ASSONAT ECHO.[31] Inhalt des "süßen Wortes" und Grund allen Trostes ist, daß Jesus Christus unser "Gnadenthron" sein will. Der mit dieser Allusion von Röm 3,25 angesprochene theologische Kontext, der *locus de iustificatione* wird in den zeitgenössischen Neujahrspredigten innerhalb der Ausführungen zur Beschneidung Jesu dargelegt. Der im Neujahrsteil des Weih-

---

machen von ihren Sünden".

25 Vgl. die weiteren Vorkommen von "Gnadenthron": BWV 55 *Ich armer Mensch, ich Sündenknecht*, Rez. 4; BWV 76 *Die Himmel erzählen die Ehre Gottes*, Arie 3.

26 Er ist vorgesehen für das Colloquium van de Koninklijke Nederlandse Akademie van Wetenschappen zum Thema "Das Blut Jesu und die Lehre von der Versöhnung im Werk Johann Sebastian Bachs" vom 15. bis 17. September 1993 in Amsterdam.

27 Martin Moller, *Praxis*, Neujahr, 150 f.; s.o. bei Anm. 9.

28 Heinrich Müller, *Schluß-Kette*, 14. S.n.Trin., 1002 b.

29 Heinrich Müller, ebda; s.o. bei Anm. 4.

30 Rez. 38, Arie 39.

31 Siehe Abb. 1.

nachts-Oratoriums scheinbar ausgeklammerte Themenkreis Beschneidung–Blut–Erlösung ist nicht nur litteraliter gegenwärtig mit der zitierten Ristschen Liedstrophe (Nr. 38), sondern der Artikel von der Sündenvergebung durch Jesu Blut ist als theologische Voraussetzung gleichsam spiritualiter gegenwärtig in der Gewißheit des Glaubens, vom ewigen Tod der Verdammnis befreit zu sein (Rez. 38, Arie 39).[32] Die *remissio peccatorum* ist auch die Voraussetzung des freudig-tätigen neuen Wandels, wie er sich in Arie 41 "Ich will nur dir zu Ehren leben" ausspricht. Haben wir die Auslegung des Evangeliums auf Neujahr, das, wie Heinrich Müller sagt, in sich die ganze Heilige Schrift, Gesetz und Evangelium begreift,[33] einmal zur Kenntnis genommen, wie sie Bach und seinen Zeitgenossen bekannt und geläufig war, dann schließt sich die umfassende theologische Bedeutung des Verses Lk 2,21 wieder im Namen Jesu zusammen. Johann Arnd:[34]

JEsu lieber Meister, erbarme dich unser. Diese armen Leute erkennen den Namen JEsu. [. . .] Last uns diesen Namen recht kennen im Glauben, in der Liebe, und in der Hoffnung, so werden wir in diesem Gnaden=Thron erhöret werden. Wer diesen Namen hertzlich lieb hat über alles, der vermag alles in demselben.

Im Namen Christi ist Erhörung, Hülffe, Gnade und Trost, ohn den Namen JEsu wird niemand getröstet,

JEsu, der süsse Name dein
Erquick im Tod die Seele mein.
GOtt hat aller Seelen Trost in diesen Namen gelegt.

Summary

This contribution demonstrates, by an examination of the substance of sermons by Martin Moller, Johann Gerhard, and Heinrich Müller, that the treatment of the Gospel for New Year's Day, Luke 2.21, in Part IV of Bach's *Christmas Oratorio*, is in accord with the general homiletic tradition of interpretation. Part IV – contrary to the *communis opinio* of Bach research – deals not only with the naming of Jesus but

---

32 Vgl. auch *Johannes-Passion* Nr. 32: "Mein teurer Heiland, laß dich fragen, [. . .]/ Bin ich vom Sterben frei gemacht? [. . .] - Jesu, der du warest tot [. . .]/ In der letzten Todesnot / Nirgend mich hinwende [. . .]"

33 Heinrich Müller, *Hertzens=Spiegel*, Neujahr, 779; s.o. bei Anm. 13.

34 Johann Arnd, *Postilla* (Anm. 7), 14. S.n.Trin., 217 a/b.

also with the passion of Jesus. This connection is made by the allusion to the key-word "Gnadenthron" ("throne of grace") of Romans 3.24f in the opening movement (No. 36), and by the use of the Rist stanza (No. 38) which presents the circumcision of Jesus as the beginning of the passion, the first-fruits ("Angeld" [Moller]) of redemption through his blood which is to be completed in the crucifixion. The name Jesus reflects ("spiegelt") the ministry of the Savior and Redeemer. The acoustic equivalent of a reflection is an echo. Thus in the echo duet (No. 39) Bach makes aesthetically conspicuous the certainty and trust-worthiness of Jesus's comforting answer to our prayer for mercy.

Contributors

FRANS BROUWER studied liturgiology in Groningen, with Casper Honders, and musicology in Utrecht. His dissertation, written under the supervision of Casper Honders, concerned liturgical and church musical developments in Denmark from the end of the eighteenth century until about 1950, and his doctorate from the Rijksuniversiteit Utrecht was awarded in 1990. He has published many articles about church music, organ building and cultural history in Scandinavia. He has also taught liturgy, hymnology and organ building at the Groningen Conservatory of Music – in succession to Casper Honders – and until 1993 was the Director of the Nederlands Instituut voor Kerkmuziek and the Faculty of Music (Utrechts Conservatorium), both within the Utrecht School of the Arts (Hogeschool voor de Kunsten Utrecht).

ALBERT CLEMENT studied organ performance at the Brabant Conservatory of Music at Tilburg, musicology at the Rijksuniversiteit Utrecht, and theology at the Rijksuniversiteit Leiden. Following his 1989 Utrecht doctorate, awarded (with highest estimation) for a dissertation on some of the organ works of J.S. Bach, he was granted a fellowship by the Royal Netherlands Academy of Arts and Sciences. In conjunction with this fellowship he currently holds a position at the Rijksuniversiteit Utrecht. Albert Clement is a member of the Internationale Arbeitsgemeinschaft für theologische Bachforschung and regularly gives lectures and recitals in the Netherlands and abroad. He is the author of many publications in the field of baroque music.

PHILIPP HARNONCOURT studied for the Catholic priesthood and, following ordination, pursued doctoral studies at the University of Graz, Austria and Munich. After completing his doctorate in 1963 he became the director of the Church Music Department of the Academy of Music and in 1972 Professor at the Institute for Liturgy, Christian Art and Hymnology, University of Graz. Philipp Harnoncourt is the author of many articles in such disciplines as liturgiology, church music, hymnology, ecumenical studies, church architecture and contemporary art. He is also a member of the Austrian Liturgical Commission, and other such bodies, and was for many years the Secretary/Treasurer of the Internationale Arbeitsgemeinschaft für Hymnologie.

MARKUS JENNY studied theology and musicology at Basle and Zurich universities (and simultaneously studied hymnology and church music with the Dutch teacher Ina Lohr). He is the author and editor of many books and articles in the areas of hymnology, liturgiology, and church music. Markus Jenny was co-founder of the Internationale Arbeitsgemeinschaft für Hymnologie, and was for many years its President. Formerly a pastor in the Swiss Reformed Church, and a Professor of Practical Theology at Zurich University, he now lives in retirement in Ligerz, Switzerland.

WIM KLOPPENBURG studied church music with Frits Mehrtens and organ performance with Piet Kee at the Amsterdam Conservatory of Music (Vereeniging Muzieklyceum). He is active as a teacher, the organist-choirmaster of the Kruiskerk, Amstelveen, and produces the weekly radio program "Liturgy and Church Music" for IKON – Interchurch Radio. From 1985 to 1991 he was a member of the executive board of the Internationale Arbeitsgemeinschaft für Hymnologie, in succession to Casper Honders.

ROBIN A. LEAVER, hymnologist, musicologist, writer and teacher on liturgy and church music, is Professor of Church Music, Westminster Choir College, The School of Music of Rider College, Princeton, New Jersey, USA, and also teaches in the Liturgical Studies program of the Graduate School of Drew University, Madison, New Jersey. He was awarded a doctorate from the Rijksuniversiteit Groningen, for a dissertation on English and Dutch metrical psalmody in the sixteenth century, written under the supervision of Casper Honders. Robin Leaver is a past-President of the Internationale Arbeitsgemeinschaft für Hymnologie, and a member of the Arbeitsgemeinschaft für theologische Bachforschung. He has published 25 books, contributed to 30 others, and more than 200 articles, reviews, etc., for publications and journals issued in four continents.

ALAN LUFF studied classics, philosophy and theology at Bristol, Oxford, and Cambridge universities. Following ordination into the Church of England he served in the Manchester Diocese, including six years at the cathedral as Precentor. After eleven years of parish ministry in Wales he became Precentor of Westminster Abbey, London (1979-1992). In 1992 he became Canon of Birmingham Cathedral. Alan Luff became Secretary of the Hymn Society of Great Britain and Ireland in 1973 and its Chairman in 1987; he is also the Warden of the Guild of Church Musicians. He has written a book on Welsh hymnody and has contributed many articles on church music, hymnody and carols to a number of journals published in the United Kingdom and the United States.

JAN R. LUTH studied theology, musicology and organ performance, and since 1980 has been tutor (universitair docent) of the Instituut voor Liturgiewetenschap, Rijksuniversiteit Groningen. He was awarded his doctorate from the Rijksuniversiteit Groningen in 1986 for a dissertation, supervised by Casper Honders, on the history of congregational singing and its accompaniment in Dutch Reformed churches. A noted organ recitalist in Europe, Jan Luth is also the author of many articles on hymnody and the role of the organ in worship, and is currently the editor of the *IAH Bulletin*, a position he took over from Casper Honders in 1987.

ANDREAS MARTI studied organ and harpsichord performance at the Conservatory of Music, Bern, Switzerland, and theology at Bern University. His dissertation was a study of rhetoric in the cantatas of J.S. Bach. Andreas Marti is currently Professor of Church Music, Bern University, and also teaches hymnology and church music at the Conservatory of Music, Bern. He is a member of various commissions on church music and hymnody in Switzerland, the hymnology editor of the *Jahrbuch für Liturgik und Hymnologie*, and was the President of the Internationale Arbeitsgemeinschaft für Hymnologie from 1989 to 1993.

DANIEL MEETER, a pastor in the Reformed Church in America, has served Hungarian and Dutch immigrant congregations in the United States and Canada, and now serves an ecumenical and interracial congregation in Hoboken, New Jersey. He earned his doctorate from Drew University, studying liturgy with Bard Thompson, and completing a dissertation on the 1793 liturgy of the Dutch Reformed Church in North America, under the supervision of Casper Honders, with whom Meeter had studied privately in Groningen. He is a member of the Consultation on Common Texts, and the author of a number of forthcoming articles in the area of Reformed liturgiology.

BERNARD SMILDE studied theology at the Free University, Amsterdam, and the Rijksuniversiteit Groningen, where he was awarded his doctorate in 1986 for a dissertation, supervised by Casper Honders, on "Hasper and the Church Hymn." An ordained minister, Bernard Smilde worked on Dutch and Frisian Bible translations (1968-1977), and more recently was involved in the Commission for a New Service Book on behalf of the cooperating Reformed Churches in the Netherlands (1985-1990). He has taught the history of music, liturgy, hymnology, and Gregorian chant at the Leeuwarden School of Music, and has published numerous hymnological articles. He also contributed texts and melodies to the Dutch *Liedboek voor de Kerken* (1973), and its Frisian edition, the *Lieteboek foar de Tsjerken* (1977).

RENATE STEIGER studied music at the Staatliche Hochschule für Musik, Cologne, and musicology, philosophy, mathematics and theology at the universities of Cologne, Bonn and Tübingen, receiving her doctorate in 1962. Since 1958 Renate Steiger has been involved in preparing critical editions of theological and philosophical texts of the 15th century; from 1969 this work has been continued in association with the Akademie der Wissenschaften, Heidelberg. She is currently the President of the Internationale Arbeitsgemeinschaft für theologische Bachforschung, the principal editor (since 1981) of the journal *Musik und Kirche*, and is the author of numerous articles and books on J.S. Bach, some co-authored by Lothar Steiger.

Addendum

Bibliography

The publications of Casper Honders

1950

Bach's Music. In: *Pioneer: The Organ of the Reformed Church in Canada* (Dec. 1957), 12-13.

1960

Het Instituut voor Liturgiewetenschap to Groningen. In: *Jaarboek voor de Eredienst van de Nederlandse Hervormde Kerk 1965-1966* (The Hague 1966), 195-200

1970

De inzettingwoorden van het Avondmaal. In: KT 23 (1972), 73-78.

Tien jaren Instituut voor Litugiewetenschap. In: MILW 8 (1973), 4-11.

Enkele opmerkingen over biecht en boete in de reformatorische kerken. In: *Tijdschrift voor Liturgie* (1974), 120-127.

Avondmaal op Goede Vrijdag. In: *Eredienst* 10 (1976), 69-72.

Het oude testament en de kerkzang. In: *Organist en Eredienst* (1977), 196-198.

Een eeuwenoud wonder. In: *Klinkend Geloof*, ed. W. Dankbaar, et al. (The Hague 1978), 9-15.

Het Liedboek Compedium. In: MILW 12 (1978), 15-18.

Internationale en Interconfessionele Hymnologie. In: *Organist en Eredienst* (1979), 166-168.

Hymnology in Europe. In: *The Hymn* 30 (1979), 196-199.

1980

Gemeetezang in diskussie. In: *Het Orgel* 76 (1980), 274-276.

Die musikalische Rhetorik bei J.S. Bach. In: MuG 36 (1982), 161-163.

R. Bennink Janssonius; B. ter Haar; H.J. Honders. In: *Biografisch Lexicon voor de Geschiedenis van het Nederlandse Protestantisme*, Vol 2 (Kampen 1983), 58-60, 229-231 & 254-255 respectively.

Johann Sebastian Bach. In: *Bewogen Grensgangers*, ed. A. Bakker, et al. (Hilversum 1987), 130-132.

1990

Oikumene. In: *Sursum Corda: Variationen zu einem liturgischen Motiv für Philipp Haarnoncout zum 60. Geburtstag*, ed. E. Renhart & A. Schnider (Graz 1992), 22.

The book, *Mijn Lief is mijn . . . : Over het Hooglied in het werk van J.S. Bach* (Voorburg 1988) will be published in an English edition in 1994: *"My Beloved is Mine" : The Song of Solomon in the Work of J.S. Bach*.